CROMWELL TANK
VEHICLE HISTORY AND SPECIFICATION

David Fletcher

© The Tank Museum 2022.

All rights reserved. No part of this publication may be reproduced or stored in a retrieval system or transmitted, in any form or by any means, electronic, mechanical, photocopying, recording or otherwise, without prior permission in writing from The Tank Museum.

First published in 1983 by HMSO.
This edition published in 2022 by The Tank Museum.

British Library Cataloguing in Publication Data.

A catalogue record for this book is available from the British Library.

Printed book ISBN 978 1739902704

Designed and produced for The Tank Museum by JJN Publishing Ltd.
Printed and bound in Malta.

CONTENTS

INTRODUCTION
SERIES INTRODUCTION 4
THE CRUISER TANKS 6

THE MANUAL
INTRODUCTION 35
VEHICLE SPECIFICATION 37
DRIVING INSTRUCTIONS 39
THE ENGINE, LEADING PARTICULARS 48
THE ENGINE, INTRODUCTION 50
CARBURETTOR AND INDUCTION ASSEMBLY 51
AIR CLEANERS 51
FUEL SYSTEM 52
OIL SYSTEM 56
COOLING SYSTEM 58
IGNITION SYSTEM 60
BEVEL GEARBOX 60
THE FINAL DRIVE 65
TRACKS AND TENSIONERS 65
SUSPENSION 69
STEERING BRAKES AND TRACK BRAKES 72
THE HULL 75
THE TURRET 84
THE QF 6-POUNDER 7CWT GUN 88
GUN, MACHINE, BESA 7.92MM 91
2-INCH BOMBTHROWER 97
TOOLS CARRIED IN THE AFV 98
AMMUNITION 100
SIGHTING TELESCOPES 105
INSTALLING AND REMOVING BESA MACHINE-GUN 107
6-POUNDER AND BESA MG CO-AXIAL MOUNTING 108
MACHINE-GUN NO 20 MOUNTING 111
PLATE THICKNESS DIAGRAM 112
INTERNAL STOWAGE DIAGRAMS 113
EXTERNAL STOWAGE DIAGRAMS 116
SCALE DRAWINGS 122

CROMWELL TANK

SERIES INTRODUCTION

This publication consists largely of a selection of material from the pages of the official War Office Service Instruction Book for the Cromwell Mark I Cruiser Tank. It is supplemented by various other original diagrams and scale drawings associated with the tank, while a newly written introductory chapter recounts the history of its creation and explains its genealogy. A selection of photographs from The Tank Museum archive completes the work.

Although the original Service Instruction Book has been abridged, this has only been done to avoid duplication of content, or to exclude sections of very limited interest. At the same time many useful diagrams have been inserted out of numerical sequence in order to place them alongside the relevant text. The original figure numbers have been retained to maintain authenticity. New consecutive page numbering has been adopted throughout to assist the reader. For this reason, a new contents page has been compiled to cover the entire book.

Besides giving enthusiasts ready access to an out-of-print and much sought-after volume, it should prove

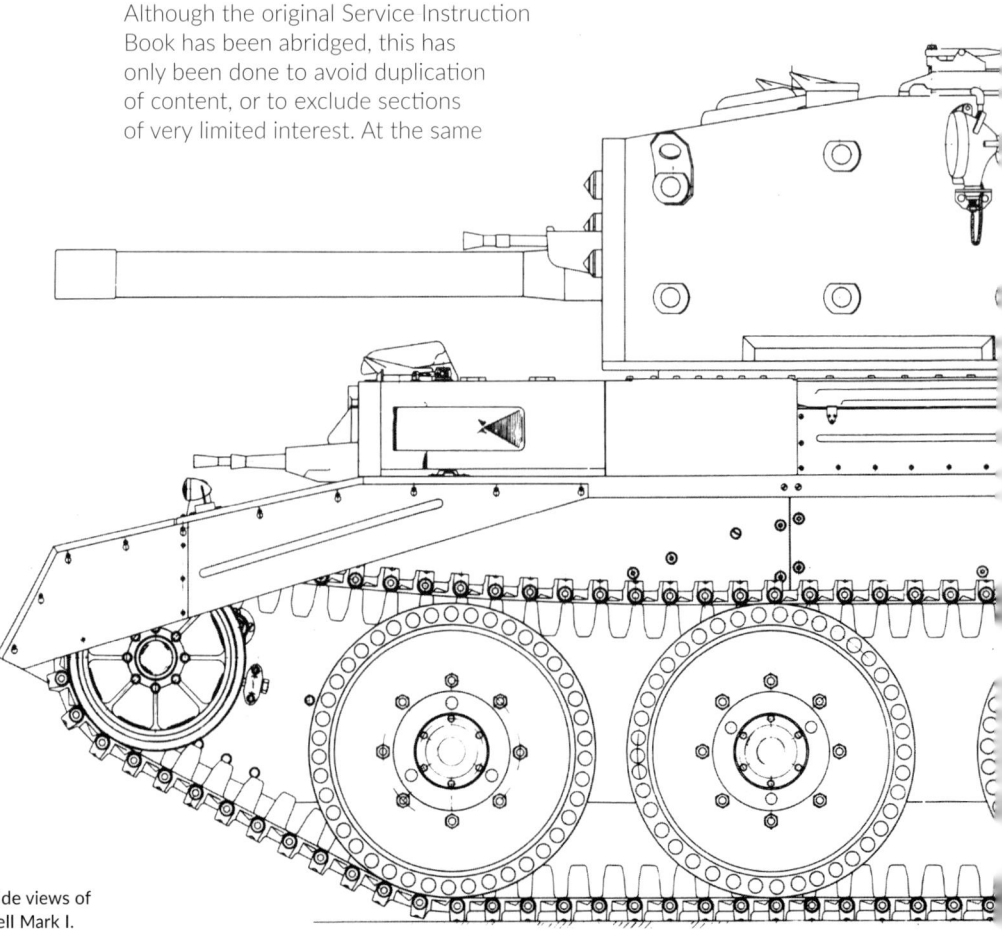

Front and side views of the Cromwell Mark I.

INTRODUCTION

of great value to modellers, military vehicle historians and anyone lucky enough to have the chance of restoring a surviving machine.

Interested readers are invited to inspect a preserved Cromwell tank, along with some of its predecessors, contemporaries and derivatives in The Tank Museum at Bovington, Dorset.

The data on the various marks of Cromwell is based on the work of Richard Harley, to whom our thanks are due.

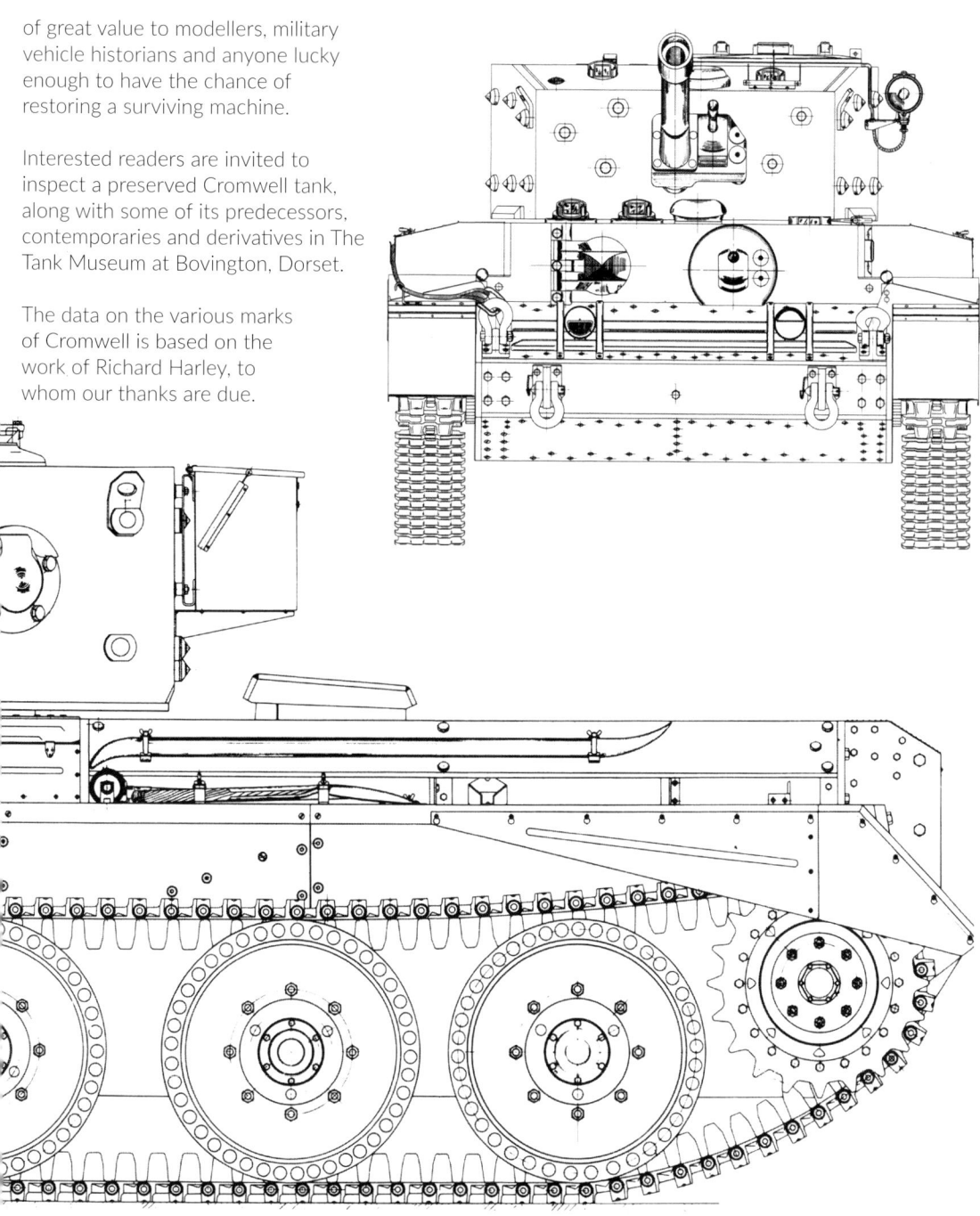

THE CRUISER TANKS

The purpose of the cruiser tank in battle is one of exploitation. In this it echoes the role of the horsed cavalry, which was launched at a weak point in the enemy line, to break through and destroy the cohesion of the opposing troops. The appearance of the cruiser tank in the British Army towards the end of the 1930s followed a period when almost all the functions of the tank on the battlefield, aside from the scouting activities of the light tanks, were undertaken by the multi-purpose Medium Tank. However, immediate pre-war thinking on the subject tended towards diversification. On the one hand the exploitation role was appreciated, but it was also felt that the infantry needed a tank to accompany them, to knock out machine-guns and neutralise field artillery. A tank that would do this must be well protected to absorb punishment, and the fact that this also made it relatively slow was of no consequence, since it was tied to the pace of the infantry anyway. By contrast, the cruiser must be fast, it had to find the weak spot and charge through. It need not be so well armoured since its very speed should make it harder to hit, and the lighter it was, the faster it could go.

Although the theory held some sway in most pre-war armies, it was in Britain in particular that it was adopted most rigorously, and pursued most doggedly, until in due course it reached the ultimate conclusion in the shape of the medium, or main battle tank, that once again combined both roles in one vehicle.

The parting of the ways caught two tanks in the early stages of development, the A9 and A10. Prototypes of both were building as cheaper, lighter mediums and both were shortly reclassified as cruisers, becoming the Mark I and Mark II respectively. But despite a robust suspension they lacked a prime ingredient – speed. In the meantime, two influential officers, General A.P. Wavell and Lt-Col G. Le Q Martel, returned from a visit to Russia where they had witnessed exciting high-speed manoeuvres undertaken by the latest Soviet BT tanks, which were

INTRODUCTION

quite capable of doing 40mph. The key to the Russian success lay to a large extent in their choice of suspension. It consisted of large rubber-tyred road wheels on long trailing arms, which acted on equally long helical springs sandwiched between the inner and outer skins of the hull sides. This was the renowned Christie system, named after the abrasive American genius J. Walter Christie. He had developed the principle in 1928, and had spent the intervening years trying to sell it to the United States Army. An unfortunate combination of official parsimony, and Christie's personal obduracy spelled doom, and in 1930 he took the technically illegal step of selling some samples to the Russians. Impressed by what they had seen, Wavell, and particularly Martel, pressed the War Office to investigate, and in the November of 1936 a turretless Christie tank arrived at Farnborough from the USA.

Pilot model of the Cromwell Mark IA, built by Birmingham Railway Carriage and Wagon Company.

CROMWELL TANK

Although the basic hull design was not suited to British requirements, the suspension was found to be ideal, and in conjunction with another American product, the modified V12 Liberty aero engine of 1916 vintage, it produced an unequalled performance. The agent for the Christie deal was Lord Nuffield, and it was to his firm that a contract was awarded for the construction of a series of production models based on the Christie design. Known to the War Office as the A13 or Cruiser Mark III, it passed through a process of evolution, which culminated in the last of the A13's, the Cruiser Mark V or Covenanter, and its successor the A15 Crusader. Despite a steady improvement in armour thickness, hull and turret shape, and latterly gun power, the last of the line, the Crusader Mark III was still fundamentally a combination on the Christie suspension and the Nuffield Liberty engine.

Wartime progress

Before the Second World War was a year old, Britain's fortunes as a tank producer were approaching rock bottom. While the more successful survivors of the pre-war policy were wearing themselves out in action, many of the new designs were found to be either totally unsuitable for combat, like the Covenanter, or at best in need of a long period of development to bring them up to scratch, like the Churchill. Faced with the choice of concentrating hard on a totally new design with a bigger gun and a more powerful engine, or

INTRODUCTION

Side view of the Mark IA pilot. It was built from mild steel rather than armour plate.

continuing production of the better existing designs like the Matilda, Valentine and Crusader, with little more than detail improvements, the War Office chose the latter. While this course sought parity with the enemy in numbers, it stifled progress in design, and clogged up production lines with masses of fighting vehicles, which were obsolete before they were delivered. Such progress as was made tended to dissipate itself on outlandish schemes for massive siege engines like TOG and A20. Likewise, in the case of armament the development of a more powerful all-purpose tank gun was retarded by an incredible scheme to fit each tank with a complex triple mounting of existing weapons; the 2-pounder anti-tank gun, 3-inch howitzer and Besa machine-gun.

The responsibility for this unhappy situation lay at many doors: the traditional independence of the various manufacturers, who often resisted progressive change in the interests of smooth production runs; a lack of positive direction from the War Office; the sometimes-unwarranted interference of government leaders; and the oft times muddled deliberations of a body called the Tank Board. This latter was a weekly sitting of interested parties from the manufacturing and service factions who were supposed to direct production and development by coordinating user requirements with the practical limitations of production.

By the summer of 1940 it was clear that a new cruiser tank was urgently

CROMWELL TANK

Cromwell Mark IIIA T189577, originally built as a Centaur by English Electric and subsequently reworked.

required. The existing 2-pounder gun was meeting its match in the thicker armoured German tanks, and although a new 6-pounder gun was in the offing it was hardly suited to any of the tanks in service. A temporary expedient was sought by fitting it into a modified Crusader, but this involved the removal of a member of the turret crew, which in turn limited the effectiveness of the tank in action. Preliminary specifications for a new cruiser were issued by the Department of Tank Design in November 1940, and by the middle of January 1941 two firms had submitted proposals. Nuffield Mechanisation and Aero, the tank building branch of the Morris group, suggested a design based on the mechanical features of the Crusader, while Vauxhall Motors offered a lighter version of their new Churchill tank.

The new Cruiser

The Vauxhall tank was given the General Staff specification A23, but it quickly dropped from the scene in favour of the Nuffield version. This was A24, and by the end of the month the firm was given the go-ahead to complete the detailed design and produce six pilots. The main specifications of the tank indicated a choice of armament between the new 6-pounder with a co-axial Besa, or the monstrous triple mounting mentioned above. In addition, a Bren or Besa machine-gun was to be carried for anti-aircraft use, and for

INTRODUCTION

close-in defence a series of portholes were suggested for the turret and hull through which a Thompson sub machine-gun could be fired. Armour thickness was to be a maximum of 65mm on the hull front, and up to 75mm on the turret, which was a considerable improvement on the Crusader. Total weight was calculated at 24 tons, being an increase of 5 tons over the Crusader. However, much of this advantage would appear to be negated by the decision to employ the same vintage, and often troublesome engine and transmission, and the same Christie suspension, unmodified to allow for the greater weight.

Then suddenly into this relatively stagnant atmosphere there was injected a new and stimulating possibility. It was learned that Rolls-Royce and Leyland Motors had been cooperating on the design of a new tank engine based on the highly successful Rolls-Royce Merlin aircraft engine, which the summer before had powered the RAF's Spitfires and Hurricanes to victory in the Battle of Britain. This striking development was the Meteor, an un-supercharged V12 which, it was confidently predicted,

Cavalier carried over the engine, transmission, suspension and gun from the Crusader Mark III on the right.

CROMWELL TANK

would deliver 600bhp, an increase of 210bhp over the best that could be achieved with the latest mark of Liberty. On 18 April 1941, the Tank Board announced that this was to be the engine for the 1942 tank programme, and instructed that it be put into production 'relatively early'.

Now at last things began to move fast, at least on paper. In May the Tank Board firmly announced that their policy would be to concentrate on the A24 or Cruiser Mark VII, as it was now called. It was definitely stated that the Cruisers Mark V and Mark VI, the Covenanter and Crusader, were not suitable for the 1943 programme, and that progress on the Mark VII was advanced enough to begin tooling up with the two available engines in mind, the Liberty and the Meteor. Although the former was not now considered up to the General Staff requirement, it was appreciated that the Meteor would not be ready in time to fit the first tanks, so they conceded that they would be prepared to accept a number of tanks fitted with the Liberty. Further, it was agreed that the production capacity at present committed to the Covenanter, Crusader, Matilda and Valentine should all be turned over to Mark VII production as soon as existing orders were filled.

Since early 1941 the Tank Board had been aware that another company, the Birmingham Carriage and Wagon Co, were working on a design for a heavy cruiser tank. Steps were therefore taken to involve them in the A24 project. Meanwhile, Meteor engines were installed in two Crusader hulls for practice trials, and to convince the sceptics that a modern aircraft engine could successfully be adapted to tank work. In April one of these modified tanks was subjected to a speed test at Aldershot. A three-quarter mile stretch was marked out, and timekeepers stationed, while the driver was instructed to keep his foot down. Despite a warning that the course was too short, the trial went ahead. The tank sped by so fast that the timekeepers forgot their task, and the driver, unable to brake or turn in time, vanished into the trees. A conservative

Cruiser Mark VII, A 24 Cavalier.

T189679 is a Cromwell Mark IVB built by English Electric.

estimate put the speed at 50mph. In order to evaluate other proposed options of engine and transmission, four of the pilot machines were planned to be tested with different systems.

The matter of transmission was a thorny one. The early cruisers had relied on a simple clutch and brake system, which was wasteful of power. Some experimental prototype tanks had been used to test more advanced systems designed by W.G. Wilson and Dr Merritt, but these had been rejected on the grounds of over complication. Instead the Covenanter and Crusader had been fitted with simplified Wilson epicyclic systems not that much different from the type employed on the later First World War tanks. Design work on the Merritt version continued, and, in a developed form, as the Merritt-Brown 301c it was adopted for the A22 Churchill, although in the initial stages it proved troublesome.

Nuffields, with ease of production in mind, were naturally inclined to retain the epicyclic system for the A24, but the Tank Board felt that they had good reason to employ the Merritt-Brown, and proceeded accordingly. At the same time the Leyland/Rolls-Royce design team offered a new five-speed synchromesh gearbox with controlled differential steering to suit the Meteor engine, and it was to settle the final choice that the modified A24 pilots were ordered.

At first it seemed that the inclusion

CROMWELL TANK

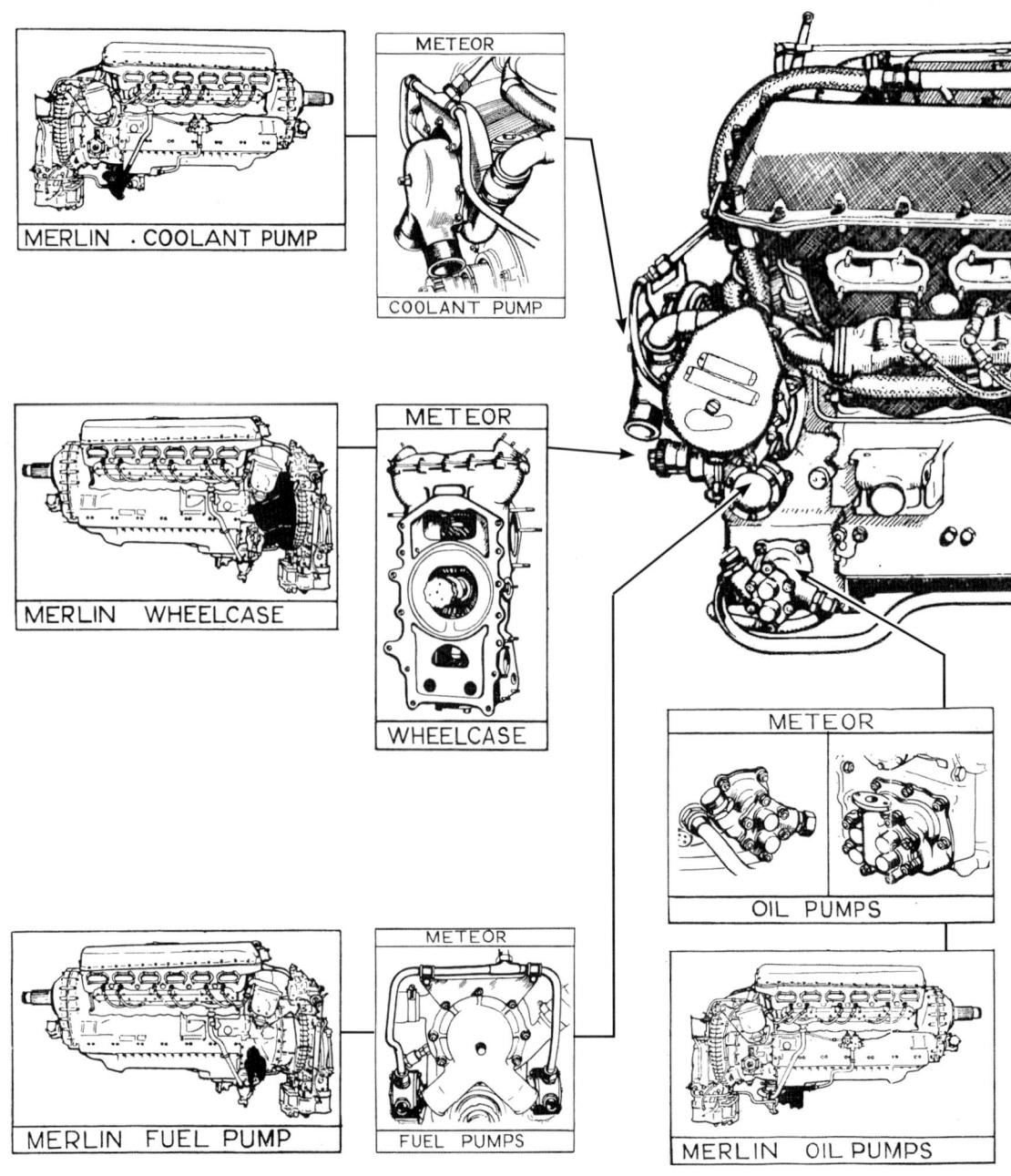

MAIN DESIGN DIFFERENCES BETWEEN METEOR TANK ENGINE AND MERLIN AERO ENGINE

Lov/DNL. DRG No.121.

INTRODUCTION

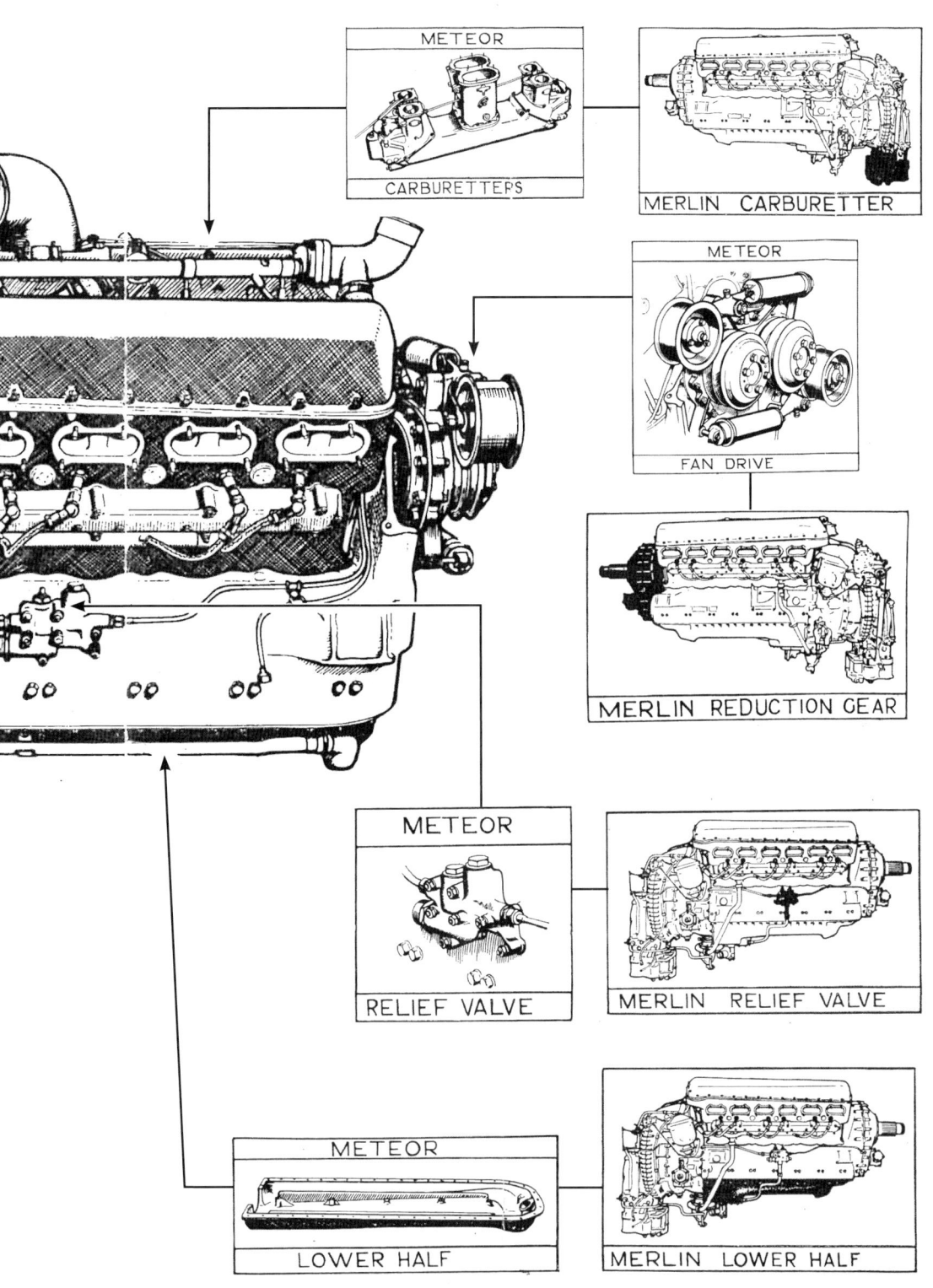

Photographed at Pickering on 31 March 1944, this is a Cromwell Mark VB of the 2nd Battalion, Welsh Guards.

of the Birmingham and Wagon Co in the A24 programme would help to speed it up, but it soon became clear that they were unable to standardise their production methods with those of the Nuffield concern. Thus, by September 1941, it was agreed that the heavy cruiser programme must take two divergent paths. Nuffields would continue with an order for 500 A24 cruisers, while the main effort was diverted to the Birmingham and Wagon Co, who would continue to develop the Meteor/Merritt heavy cruiser under the new designation A27, the cruiser Mark VIII. This effectively released Nuffields from the need to modify their design for the Merritt gearbox.

In a progress report dated 8 January 1942, the Tank Board spelled out the position. Nuffield Mechanisation and Aero were in the throes of building 500 new tanks to GS specification A24. Mechanically, these would be based on the A15 Crusader, with the same engine, transmission and suspension. The Birmingham Carriage and Wagon Co were working on the pilot A27, which would retain the same hull and turret shape of the A24, but with a stronger suspension and a Rolls-Royce Meteor engine coupled to the Merritt-Brown transmission. The opportunity was also taken to revise the cooling system. This had been a noted source of trouble in both the Covenanter and Crusader, and was certainly not suited to the more powerful engine. Rolls-

INTRODUCTION

themselves in the engine bearings, the cooling and the fan drive, all of which it inherited from the Crusader. By contrast, the A27 pilot had completed its 1,000 miles over February and March with such little trouble that it had gone on to amass 2,200 miles on the clock. At this stage a fault appeared in the clutch shaft, but the overall verdict spoke of a good performance.

The main problem now was the supply of Meteor engines. Early teething troubles, especially over cooling, had given the Leyland faction cold feet and in July 1941 they opted out, leaving Rolls-Royce to continue alone. Despite a massive prior commitment to supply Merlins to the RAF, the company accepted the extra work associated with the Meteor, and in due course both Meadows and the Rover Company joined the programme. In fact, the latter took over the lion's share of production after 1943 when they exchanged projects with Rolls-Royce, who then undertook development of the Welland jet engine. Delays were inevitable in this situation and the Tank Board decided that in addition to the A24 series, some A27s could be built with the Liberty power unit, too. This would, in any case, produce a more serviceable tank than the A24 since it would have the improved cooling, and a suspension better suited to the weight. At the same time, since all the other mechanical

Royce engineers therefore devised a new scheme, which still fitted into the limited space available in the engine compartment, and at the same time they introduced a more efficient type of air cleaner, and improved petrol stowage. By 20 January, 1942 the Tank Board was able to report that the first cruiser Mark VIII was nearing completion at Birmingham, and at about this time the codename Cromwell was adopted for both the A24 and the A27 series.

Towards the end of May 1942, the Cromwell I, or A24 pilot, was at Farnborough, where it was said to be in its 'final form'. In March it had completed 1,000 miles and had then been returned to the makers for complete stripping and inspection. Faults manifested

Cromwell Mark IV or Mark V with Type B hull, photographed on 14 August 1944.

17

features would be those of the A27, there would be no foreseeable problem in fitting Meteor engines when they became available. Thus, what had been one became three: A24 Cruiser Mark VII was Cromwell I; A27L Cruiser Mark VIII was Cromwell II; A27M Cruiser Mark VIII was Cromwell III. In August 1942, this confusing nomenclature was hopefully simplified in a rechristening process by which, Cromwell I became Cavalier, Cromwell II became Centaur, and Cromwell III became just Cromwell.

There were but two notes of caution; in a memo of July 1940, the Tank Board pointed out that with a final weight of 26 tons 8cwt the A27M was close to the limit of the safety margin of the strengthened suspension, and a body of opinion had built up, which still thought that a modified aircraft engine would not work in a tank. This theory was also backed by American interests, which wanted both nations to standardise on a new Ford V12. The matter was finally settled with a handicap race on a circular course at Farnborough, in which the Cromwell beat all comers handsomely.

Until now all three designs had been developed with a view to mounting the 6-pounder gun, but once again the progress had been slow and

The A30 Challenger featured an enlarged Cromwell derived hull fitted with a new turret mounting the 17-pounder gun.

INTRODUCTION

The Royal Marines Armoured Support Group used the 95mm howitzer-armed Close Support variant of the Centaur. They were the only unit to use the tank in combat.

CROMWELL TANK

Around 100 Centaurs were converted to Anti-Aircraft tanks, but none saw service.

complicated. By the time they entered service, the requirement at the battlefront had changed drastically, and the 6-pounder was of little more use than the 2-pounder had been against the latest German tanks in 1941. In answer, Britain had developed a weapon with characteristics that placed it on a par with the latest German gun, the 88mm. The new British piece was the 17-pounder, but such a large gun was out of court in a tank the size of Cromwell. Thus, a small proportion of the A27 effort was diverted once again to produce a vehicle suited to the bigger gun. This finally appeared as a longer, wider Cromwell, the A30 Challenger. At the same time a new 75mm gun was also designed, based on

INTRODUCTION

American equipment but suited to the existing 6-pounder mounting. By December 1942, it had been decided to aim for a situation whereby all Centaur and Cromwell machines would ultimately appear with the new weapon, while the Cavalier, which would never now be more than a training machine, would retain the 6-pounder. Production delays, however, would once again mean that initially many Centaurs and Cromwells would be completed with the 6-pounder gun, although the facility was there to replace it in due course. The 75mm was the first wartime British tank gun that could deal out a respectable high explosive shell as well as the armour-piercing type, but a need was still felt for a more powerful close-support weapon, and in February

The Cromwell Mark VI carried the 95mm Close Support howitzer.

1943 it was agreed that a 95mm howitzer would be carried in a few A27s. The proposed ratio was 10 per cent in the Cromwell, 12 per cent in the Centaur and none on the Cavalier.

Meanwhile, the Tank Board issued another progress report in January

Wounded German soldiers are ferried to an aid post by Cromwell T188169, a Mark IVF, on 3 September 1944.

CROMWELL TANK

1943 that disclosed the following state of affairs: priority had been completely reversed since the previous year and it was stated that the Cromwell had completed its acceptance trials and production had begun. On the other hand the Centaur had not yet been submitted for acceptance trials although production had begun anyway, and Cavalier had neither completed its trials, nor had production yet begun.

This, then, is roughly the state of affairs that applied when the Handbook for the Cromwell Mark I was published. In due course the type would run to eight marks, many of which would be up-gunned re-engined Centaurs. There would be numerous detail improvements over the next two years, notably to the driver's and front gunner's hatches, and the adoption of welding techniques to improve construction and reduce weight. Because of the long gestation period the Cromwell arrived on the scene at a time when the vast productive capacity of the United States was also making itself felt. Thus, the new tanks did not see any action until June 1944 when both Cromwells and Centaurs rolled down the ramps of the landing craft on to the Normandy beaches. By this time both the gun and the armour protection had been surpassed by the latest German developments, although the factors of speed and reliability remained as potent as ever. Centaurs served with the Royal Marines while the majority of Cromwells formed the armoured reconnaissance regiments of the British armoured divisions, backed up by the mass of Shermans.

INTRODUCTION

Cromwell Mark IVD or IVE, T187740, of 2nd Northamptonshire Yeomanry passes through Hérouvillette on 14 June 1944.

Cromwell Mark IVs of 2nd Battalion Welsh Guards, the Armoured Reconnaissance Regiment of the Guards Armoured Division, in July 1944.

CROMWELL TANK

Later developments

Most tanks that enter service continue to develop through a succession of marks in an attempt to keep pace with the latest requirements, and as a result of user experience. The Cromwell was no exception, but it reached a new peak in complication at the same time. This was due to a decision to classify some modifications by mark, and others by type. Since any one mark could appear in up to four different types, and some types applied to at least six different marks, the permutations were numerous and not a little confusing. This was further complicated by those Centaurs that exchanged their Liberty engines for

INTRODUCTION

Meteors, and thus became Cromwells.

A Centaur tank could be constructed as a Mark I or II with a 6-pounder gun, a Mark III with a 75mm or a Mark IV with a 95mm howitzer. If a Meteor engine was fitted, the tank became a Cromwell with a mark number appropriate to the latter. Cromwells were built as Marks I, V, VI and VII, but they too could change identity with a change of armament, or the addition of extra armour in some cases. The Type system followed an alphabetical progression, but it remained constant. No tank of one type would change into another. The features associated with these types were:

In mid-1943, this Cromwell Mark I was fitted with appliqué armour as part of an abortive project that looked at increasing the tank's protection.

CROMWELL TANK

Cruiser Mark VIII, A27L Centaur. This 6-pounder-armed Mark I has a Type B hull.

Centaurs of 5th Independent Armoured Support Battery, Royal Marines Armoured Support Group.

A Cromwell Mark IV in a prepared hull-down position is resupplied with ammunition near Sittard in Holland on 30 December 1944. The tank's unit markings have been obscured by the censor.

Type A
The earliest Cavaliers, Centaurs and Cromwells as built.

Type B
Centaurs and Cromwells fitted with the front gunner's escape hatch.

Type C
Centaurs and Cromwells with thinner (25mm) rear hull top plates and a revised pattern of air intake.

INTRODUCTION

Type D
Centaurs and Cromwells with a revised layout of engine compartment cover plates.

Type E
Late model Cromwells with modified final drive gear ratios to reduce top speed.

Type F
Late model Cromwells with a matching side escape hatch for the driver.

The various marks of Cromwell were as follows:

Mark I
The original version with the 6-pounder gun.

Mark II
A reworked tank with the hull machine-gunner and his weapon removed,

Vauxhall had planned to build the Cromwell Mark II, with this distinctive cast turret. It was cancelled and Vauxhall focused on Churchill production instead.

CROMWELL TANK

Cromwell Mark VI with Type F hull, showing driver's side-opening hatch and turret storage bins.

running on wider 15½in-wide tracks.

Mark III
A re-engined Centaur I.

Mark IV
A re-engined Centaur I or III with 75mm gun. Or a newly built model to this configuration.

Mark V
A reworked Cromwell I with the 75mm gun.

Mark Vw
A newly built Cromwell using welded construction and mounting a 75mm gun.

Mark VI
A reworked Centaur I or IV with 95mm howitzer, or a newly built Cromwell with the same weapon.

Mark VII
A reworked Cromwell IV with thicker (101mm) frontal armour and 15½in-wide tracks.

Mark VIIw
A reworked Cromwell Vw with thicker frontal armour and wide tracks, or newly built to the same standard.

Mark VIII
A reworked Cromwell IV with thicker frontal armour, wider tracks and mounting a 95mm howitzer.

T188257 is a Cromwell Mark IVF. This photograph shows it in use with 4th RTR in 1947/48.

A whitewashed Cromwell of 7th Armoured Division (The 'Desert Rats') moves through the Dutch town of Roermond on 16 January 1945.

CROMWELL TANK

A24 Cavalier Armoured Recovery Vehicle fitted with trunks for deep wading.

The 'w' suffix indicates those tanks in which welding techniques were employed instead of riveting. This allowed a reduction in the overall weight, and thus the opportunity for thicker armour.

Cromwells were also modified in more specific ways to undertake particular tasks, or to suit local requirements. In Normandy, the Culin Prong device fitted to some tanks was used to slice away the top of an earthen bank, avoiding the risk of exposing too much of the frail underside to anti-tank fire. Other tanks were equipped as

Cromwell ARV. These were conversions of existing tanks, mostly Mark IVs with Type C hulls. This vehicle began life as T189913.

Command Posts or Artillery Observer's Vehicles, carrying extra wireless equipment, so the main armament was removed. There was also an Armoured Recovery Vehicle version without a turret, which was equipped with the specialised gear needed to salvage tanks and repair them in the field.

The tanks were built by a variety of firms, among which Morris Motors, English Electric, the London Midland and Scottish Railway, and Leyland Motors are the best-known. Special prototypes were also built by Vauxhall Motors and Rolls-Royce themselves.

Cromwell ARV of 11th Armoured Division recovers a German Panzer IV, Normandy, July 1944.

Camouflaged Cromwell Mark IVF of 5th RTR.

Centaur Mark IIIC fitted with a Culin Prong hedgerow cutter for tests in September 1944. Production of the Prong did not begin until November by which time it was too late to be of any use.

31

CROMWELL TANK

'A tank in the field is worth ten in the shop'

CROMWELL I

SERVICE INSTRUCTION BOOK

This Publication has been produced to the instructions of
THE CHIEF INSPECTOR OF FIGHTING VEHICLES
to whom all communications should be addressed.

FIRST EDITION—1943

Note: The Service Instruction Book is an abridged version of the original and therefore any cross-references to pages and figure numbers contained in the text are no longer relevant.

VEHICLE HISTORY AND SPECIFICATION

Cromwell I Left-hand side view from front.

CROMWELL TANK

Cromwell I.—Front view.

Cromwell I.—Left-hand side view from rear.

INTRODUCTION

The Cromwell I is a heavy-weight fighting vehicle. The front part of the hull accommodates the crew of five, while the rear part houses the engine and transmission. The front part is further subdivided into a fighting compartment, a driver's compartment and a forward gunner's compartment. A partition, with access holes cut in it, separates the personnel in the fighting compartment from the driver and front gunner, while a similar partition, also with an access hole, separates the driver from the front gunner.

Single armour plate is used at the front and rear of the vehicle, but a double plate is placed at the sides, the outer plate of which affords protection to the suspension. The inner plate, on each side, carries five main suspension spring housings, each of which is attached to an axle arm (*see* Fig. 186). These arms are pivoted in bushes housed in the main suspension tubes which are attached to the floor plates (*see* Fig. 187).

The axle arms project through the outer side plates to carry five road wheels on each side of the vehicle, which run on tracks. The tracks are driven by double-toothed sprocket wheels at the rear of the vehicle and have tensioner wheels at the front.

The turret consists of double armour plated sides, the outer plates of which are bolted to the welded inner structure, and a single plate roof. It is rotated hydraulically.

Three main cooling air intakes are fitted, one at each side of the engine compartment roof and another on top of the roof. The air outlet louvres, of which there are three, are at the rear.

The hull is sealed against water ingress to a depth of 4 ft., by means of a fording flap in the lower air outlet louvre.

There are four external access doors, one to the driver's compartment, two in the turret roof and one to the front gunner's compartment, which can also be used as an emergency escape door.

For fire fighting, $C.O._2$ carbon dioxide apparatus is provided.

A 12-cylinder V-type engine is installed, which is connected to a dry twin-plate clutch. From this clutch the power is transmitted through a five-speed gearbox to the final drives on which the driving sprockets are mounted.

The main oil and fuel tanks are located on each side of the engine, while the coolant radiators are installed at the rear of the engine compartment.

Steering is accomplished through controlled epicyclics and the turning circle is dependent upon the gear ratio selected by the driver. The clutch, steering and track brakes are all hydraulically operated.

It is important to remember that the vehicle will turn about its axis with the gear in neutral (see Fig. 5).

The vehicle has been designed so that the crew can be as comfortable as practicable, and yet at the same time all available space has been used to the maximum advantage. In this way, the vehicle presents the smallest possible target for its fire power and weight.

CROMWELL TANK

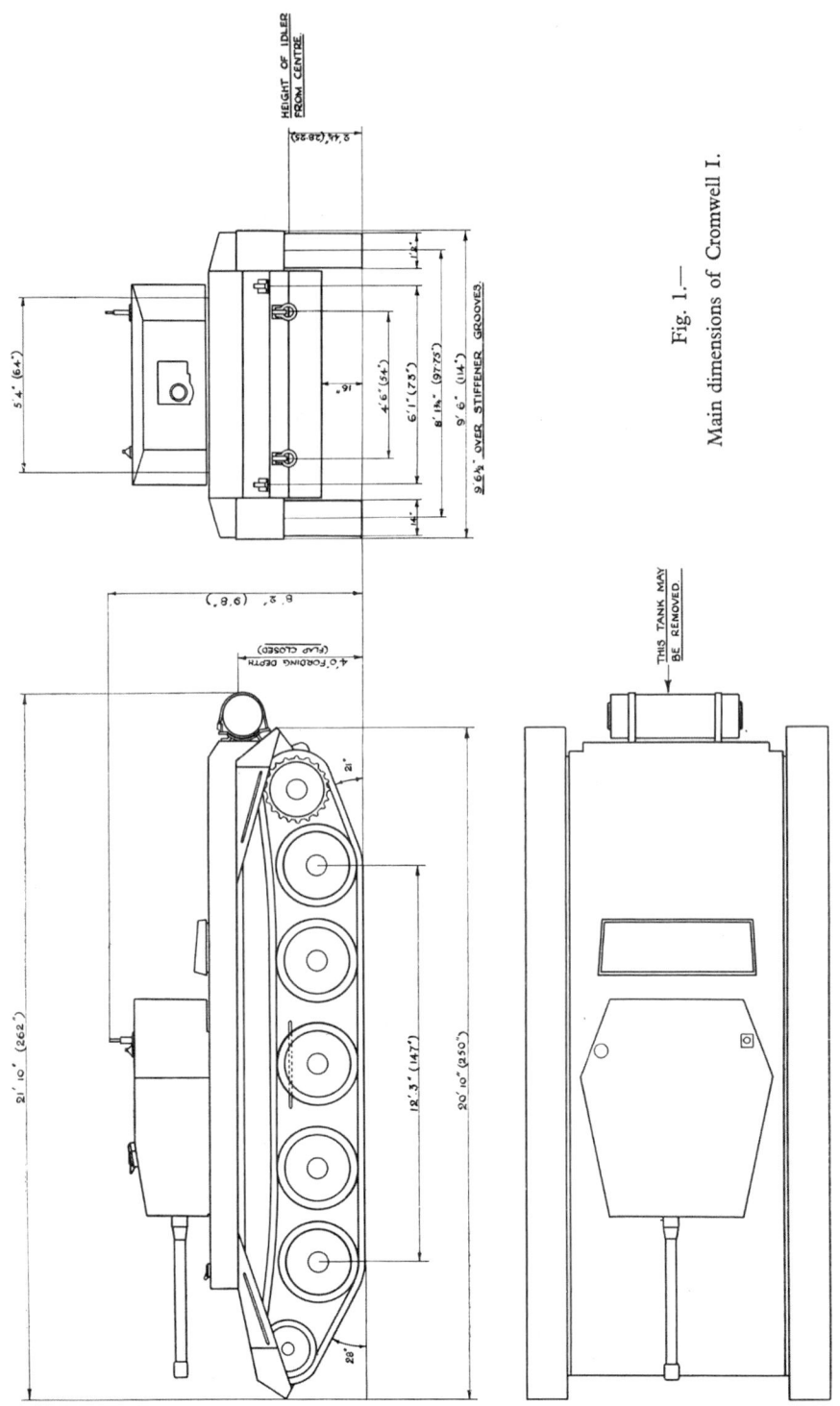

Fig. 1.— Main dimensions of Cromwell I.

VEHICLE SPECIFICATION

Weight	27 tons (approx.) fully stowed, including crew.
Power weight ratio	22 to 1 b.h.p./tons.
Overall length	20 ft. 10 in.
Overall width	9 ft. 6½ in. (over stiffener grooves).
Overall height	8 ft. 2 in. (maximum over aerial mounting).
Crew	Total 5 (commander, two gunners, loader and driver).
Armament	One 6-pdr. ⎫ co-axially mounted in turret. One 7·92 mm. Besa M.G. ⎭ One 7·92 mm. Besa M.G. (in front gunner's compartment). One P.L.M. mtg., with twin Vickers A.A. guns. One Thompson sub-M.G. One 2 in. smoke bombthrower.
Ammunition	6-pdr. ... 75 rounds. Besa M.G. ... 4,950 " Vickers A.A. guns ... 2,000 " Thompson sub-M.G. ... 320 " Bombthrower ... 30 "
W/T set	No. 19 set (in rear of turret).
Suspension	10 road wheels independently sprung; 8 shock absorbers (four each side).
Engine	12-cyl. 60° V-type, pressure liquid cooled petrol engine.
Clutch	Dry twin-plate, hydraulically operated, 16 in. diameter (O.D. of driven plates).
Fuel tanks	2—capacity { R.H., 60 galls. } 1 auxiliary—capacity 30 galls. (if fitted). { L.H., 56 galls. }
Oil tanks	2—capacity { R.H., 8½ galls. { L.H., 6 galls.
Cooling	1 header tank ⎫ capacity 14 galls. (approx). 2 radiators ⎭
Engine starting	Electric starter motor mounted on bevel gearbox.
Range (on acceptance test)	Road, 87-174 miles ⎫ without auxiliary tank. Cross country, 58-87 miles ⎭
Road speed	40 m.p.h. at 2,550 r.p.m.
Turret traverse	Hydraulic pump driven through bevel gearbox from engine. Traverse motor mounted in turret and geared to turret ring. Auxiliary hand traverse.
Gearbox	Z.5 type. Five forward speeds and reverse. Ratios:—Reverse 22·894 to 1 3rd ... 2·855 to 1 1st ... 11·643 to 1 4th ... 1·807 to 1 2nd ... 4·593 to 1 5th ... 1·343 to 1
Final drive	Twin-type sprockets each side of hull at rear. Ratio 3·71 to 1.
Steering gears	Epicyclic gears, controlled by hydraulically operated brakes.
Road brakes	Internally expanding type, hydraulically operated by foot pedal.
Length of track on ground	12 ft. 3 in.
Track centres	8 ft. 1¾ in.
Track pressure	13·27 lb. per sq. in.—15½ in. tracks. 14·7 lb. per sq. in.—14 in. tracks.
Vertical obstacle crossed	3 ft. 0 in.
Gap crossed	7 ft. 9 in. (with flat approach).
Height of idler from centre	2 ft. 4¼ in.
Ground clearance	16 in. (approx.).
Fording depth	4 ft. 0 in. (still water with flap closed).
Access doors	Turret roof ... 2 Driver's roof ... 1 Front gunner's roof ... 1
Battery charging	Dynamo, driven through bevel gearbox from engine. Auxiliary charging set in fighting compartment.
Water tanks	12 galls. (fitted in turret).

CROMWELL TANK

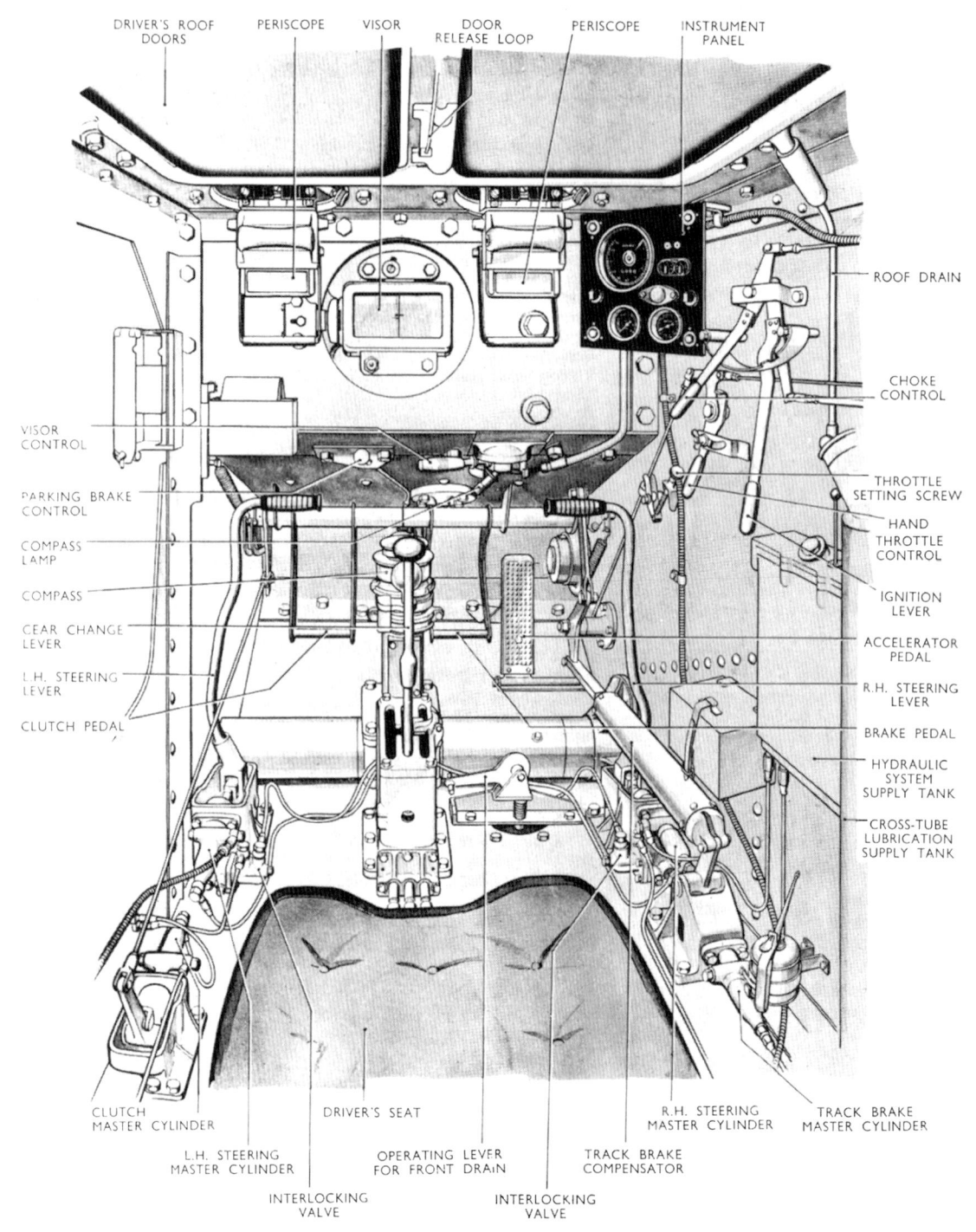

Fig. 3.—Driver's compartment and controls.

DRIVING INSTRUCTIONS

The driver's compartment is situated in the right-hand side of the nose of the vehicle. Access to it is either by the doors in the roof above the seat, or, should these be shut, through the doors in the fighting compartment roof and the hole in the forward compartment bulkhead.

The controls can be brought within easy reach of any driver, by adjustment of the seat position (*see* Chapter VI A). A general view of the compartment is given in Fig. 3, which should be carefully studied by all new drivers.

PREPARATION OF VEHICLE BY CREW.

When starting up each morning, certain duties must be performed by the crew, and, as these duties are closely connected, the complete procedure is given below:—

(*a*) **The Tank Commander.**
  (1) Ensure that the vehicle is correctly stowed and that water, rations, ammunition and other equipment are carried as ordered.
  (2) Check that fire extinguishers are full.
  (3) Assist operator to check external communications on W/T set, etc.
  (4) Inspect vehicle to make certain that all is correct before moving off.

(*b*) **The Driver.**
  (1) Check that main and auxiliary (if fitted) fuel tanks are full.
  (2) Test that coolant and engine oil levels are correct.
  (3) Test that the five flame switches are operating.
  (4) Inspect engine and transmission compartments for oil, fuel and coolant leaks. The floor must be clean and dry. Rectify any leaks and report if normal tightening will not cure.
  (5) Make sure that no paper, rags, waste, etc., is left on track guards on engine compartment roof.
  (6) Instruct front gunner to start engine.
  (7) While engine is running inspect engine again for oil, fuel and coolant leaks. If any leaks are detected, stop engine and proceed again as at (4).
  (8) Listen carefully for faulty running. Check both magnetos by instructing gunner to switch off each in turn.
  (9) When engine is warm instruct gunner to stop by switching OFF ignition.
  (10) Re-check engine oil level and top up if necessary.
  (11) Close all engine and transmission covers, make certain that wire handles on front covers are fully down to prevent fouling the turret.
  (12) Check that all plates and plugs are in position in hull floor. Instruct wireless operator to open and close rear sump valve, and gunner to work rota-trailer release and auxiliary fuel tank release (if fitted). Check external stowage.
  (13) Enter driver's seat, switch OFF exterior lights and close flaps. Start up engine and instruct gunner to traverse turret in both directions by hand and power. Set hand throttle to correct idling speed and switch off engine.
  (14) Inspect Triplex block and operation of visor and seat.

(*c*) **The Wireless Operator.**
  (1) Start up auxiliary charging set if necessary.
  (2) Check W/T sets as instructed in Wireless Manual.
  (3) Test turret lights and ventilating fan for correct operation.
  (4) Operate rear sump valve when instructed by driver.
  (5) Check operation of periscopes and revolver ports. Also test 2-in. bombthrower by cocking and pressing trigger. Dry clean bore if firing is expected.
  (6) Stow waterproof sheets and camouflage nets.
  (7) Instruct front gunner to switch ON exterior lights and check that all lights are operating correctly.

CROMWELL TANK

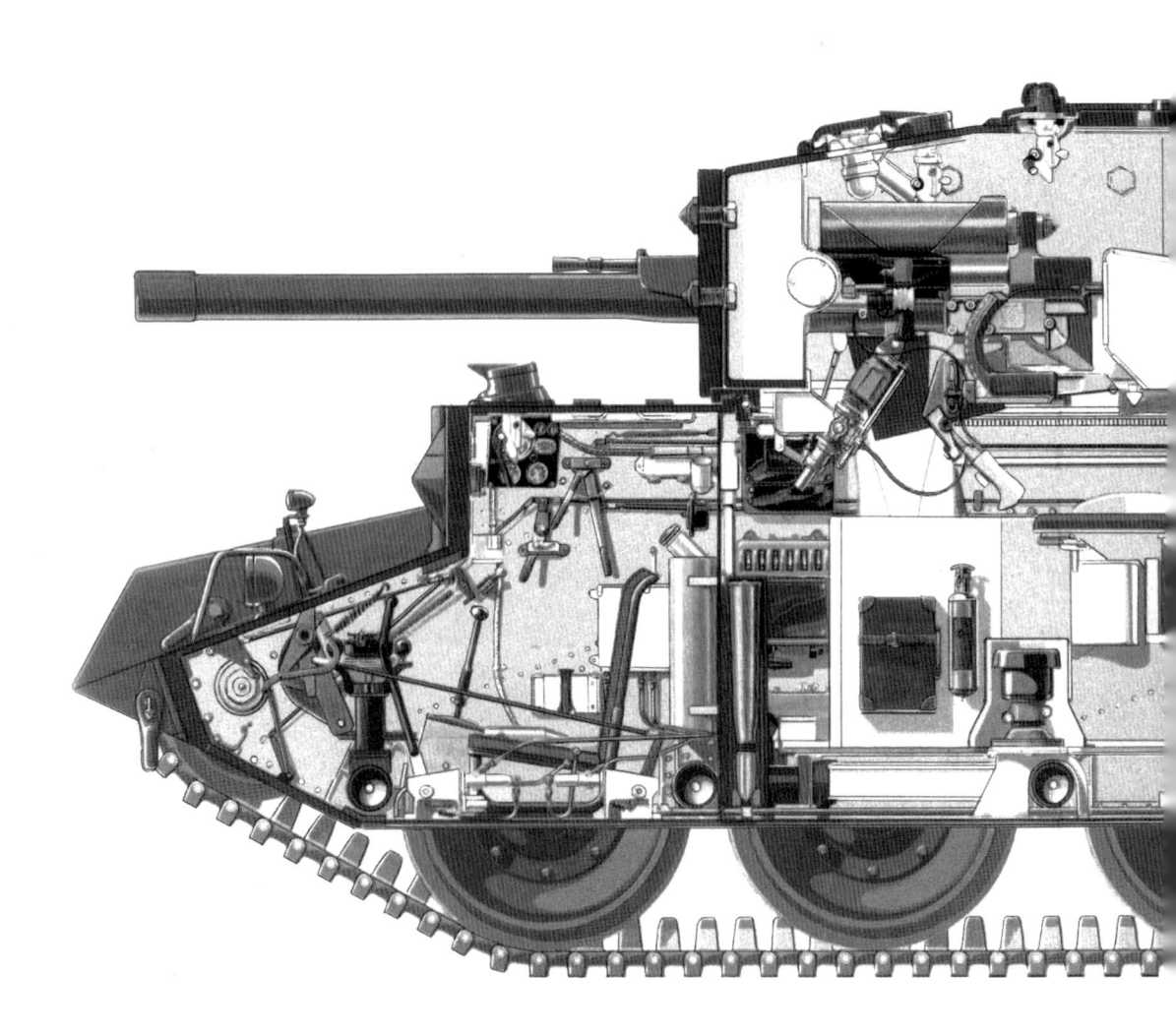

VEHICLE HISTORY AND SPECIFICATION

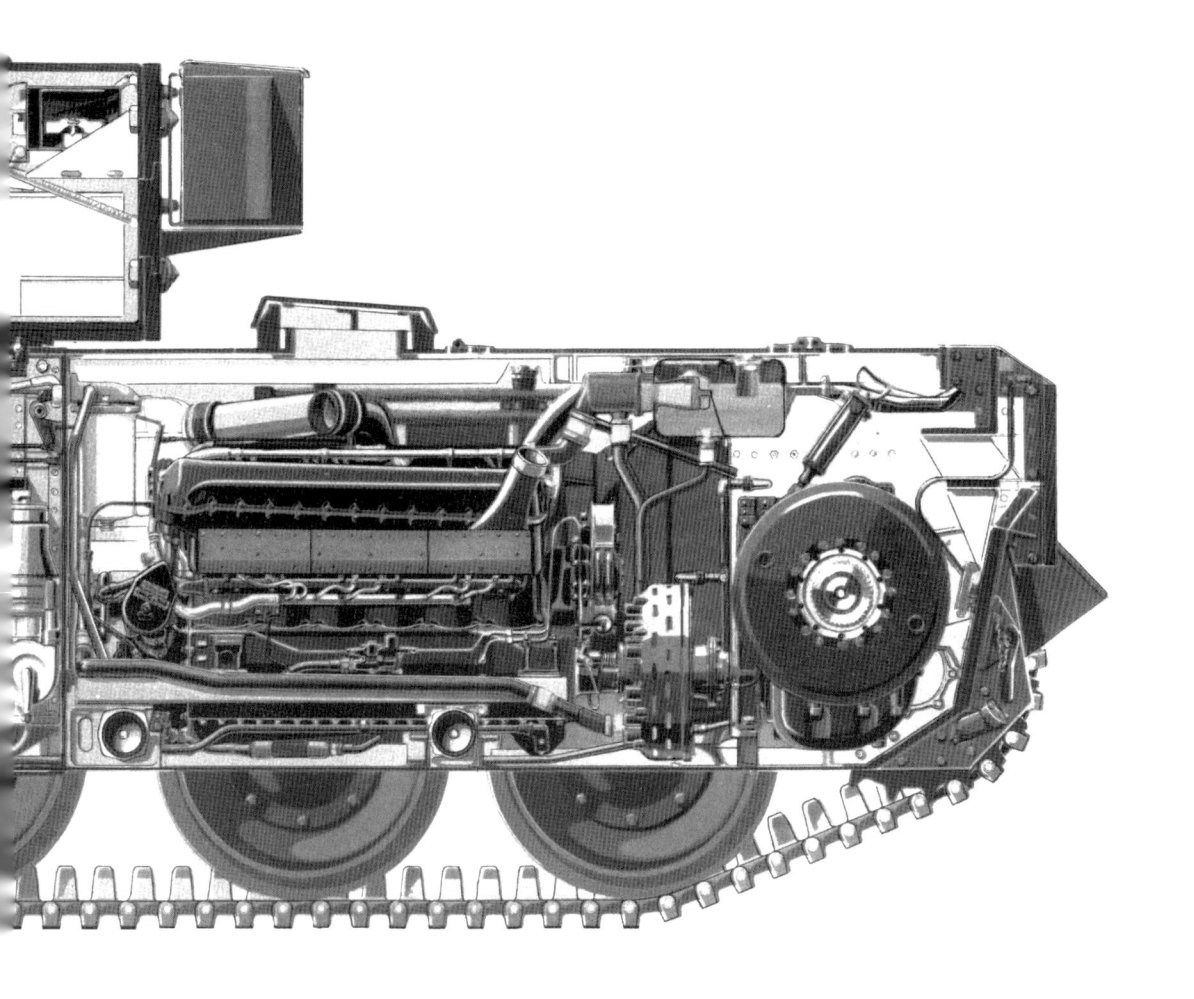

CROMWELL TANK

(d) **The Front Gunner.**

   (1) Switch ON battery cut-off switch and yellow warning light will glow.
   (2) Remove safety screws from pins of both CO_2 bottles.
   (3) Check level of fluid in hydraulic reservoir, and level of oil in suspension tube lubrication reservoir.
   (4) Test operation of sump valve in driver's compartment and free movement of both steering levers, clutch pedal and brake pedal.
   (5) Test operation of each steering interlock valve, by holding one lever fully back and checking that the movement on the opposite lever does not exceed $\frac{5}{8}$ in.
   (6) Apply foot-brake and engage locking ratchet.
   (7) Make certain that gear lever is in neutral and steering levers fully forward.
   (8) Move carburetter strangler control lever *fully* back.
   (9) Switch ON ignition, depress clutch pedal and instruct gunner to operate Ki-gass priming pump.
   (10) Press starter button and red warning light will glow. Release as soon as engine fires. If engine does not start, release starter button and try again. *When engine is running do not touch steering levers.*
   (11) As soon as engine will run without strangling, return carburetter strangler control lever to forward position. *Never use Ki-gass pump on a warm engine, but careful use of the carburetter strangler control lever is permissible provided care is taken to avoid excess rich mixture.*
   (12) Engage clutch pedal, being prepared to switch OFF immediately should vehicle start to "swing" in neutral.
   (13) Warm up engine by setting hand throttle to give medium speed.
   (14) Check all gauge readings. Engine oil pressure should rise immediately when the engine starts. Test panel and compass lights, also front gunner's light and fan. Set speedometer trip to zero.
   (15) When instructed by driver, switch OFF engine, and when instructed by wireless operator, switch ON all exterior lights and open driver's flap.
   (16) Enter front gunner's compartment and carry out first parade on gun, ammunition and stowage.
   (17) Check that machine gun is secure on its mounting. Prove gun and then test firing gear and oil frictional surfaces as necessary. See that deflector and chute are secure. Dry clean bore if firing is expected.
   (18) Test seat and brow-pad and check that telescope and periscope are clean.
   (19) Check that all spares, tools, M.G. oil can and plugs are clean and stowed, also that all stowage and ammunition are correct in this compartment.

(e) **The Gunner.**

   (1) Turn on light above powered traverse filter, check oil level in recuperator and pump handle until indicator shows "full".
   (2) Check that control handle of variflow pump is in OFF position.
   (3) Turn ON fuel tap, and when instructed by front gunner, unscrew the Ki-gass knob and inject three pumpfuls of fuel into induction system. *Screw up knob tightly after use.* The use of this pump is only necessary under very cold conditions.
   (4) When instructed by driver, depress each magneto emergency stop switch in turn. Set turret speedometer trip to zero.
   (5) When instructed by driver, operate rota-trailer release and also auxiliary fuel tank release (if fitted).
   (6) Examine 6-pr. breech mechanism for dirt, rust or other defects. Oil lightly, frictional surfaces if necessary. See that all nuts and bolts and pins on the mountings are tight. Test firing gear. See that deflector and chute are secure, also test elevation and depression. See that S.A. cam is at S.A. Examine level of oil in buffer cylinder and top up if necessary, examining for leakage. Dry clean bore if firing is expected, and replace muzzle cover.
   (7) Check that co-axial gun is secure in its mounting, prove the gun, then test the firing gear and oil frictional surfaces if necessary. See that deflector and chute are secure. Dry clean the bore if firing is expected.

(8) Test seat, brow-pad, commander's hatch and mounting lock. Check that telescope and periscope are clean.

(9) Prove first, then test action of A/A machine gun. Prove and test Thompson machine gun by cocking and pressing trigger, controlling bolt action. Oil frictional surfaces if necessary. Check the elevation and traverse of the P.L.M. mounting and finally clamp with handle bars horizontal. Dry clean the bore of these weapons if firing is expected, and slightly oil the chamber of the carbine.

(10) See that spare parts and tools, especially the spare striker case, Wesco and M.G. oil cans, clearing plugs and cleaning rods are clean and correctly stowed.

(11) Test powered traverse system for air, and bleed if necessary. Remove all obstructions and, when instructed by driver, traverse once by hand and in each direction by power. With aid of wireless operator, test operation of depression stop while traversing.

(12) Inspect front of engine compartment and bevel gearbox for leaks.

When parking the vehicle, turn OFF the fuel tap and switch OFF the battery cut-off switch.

DRIVING THE VEHICLE.

Learn to handle the vehicle properly on a good road before venturing into rough and open country.

With the engine running:—

(1) See that the carburetter strangler control lever is in the forward position.

(2) Release the parking brake by pressing fully on the brake pedal and pulling ratchet control knob.

(3) Depress clutch pedal, and when this is right down, engage gear required. If any difficulty is experienced in engaging the gear, ease one of the steering levers just sufficiently to take up the free movement only. The gear can then be engaged easily.

> *Note.*—First gear should only be used in confined spaces, on steep inclines or when sharp turns are required. Otherwise always start in second gear.

(4) Slowly accelerate the engine and, at the same time, release clutch pedal. The clutch should be engaged at low engine revs., whenever possible.

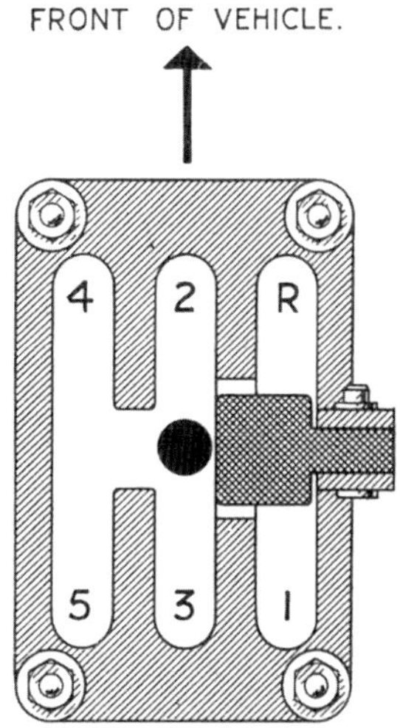

Gear-changing:—

Fig. 4.—Gear change gate.

Normal double-declutching methods must be used for all gear changing.

When the vehicle is moving, accelerate the engine until the vehicle speed is 5 m.p.h., and engage the next (third) gear. When driving on a level surface the vehicle should be in third gear within 6-10 yards of the starting point. While driving on hard ground make the slightest pause in the gate, but when crossing soft ground move straight through the gate without hesitation. Always use sharp, clean movements when going through the gate.

Do not attempt to change gear when steering. To change from third to fourth gear proceed as above with the vehicle running at 10 m.p.h., and finally change from fourth to top at 15 m.p.h.

Before changing-up while driving across country, and particularly on soft ground, depress the accelerator; then change gear. When stopping on an incline for any period, do not rely solely on the brakes. Stop the engine and engage a gear.

Ignition lever.—This lever is not required for use with the Meteor engine and is therefore disconnected.

Accelerator hand lever.—This enables the driver to control the engine speed by hand. The lever can be fixed in any given position by tightening the thumb-screw, as when using the power traverse gear with the vehicle stationary.

Slow-running screw.—This is provided for increasing the idling speed of the engine which, for normal running, is governed by the carburetter jet settings.

CROMWELL TANK

To check oil pressure.—The only definite method of checking the minimum engine oil pressure is to drive the vehicle at 9 m.p.h. in second gear when the engine is hot. The oil gauge should then show a pressure of at least 25 lb. per sq. in.

STEERING.

Do not snatch the steering levers, but use a firm steady pull.

Do not steer and use your main brake at the same time.

Do not touch either lever when the engine is idling.

STEERING FORWARD.

The vehicle is steered by altering the relative track speeds, and it follows, therefore, that by increasing the forward speed of the right-hand track the vehicle will turn to the left, and vice versa.

Steering control is by means of right and left-hand steering brake levers, one on each side of the driver's seat (*see* Fig. 3).

To turn the vehicle to the *left*, pull back the *left*-hand steering lever. To turn the vehicle to the *right*, pull back the *right*-hand steering lever.

Should the vehicle be moving forward on the higher gears and a sharp turn is required, the driver must change down to a lower gear.

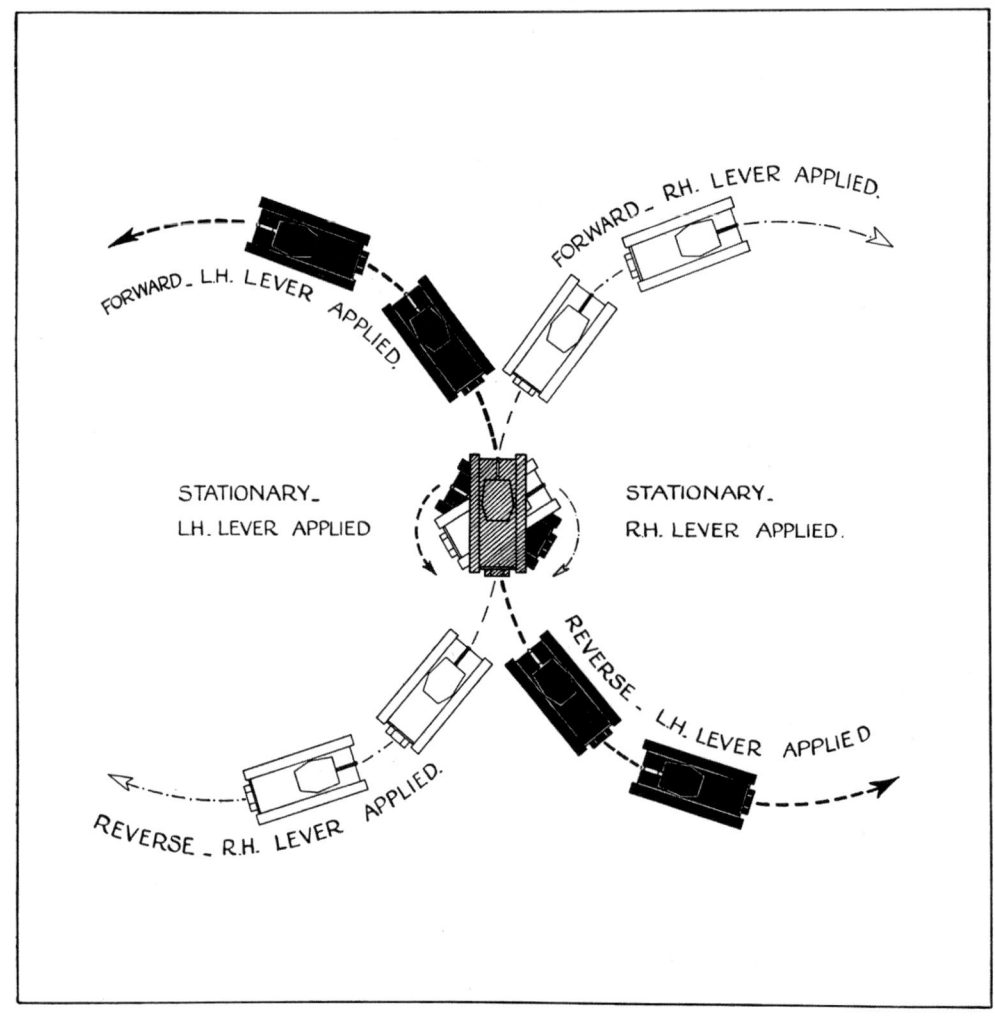

Fig. 5.—Diagram showing operation of steering levers.

STEERING IN REVERSE.

Remembering that you are seated *facing forwards*, to cause the rear end of the vehicle to turn to *your* left, pull the *right*-hand lever. For the rear end of the vehicle to move to your *right*, pull the *left*-hand lever. This can more readily be understood on referring to Fig. 5 which shows that no matter in what direction the vehicle is moving, pulling the *right*-hand lever turns its nose to the right and its tail to the left, while pulling the *left*-hand lever turns its nose to the left and its tail to the right.

BRAKING AND STOPPING.

To slow down or stop, apply the foot brake, which actuates the hydraulically operated track brakes fitted between the gearbox output shaft and the final drive. When stopping, declutch and move the gear lever into neutral.

Before getting out of driver's compartment:—
    (1) Apply the parking brake (*see* Fig. 3).
    (2) Switch OFF engine ignition.
    (3) Switch OFF battery cut-off switch.
    (4) Turn fuel tap handwheel (in fighting compartment) to OFF position.

STEERING CHARACTERISTICS.

(1) **In gear, clutch disengaged.**—Steering effective as long as vehicle is moving, but steering effort will slow down vehicle.

(2) **In neutral, clutch engaged.**—Steering effective according to engine r.p.m., whether vehicle stationary or moving. Steering effort will tend to stall engine unless the latter is accelerated.

(3) **In neutral, clutch disengaged.**—No steering under any conditions.

Note.—If steering is applied while changing gear, it becomes operative immediately the gear is engaged, i.e. before the clutch is engaged (*also see* Chapter IV A).

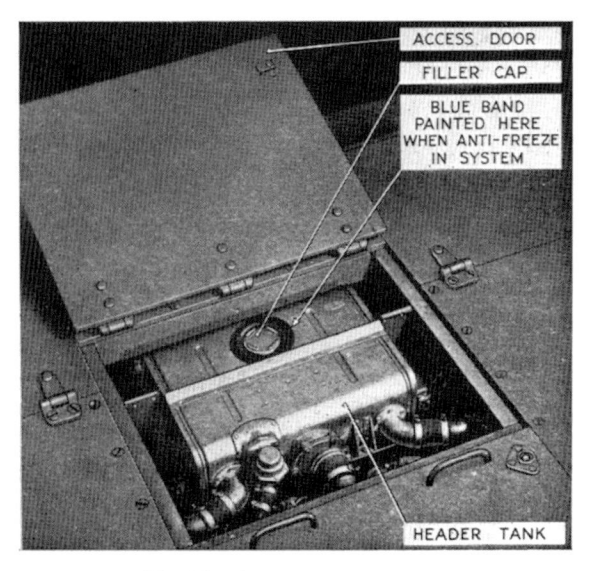

Fig. 5A.—Access to header tank.

CROMWELL TANK

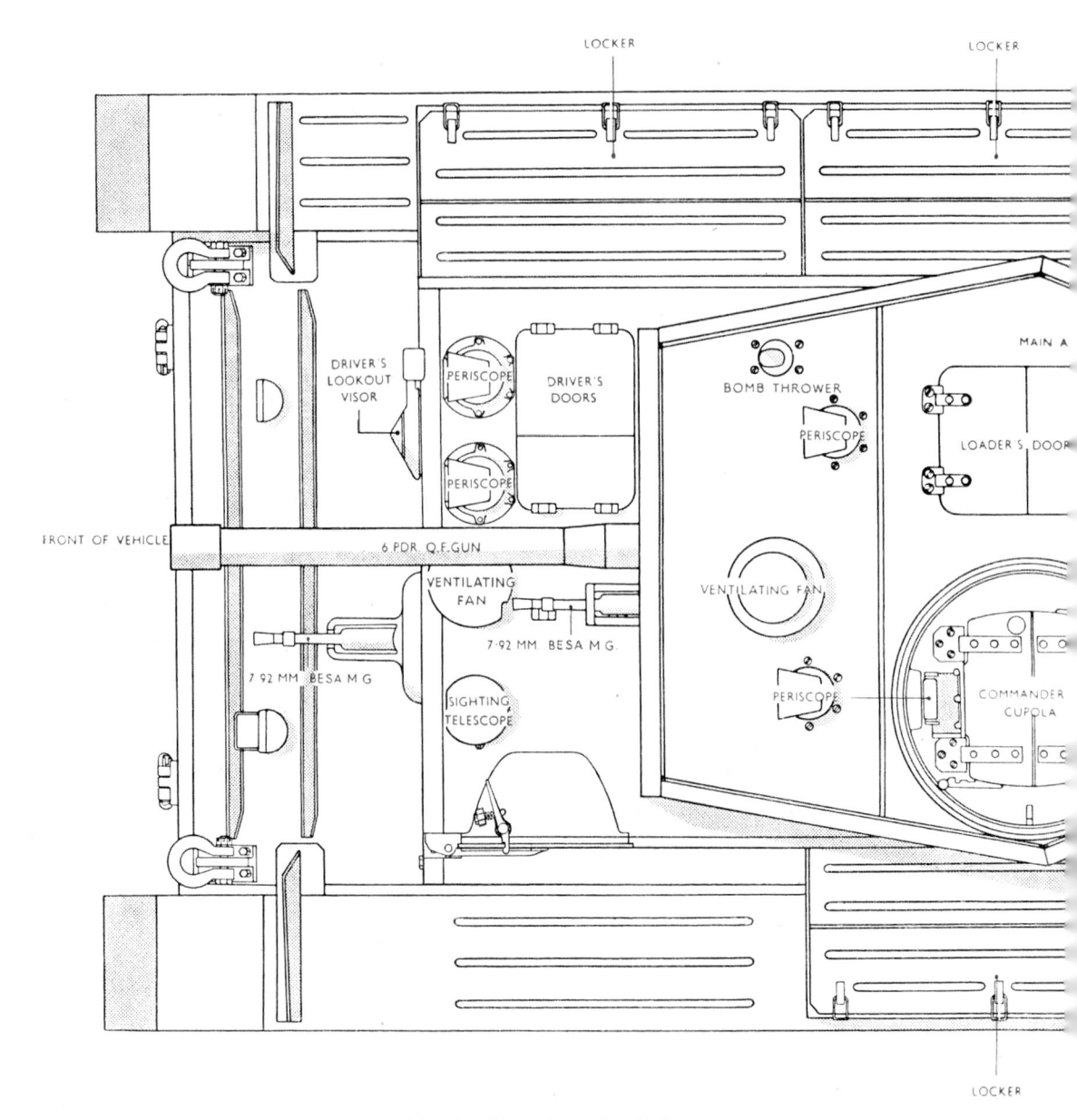

Fig. 6.—Plan view of vehicle.

VEHICLE HISTORY AND SPECIFICATION

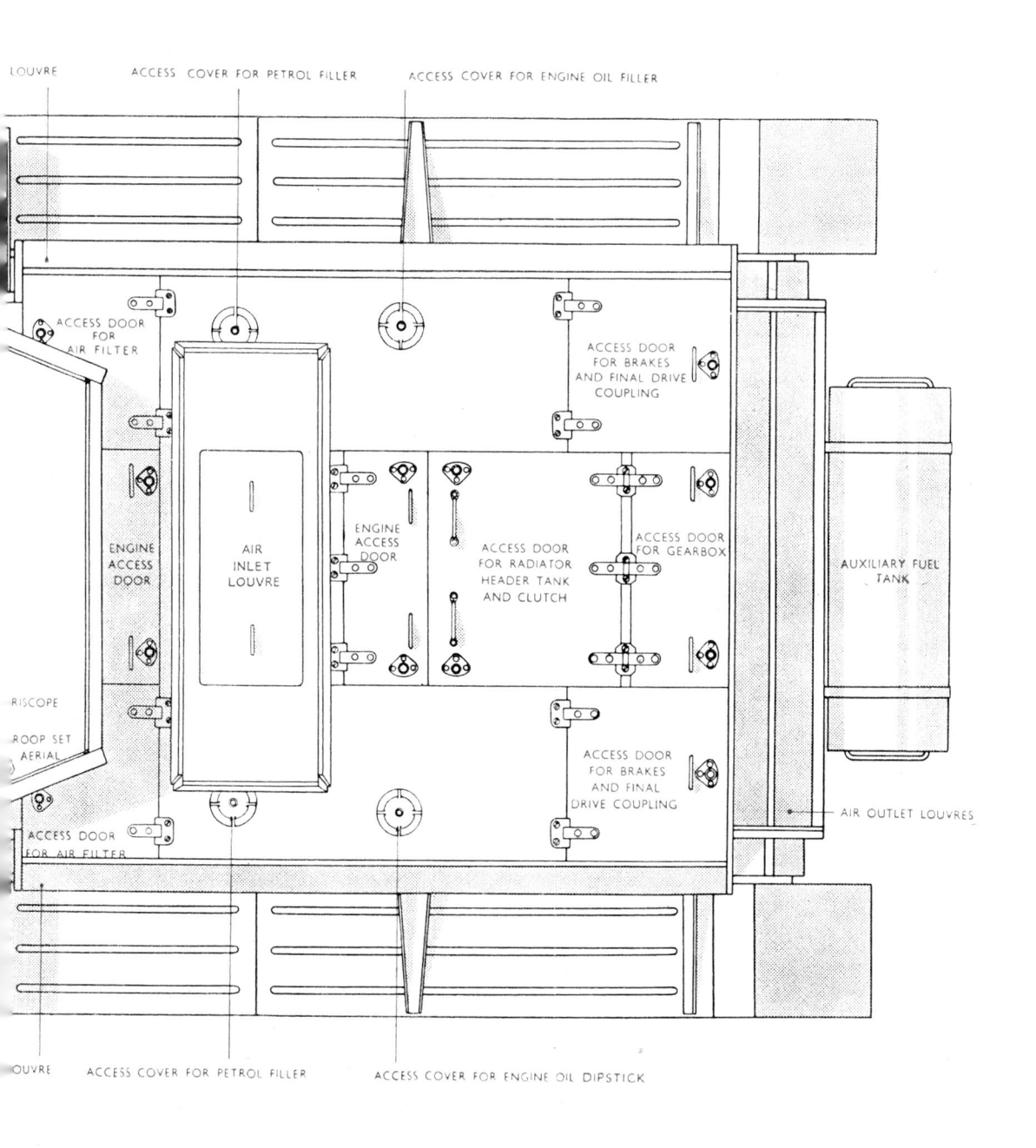

[Engine deck plan view with labels:]

- LOUVRE
- ACCESS COVER FOR PETROL FILLER
- ACCESS COVER FOR ENGINE OIL FILLER
- ACCESS DOOR FOR AIR FILTER
- ACCESS DOOR FOR BRAKES AND FINAL DRIVE COUPLING
- ENGINE ACCESS DOOR
- AIR INLET LOUVRE
- ENGINE ACCESS DOOR
- ACCESS DOOR FOR RADIATOR HEADER TANK AND CLUTCH
- ACCESS DOOR FOR GEARBOX
- AUXILIARY FUEL TANK
- PERISCOPE
- TROOP SET AERIAL
- ACCESS DOOR FOR BRAKES AND FINAL DRIVE COUPLING
- AIR OUTLET LOUVRES
- ACCESS DOOR FOR AIR FILTER
- LOUVRE
- ACCESS COVER FOR PETROL FILLER
- ACCESS COVER FOR ENGINE OIL DIPSTICK

CROMWELL TANK

THE ENGINE

LEADING PARTICULARS

1. **GENERAL.**
   - Type of engine ... ... Normally aspirated, pressure-liquid-cooled V-engine.
   - Number of cylinders ... ... 12.
   - Arrangement of cylinders ... ... Two lines of six cylinders forming a 60° V.
   - Bore ... ... 5·4 in. (137·16 mm.).
   - Stroke ... ... 6·0 in. (152·4 mm.).
   - Capacity ... ... 1,649 cu. in. (27 litres).
   - Compression ratio ... ... 6 to 1.
   - R.A.C. rating ... ... 140 h.p.
   - B.H.P. ... ... 570 to 600 at 2,550 r.p.m.
   - Torque ... ... 1,450 lb./ft. at 1,500 r.p.m.
   - Cylinder numbering ... ... From fan drive end—1A, 2A, 3A, 4A, 5A, 6A, 1B, 2B, 3B, 4B, 5B, 6B.
   - Firing order ... ... 1A, 2B, 5A, 4B, 3A, 1B, 6A, 5B, 2A, 3B, 4A, 6B.
   - Nominal governed speed ... ... 2,550 r.p.m.

2. **FUEL.**
   - Type ... ... 67 octane upwards (Pool).
   - Consumption ... ... Road—·75 to 1·5 miles per gallon.
   - Cross country—·5 to ·75 miles per gallon.

3. **OIL.**
   - Type ... ... 10 H.D. (M.160).
   - Consumption ... ... 40 miles per gallon (approx.).
   - Pressures—
     - Main ... ... Minimum—35 lb. per sq. in. at 2,550 r.p.m.
     - Auxiliary ... ... Minimum—3 lb. per sq. in.

4. **IGNITION.**
   - Number and type of magnetos ... ... Two F.S.T./12/R, G/2.
   - Number per cylinder and type of sparking plug Two RC76/2.
   - Magneto timing—
     - Fully retarded ... ... Inlet 5° before T.D.C.
     - Exhaust 10° before T.D.C.
   - Contact breaker gap ... ... 0·012 in.
   - Sparking plug gap ... ... 0·012 in.

5. **CARBURATION.**
   - Carburetters ... ... Two 56 – DC.

6. **VALVES.**
   - Valve timing ... ... Inlet opens 7° before T.D.C.
     - Inlet closes 45° after B.D.C.
     - Exhaust opens 45° before B.D.C.
     - Exhaust closes 7° after T.D.C.
   - Valve clearance ... ... 0·030 in. for timing.
     - 0·020 in. for running.

7. **COOLANT.**
   - Type ... ... 100% pure water or pure water plus ethylene-glycol (see "Frost Precautions").
   - Maximum outlet temperature ... ... 110° C. – (230° F.).

8. **STARTING SYSTEM.**
   - Type ... ... Electric turning gear.

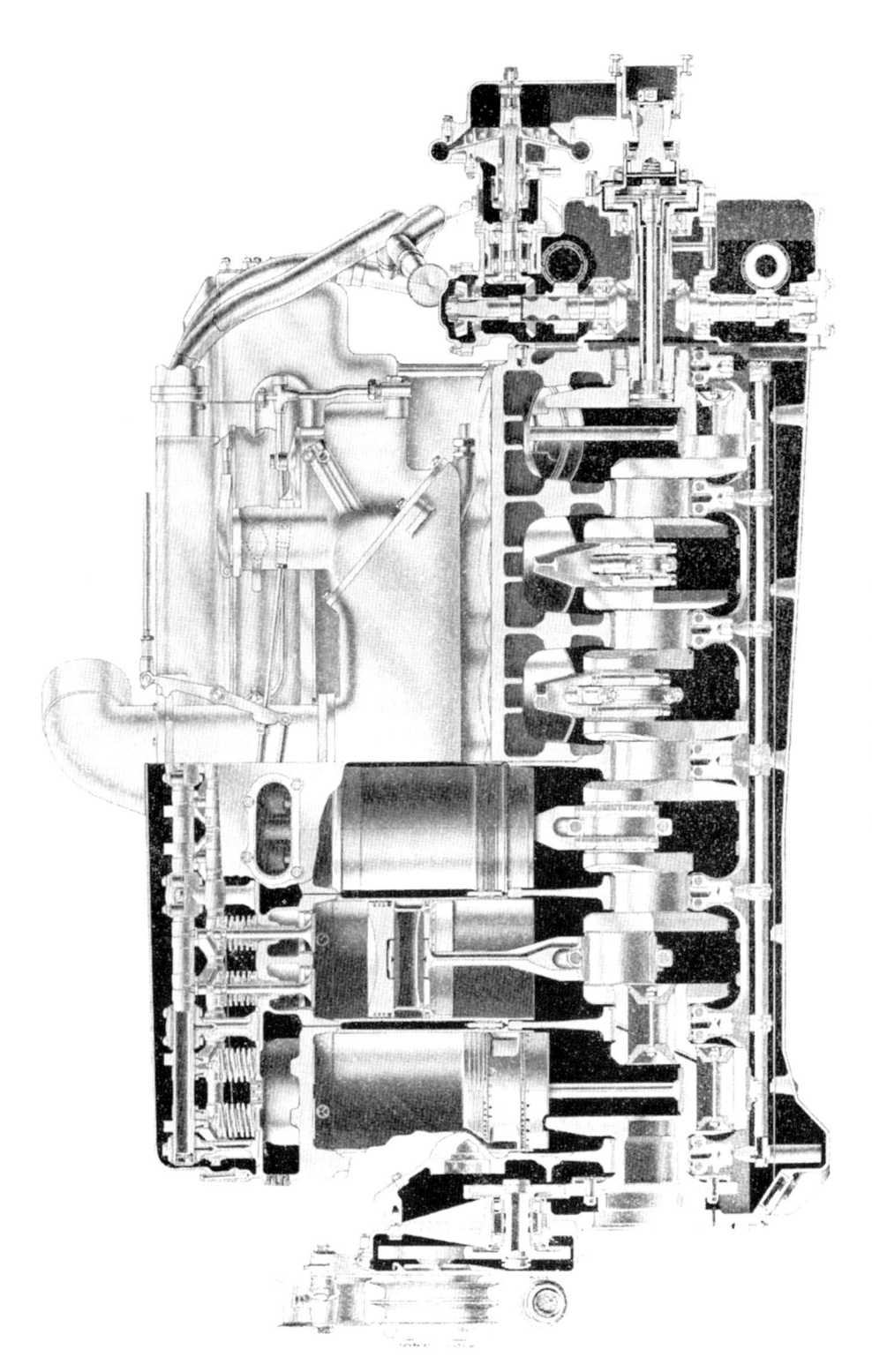

Fig. 9.—Section through engine.

INTRODUCTION

The Meteor tank-engine (*see* Figs. 9, 10 and 11) is of the 12-cylinder type, having two integral pressure-liquid-cooled banks of six cylinders forming a 60° V, and is designed to operate on 67 octane fuel.

The two monobloc non-detachable-head cylinder blocks are mounted on inclined upper faces of the crankcase, and are designated "A" and "B" banks respectively, the "A" bank being on the left-hand side of the engine when viewed from the fan drive end. The "A" (left-hand) side camshaft cover bears the cylinder firing order plate. The separate steel liners are of the wet type and are provided with shoulders at each end which abut against the cylinder block and crankcase respectively. Each cylinder has *four* valves—two inlet and two exhaust valves and two sparking plugs. The valves of each cylinder block are operated from single centrally-disposed overhead camshafts through a system of individual tappet fingers.

The balanced six-throw crankshaft is supported within the crankcase in seven lead-bronze lined main bearings. The connecting rods are H-section steel forgings and are of the plain type on the "A" (left-hand) side, and of the forked type on the "B" (right-hand) side. A divided steel block is bolted to the forked rod and retains a flanged thin lead-bronze lined steel shell in

Fig. 10.—Meteor I—left-hand or "A" side.

Fig. 11.—Meteor I—right-hand or "B" side.

its bore, which works directly on the crankpin. Similar split bearing shells are fitted to the plain rod, working on the outer surface of the forked rod block.

Bolted to one end of the crankcase is the fan drive unit and mounted at the other end of it is the wheelcase which houses the gear wheel assemblies transmitting the drive to the camshafts and wheelcase accessories. The gears are driven from the crankshaft through a torsionally flexible shaft which acts as a spring drive. Twisting of this shaft is positively limited, and torsional oscillations are damped by a special friction drive. The shaft also serves to smooth out irregularities in angular velocity and torque in the drive between the crankshaft and auxiliary components. The wheelcase provides mountings for the magnetos, coolant pump, fuel pumps and oil pumps. An electric starter, mounted vertically in the Fighting Compartment adjacent to the engine bulkhead, is connected to the outer end of the spring drive shaft by a circular flanged coupling.

Carburation is provided by two twin-choke up-draught type carburetters, located below the induction manifolds between the cylinder blocks, fuel being supplied to them from the pumps mounted one on each side of the wheelcase.

The lubrication system is of the dry sump type, and one pressure pump and two scavenge pumps are employed. These three pumps are mounted on the wheelcase, the two scavenge pumps on the "B" (right-hand) side and the pressure pump on the "A" (left-hand) side of this unit. One scavenge pump drains the crankcase and the other the wheelcase. A proportion of the main pressure oil is transformed by a reducing relief valve to low-pressure, for the purpose of lubricating the fan drive unit, camshafts and wheelcase drives.

The final drive is transmitted by means of a shaft, the forward end of which is splined to the crankshaft. Midway along this shaft is a circular flange to which is bolted the clutch. An electrical governor incorporated in each magneto prevents the maximum engine speed from being exceeded. The magnetos also carry an automatic timing device for advancing the spark as the engine speed is increased.

MAINTENANCE.

Maintenance on the Meteor engine has been cut to a minimum under the workshop overhaul period, and is confined to certain items of the ignition, fuel, oil and cooling systems which are dealt with under their appropriate headings. Such things as tightness of nuts, pipe unions and hose connections must be checked and engine control linkages oiled EVERY 250 MILES.

CARBURETTER AND INDUCTION ASSEMBLY

The carburetter and induction assembly consists of a complete unit which is mounted between the cylinder blocks (*see* Fig. 115), and is fully described in Part 2, Chapter I B.

MAINTENANCE.

No maintenance or adjustment is necessary under the workshop overhaul period, as the various carburetter jets have been carefully set by the manufacturers and are kept free of dirt and dust by means of a fuel filter which must be regularly serviced (*see* Part 4, Chapter I A).

AIR CLEANERS

Two oil bath type air cleaners are installed at the forward end of the engine compartment above the end of each fuel tank, being secured in position to the fighting compartment bulkhead. With the flap open, air is drawn from the fighting compartment, so providing additional ventilation for the crew. Should this become undesirable, as for instance when causing a draught in cold weather, the flap should be closed. Air is then drawn from the engine compartment, but it is recommended that air is drawn from the fighting compartment whenever possible. The cleaners are reached by opening access doors in the roof of the engine compartment.

MAINTENANCE.

This entirely depends on both climatic and geographical conditions, and may vary from 1,000 MILES under ideal conditions to DAILY under extremely dusty conditions.

Dismantling.
  (1) Remove induction pipe coupling from the cleaner outlet and plug the end of the induction pipe with clean rag.
  (2) Turn loop handle at top of cleaner in an anti-clockwise direction until free and gently lift out the cleaner. The oil bowl should come away with it. Be careful not to drop or strike the bowl on any hard surface.

CROMWELL TANK

(3) Pull slightly on the loop handle and release the two side clips holding the oil bowl. Remove the bowl.
(4) Lift off the jet sleeve and baffle, wipe clean and see that the tubes are clear.
(5) Sediment in the bowl must be scraped away and the bowl wiped out.
(6) Wash the element by pouring petrol into the air outlet with the top at a suitable angle. *Damage can be caused by flushing the element through from the bottom, as it would tend to carry dust and sand up towards the outlet and so into the induction system.*
(7) By means of a piece of rag wipe away any accumulation of dust in the centre tube and swill out with petrol.
(8) Clean out any oil or dust that has accumulated in the base casting attached to the fighting compartment bulkhead. Inspect the flap and wire mesh for foreign matter, such as clogged sand, paper or rag, and remove same.

Reassembling.

(1) Fill the oil bowl with clean engine oil up to the level indicated by means of a plate rivetted to the baffle plate which is inscribed, "FILL WITH ENGINE OIL TO LOWER EDGE OF RIM".
(2) Replace jet sleeve and baffle in the bowl and clip on top of cleaner.
(3) Lower top of cleaner into position on the base casting and screw down loop handle.
(4) Remove rag from end of induction pipe and couple it up to cleaner outlet.

Great care should be taken when reassembling to ensure that no dust or dirt enters the cleaner outlet. A short run at half-throttle will show that the oil is circulating. This can be seen through the inspection window at the top of the cleaner.

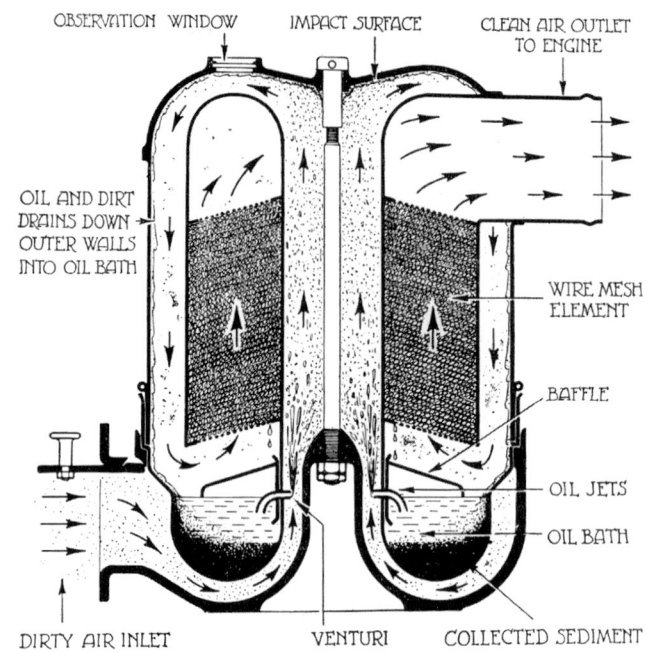

Fig. 12.—Diagram of air cleaner.

FUEL SYSTEM

MAIN FUEL TANKS.

Fuel is carried in two tanks installed in the engine compartment (*see* Figs. 124 and 125), being located one on each side of the engine. Capacities—R.H. tank, 60 gallons; L.H. tank, 56 gallons.

The filler caps are pressure-tight and are vented to atmosphere via a pipe which is led to the space between the vehicle side plates. DO NOT FILL THESE TANKS WITH OIL. The word PETROL painted in BLUE on the inclined face of the side air inlet louvre locates each filler cap, while the word OIL painted in YELLOW on the right-hand side air inlet louvre locates the oil filler cap.

Filling.—Each main fuel tank is filled in the usual manner by removing the access cover and unscrewing the filler cap (*see* Fig. 13). Insert the hose into the filler neck and carry on filling until the fuel level in each tank (no balance pipe is fitted) is up to the bottom of the filler neck. Replace filler caps and bleed the system as described on page 27.

Draining.—Fig. 67 shows the position of the fuel tank drains and outlet pipe covers. Only remove the drain plugs when it is necessary either to completely drain the tanks of fuel or to drain away any water that

VEHICLE HISTORY AND SPECIFICATION

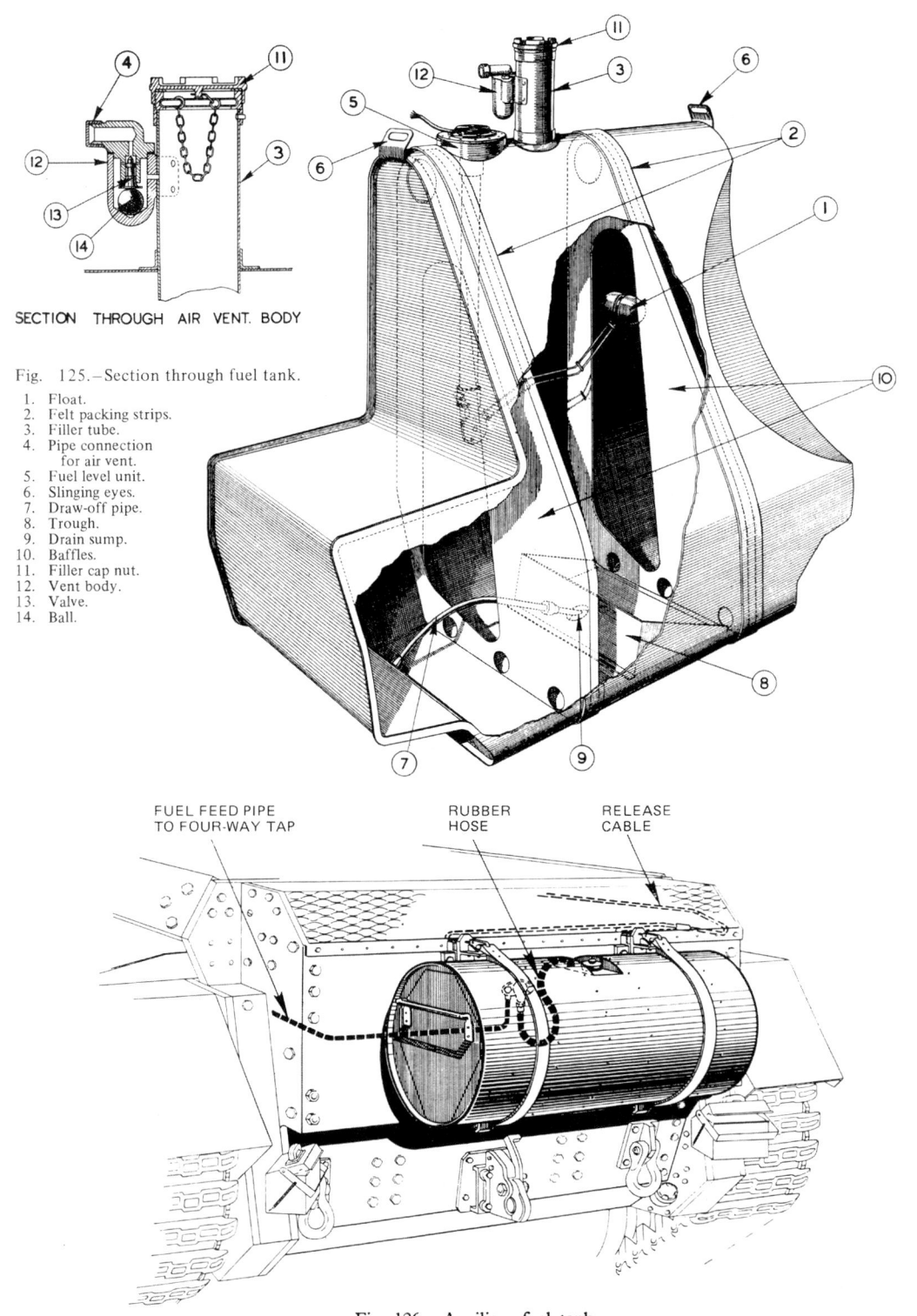

SECTION THROUGH AIR VENT. BODY

Fig. 125.—Section through fuel tank.
1. Float.
2. Felt packing strips.
3. Filler tube.
4. Pipe connection for air vent.
5. Fuel level unit.
6. Slinging eyes.
7. Draw-off pipe.
8. Trough.
9. Drain sump.
10. Baffles.
11. Filler cap nut.
12. Vent body.
13. Valve.
14. Ball.

Fig. 126.—Auxiliary fuel tank.

CROMWELL TANK

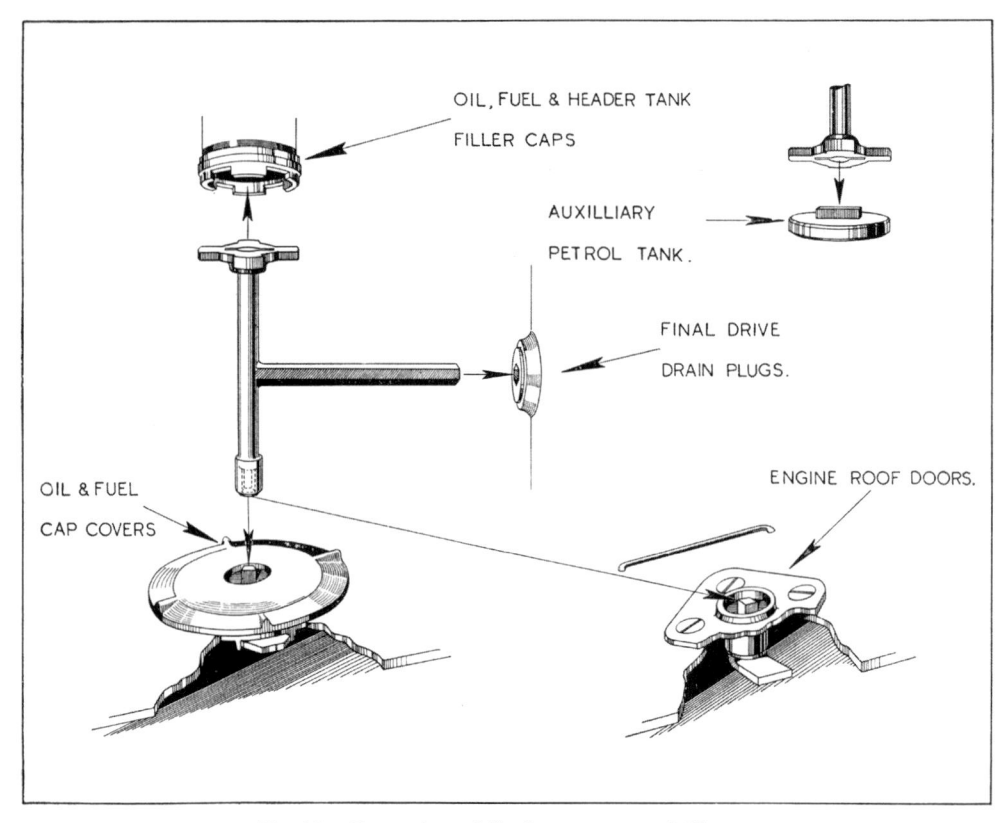

Fig. 13.—Composite tool for doors, covers and filler caps.

may have collected in them. In the latter case the plugs need not be fully unscrewed and should be screwed up again as soon as fuel starts draining from the tanks.

The outlet pipe covers are detached only when the tanks are lifted, or when for some other reason the outlet pipes require attention.

AUXILIARY FUEL TANK (if fitted).

An auxiliary fuel tank, containing 30 gallons, may be fitted to the rear of the vehicle (*see* Fig. 126), in which case the fuel in it should be used when moving to the scene of operations so that, if necessary, the tank may be jettisoned. To jettison the tank, pull the handle in the right-hand rear corner of the fighting compartment. This action releases the two straps retaining the tank in position, so that it falls away under its own weight and at the same time disconnects its supply pipe at the rubber junction.

To replace the tank, push in the handle, lift the tank into position by the handles provided and close the two straps. A pin fixed to the end of each strap fits into a catch, which is then snapped into position. Refit the rubber tube to the supply pipe.

FOUR-WAY TAP.

All three fuel tanks are connected to a four-way tap mounted on the left-hand side of the intermediate bulkhead, and is operated by a handwheel in the fighting compartment (*see* Fig. 128). This wheel is inscribed with the word **PETROL** at the bottom, and four other markings which, when turned so that they coincide with a pointer, are as follows:—

    (1) OFF—indicates fuel supply shut off.
    (2) R.H.—indicates right-hand fuel tank in use.
    (3) L.H.—indicates left-hand fuel tank in use.
    (4) AUX.—indicates auxiliary fuel tank in use.

VEHICLE HISTORY AND SPECIFICATION

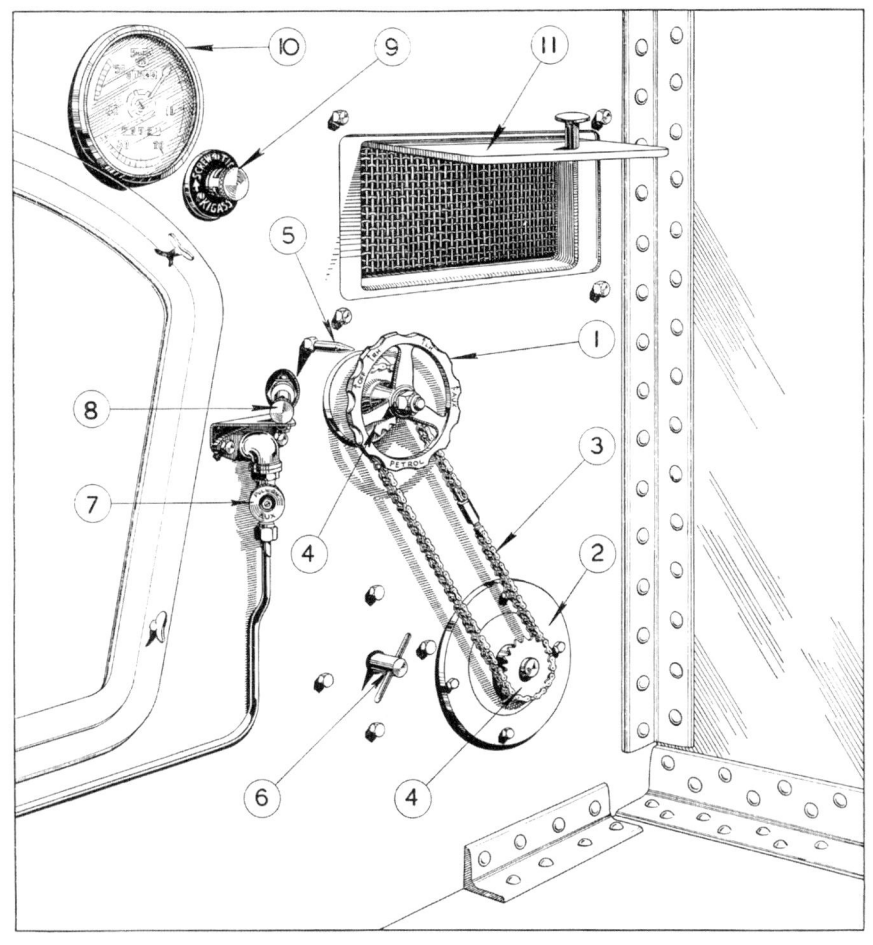

Fig. 128.—Fuel system controls.

1. Hand-wheel.
2. Four-way tap unit.
3. Bicycle-type chain.
4. Sprockets for (3).
5. Pointer for (1).
6. Filter tommy bar.
7. Fuel control for auxiliary charging motor.
8. Air-bleed control for filter.
9. Ki-gass priming pump.
10. Speedometer.
11. Intake for air cleaner.

Movement of the handwheel to the appropriate position is all that is necessary, as this makes the required connection. Fuel gauges are mounted on the driver's instrument panel for each of the main fuel tanks, but none is provided for the auxiliary tank.

FILTER.

The fuel flows from the tank, selected by the four-way tap, to the inlet side of a cloth type filter. This filter has two outlets each of which is connected to a separate diaphragm-type engine-driven pump delivering to the carburetters.

The filter should be dismantled and examined EVERY 500 MILES.

Dismantling (from fighting compartment).

(1) Turn four-way fuel tap control handwheel to OFF position.
(2) Remove inspection plate in the intermediate bulkhead, behind the bevel gearbox.
(3) Unscrew filter handle in the fighting compartment; this releases the bowl, which can then be removed with the left hand from its position on the engine compartment side of the intermediate bulkhead.
(4) Clean the bowl thoroughly with rag, using main fuel supply by opening the four-way tap for a second or two at a time, as required. Also clean the body of the filter, particularly round the cork gasket.

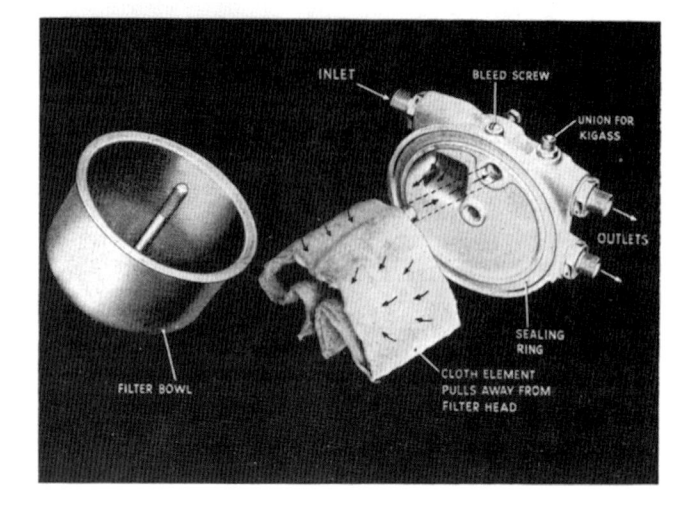

Fig. 14.—Operation of fuel filter.

(5) Remove the element and clean it or fit a new one. If in doubt, fit new element. Make sure the felt sealing ring is in position on the outlet tube of the element. The element can be cleaned by drying it and shaking off the sand or grit, or by washing it in petrol. *No attempt should be made to scrub the outside of the element with a brush.*
(6) Replace the cork gasket if necessary. This should not be removed unnecessarily, but it is readily replaced by a new one by pressing it into the groove in the filter body.
(7) Examine the fibre washer under the head of the filter handle and replace if cracked. It should not be necessary to more than hand-tighten the filter handle to obtain a fuel-tight joint. The use of excessive leverage may strain the casing or bend the filter handle.

Reassembling.

(1) Replace the filter bowl with the left hand and screw up the handle (just hand-tight).
(2) Bleed the system (see below).
(3) Replace inspection plate in intermediate bulkhead.

Bleeding is carried out by means of a special bleed tap fitted to the fighting compartment side of the intermediate bulkhead (*see* Fig. 128). Open the bleed tap until fuel begins to flow from it, then close it again. Due to the nature of the filter element, it is unavoidable that air will at times get trapped in the filter and reduce the efficiency of the system. This condition is most likely to occur when refilling the system from dry.

Oil System

The oil for lubricating the engine is stored in two interconnected tanks located one on each side of the engine (*see* Figs. 134 and 136).

A filler cap is provided in the right-hand tank which is reached after removing the access cover in the engine roof (*see* Fig. 13). The word OIL is painted in YELLOW on the inclined face of the right-hand air-intake louvre adjacent to this filler cap. DO NOT POUR PETROL INTO THIS TANK.

The two tanks are connected by means of a balance pipe so only one filler cap is provided, but a dipstick is fitted to the left-hand tank (*see* Part 5, Chapter I B).

Filling.
(1) Pour oil into the filler tube in the right-hand tank until the FULL mark on the dipstick in the left-hand tank has been reached. Pour quickly so as to ensure that the right-hand tank is full by the time the FULL level in the left-hand tank is reached.
(2) Replace filler cap.
(3) Replace dipstick.

Draining.
Each tank has a separate drain plug, and these can be reached by removing the oil tank drain covers in the floor plates (*see* Fig. 67). The plugs can then be unscrewed (*see* Fig. 136), but when doing so, be certain to have a container underneath to prevent wastage. The total capacity is 14½ gallons, so use a receptacle which is large enough. Most of the system can be drained through one tank plug, but removal of the other plug is necessary to clear the residue contained below the level of the balance pipe. Drain the system when the engine oil is *warm* and with the vehicle on *level* ground. The plugs can also be used for draining any water in the system. To do this, unscrew each plug in turn until oil starts to flow and then tighten the plugs.

Changing Oil.
(1) It is preferable to change over to the new H.D. oils while the engine is in a new condition, or as soon after an overhaul as possible. Engines which are nearing overhaul should, if possible, continue to run on the existing mineral grades of oils (*see* Lubrication Chart).
(2) When changing over to the H.D. oils, the engine must be run until the normal working temperature is attained and the existing oil drained off while hot.
(3) The engine oil tanks should then be filled (as above) with the appropriate grade of H.D. oil and the engine run at approximately half throttle for half an hour. The oil should then be drained off again while hot, and all easily removed filter elements, gauzes, pipe lines and relief valves must then be removed and cleaned.
(4) The engine oil tanks must then be refilled with the H.D. oil and a label affixed to the driver's instrument panel near to the oil pressure gauge, giving in large letters the grade of H.D. oil used, the date and mileage of the change-over; this information must also be entered in the A.B.413.
(5) Normal running should then be continued for not less than 300 or more than 500 miles, during which time special notice should be taken for evidence of low oil pressure or overheating of the engine. If a drop in oil pressure or overheating is experienced, the engine must immediately be stopped, the oil drained off, and the lubrication system cleaned as in (3) above, and replaceable filter elements renewed.
(6) If the operation of the engine has been normal during the 300-500 mile run, the oil must still be drained off while hot and the lubrication system cleaned as in (3) above and replaceable filter elements renewed. The label on the instrument panel and the A.B.413 must be endorsed to the effect that the second draining of the oil has been carried out.
(7) Normal oil changes and operation of the vehicle can then be resumed.

OIL FILTER (Pressure).
A felt-type pressure oil filter (*see* Fig. 15) is mounted on the engine compartment side of the intermediate bulkhead and cleans the oil before it passes via an oil cooler into the engine. It should be dismantled, cleaned and fitted with a new element EVERY 1,000 MILES.

Dismantling.
(1) Remove the drain plug (10) and drain the filter casing.
(2) Unscrew the six bolts securing the casing ring (5) to the cover (4) when the casing ring should drop

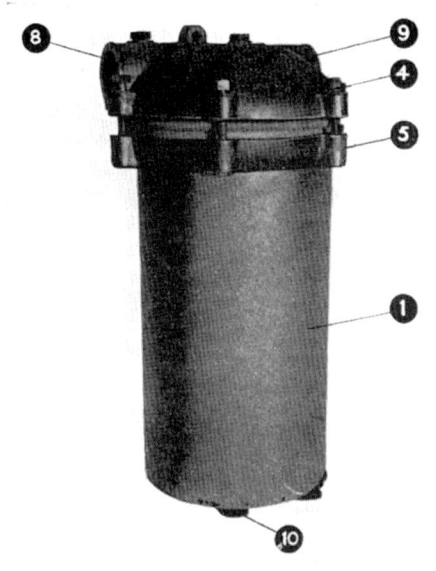

Fig. 15.—Oil filter.
1. Filter casing.
4. Aluminium cover.
5. Casing ring.
8. Oil inlet.
9. Oil outlet.
10. Drain plug.

away and the filter casing can be drawn downwards away from the cover (4). It may be necessary, after the casing has been drawn down several inches, to grip the element with the fingers, and by slightly twisting, to pull it away from the filter cover.

(3) Wash out the casing with petrol and clean the perforated tray.

If time does not permit complete dismantling of the filter, the drain plug can be removed and any accumulated sludge or water drained off.

Reassembling.

(1) Drop the perforated tray into the filter casing, followed by a new element, and then prime with engine oil (approx. 1 gal.). Finally offer up the assembly to the filter cover.
(2) Fit a new rubber washer in the casing cover.
(3) Fit the element tube into the central hole in the cover by pressing and twisting slightly. The filter casing can then be pressed home, taking care that no part of the felt element is trapped between the top of the casing and the rubber washer in the cover.
(4) Screw up the six filter casing retaining bolts, taking care to do this evenly all round. Do not over-tighten them as it will be found that no leakage will take place with the bolts just moderately tight.

If at any time the oil pipes are disconnected, the by-pass valve should be tested to see if it moves freely. This can be done by pressing on the end of the spindle seen inside the inlet port. It is not advisable to dismantle this valve, but if a spring is broken, the valve should be kept on its seat by pressing from the outlet port end and the split pin removed from the spindle. Replacing the spring is best done by making a small device rather like a bicycle tyre lever. This can be used to press down the washer and spring, the split pin being inserted by a pair of long-nosed pliers.

OIL FILTERS (Scavenge).

Two scavenge oil filters (*see* Fig. 140) are fitted at the bottom of the engine wheelcase, and these should be examined and cleaned EVERY 2,000 MILES. They can be reached after removing the appropriate cover in the floor plates of the vehicle (*see* Fig. 67). Then proceed as follows:—

(1) Remove the two dome nuts securing the filters in position, and also the nuts securing the external oil pipe which is attached to one of the filters, and gently withdraw the filter elements.
(2) Inspect for any foreign matter and wash the filters in petrol.
(3) Replace in position and carefully tighten the dome nuts and the oil pipe securing nuts.
(4) Examine the aluminium joint washers and replace if damaged.

COOLING SYSTEM

The cooling of the radiators depends entirely upon the circulation of air by two fans. These fans are built into the front of the two radiators which are installed one on each side of the rear end of the engine compartment (*see* Part 6, Chapter I B, for description and illustrations). One header tank serves as a reservoir for the system, the total capacity being approximately 14 gallons.

The coolant is circulated by means of an engine-driven centrifugal pump and is pumped through the cylinder block and induction pipe coolant-jackets, and through a thermostat with by-pass, into the header tank. From the header tank it travels downwards through the radiators where it is cooled by the forced draught of air from the fans. From the bottom of the radiators it is drawn up into the circulating pump and so to the engine again.

To work efficiently the cooling system must be kept clean and full of coolant. The level must therefore be checked DAILY. If the system has to be topped up daily, check for leaks.

Filling the system.—The system is filled through the header tank, by lifting the access door on top of the engine compartment (*see* Fig. 5A) and unscrewing the filler cap. *Do not remove the filler cap while the engine is running, and wait until the temperature falls below* 100° C. (212° F.).

When filling, the level will rise slowly until about half-way up the filter, when it will rise rapidly. At this point the system is full. Run the engine for about half a minute, then top-up.

Do not, at any time, remove the filter except for cleaning. If the coolant takes a long time to run through the filter, the gauze needs attention. Clean same by removing the complete filter cage and swilling it in petrol.

After filling.—Screw home the filler cap sufficiently tight to make a pressure-tight joint. Do not over-strain in tightening, *but it is not sufficient to have the filler cap just hand-tight.*

Draining the system.—The system is drained by means of an evacuation pump mounted at the rear of the header tank (*see* Fig. 145), thus simplifying the preservation of coolant when operating far from adequate water supplies or when using anti-freeze mixture (*see* "Frost Precautions"). The vehicle should be run on to level ground before operating the pump.

The pump is connected by piping to a three-way tap, and this in turn is connected to the sumps of each radiator. A length of flexible hose is supplied for attachment to the pump outlet, and the loose end of this pipe should be placed in a suitable clean container (*see* Fig. 16).

The tap is marked R.H., L.H. and OFF. Turn the tap to R.H. to drain the right-hand radiator and to L.H. to drain the left-hand radiator, and work the ram up and down. Great care must be taken to see that the system is pumped completely dry, with the tap in both positions. Collect the coolant in the container and keep covered until it is poured back into the system.

RADIATORS.

Remove inspection covers in fan cowls EVERY 1,000 MILES and remove foreign matter which has lodged against the matrices. Provided the radiators are free from oil, they are unlikely to become choked, but if in an oily condition they will rapidly become blocked up, in which case the only effective remedy is to have them removed and degreased.

FANS AND BELTS.

The two fans are driven by belts from the fan drive unit on the rear end of the engine (*see* Figs. 105 and 106). Each fan has eight blades and is carried on ball and roller bearings which are packed with grease on assembly.

The fan belts are of V-section and should be examined EVERY 1,000 MILES and replaced if necessary. New belts need not be paired when fitted, but if removed for any reason they *must* be replaced in pairs by removing the pulleys on the fan drive unit. *Do not attempt to stretch the belts over the pulleys.*

After removing the fan drive pulleys on the engine, remove the inspection cover in the front of each fan cowl and hook the belts over the fan pulley wheels. Place the new belts in position over the fan and engine pulleys, and replace the engine pulleys on the fan drive unit.

Lubricators were fitted on the fan drive pulley pivot arms on early-type engines, but have now been deleted. In the event of these being fitted, no greasing operation is necessary.

COOLANT PUMP.

A centrifugal type circulating pump is fitted to the wheelcase end of the engine (*see* Fig. 107). The pump spindle bush is lubricated by means of an external lubricator which must be serviced EVERY 500 MILES. This lubricator will be deleted on later type pumps.

This operation is performed from the fighting compartment and should be carried out at the same time as the servicing of the fuel filter, as the inspection plate behind the bevel gearbox will have already been removed. Screw down the cap of the lubricator 1-2 turns.

If there is any excessive leakage from the gland nut, this should be tightened by means of the tommy-bar in the vehicle tool-kit. *Do not overtighten.* A slight "weep" at this gland is necessary for lubrication purposes.

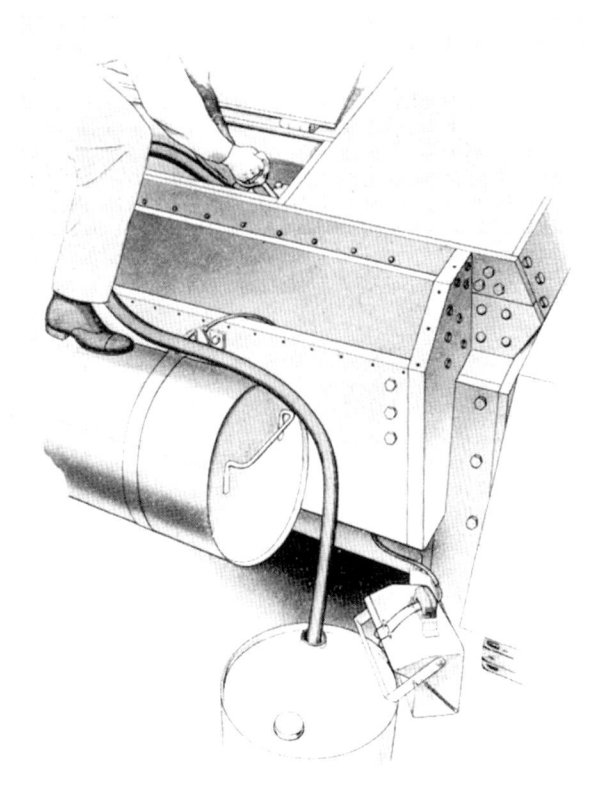

Fig. 16.—Draining the coolant system.

IGNITION SYSTEM

The ignition system is specially designed to ensure that it will not cause interference with the wireless equipment. The magnetos are completely screened and all cables are of the shielded metal braided type.

The magnetos are mounted on the sides of the engine wheelcase, being driven by coupling shafts contained in the wheelcase. Automatic timing devices and electrical governors are incorporated with the magnetos, the whole system being described in Part 7, Chapter I B.

MAINTENANCE.

The only maintenance to be carried out concerns the magnetos and consists of replacing the cam lubricating pads, greasing the contact breaker pivot pins and checking the gaps of the contact breakers (*see* Fig. 17). These operations must be carried out EVERY 2,000 MILES. Proceed as follows:—

(1) Remove the distributor block and screen by unscrewing the two long securing bolts.

(2) Remove the distributor rotor by unscrewing the two securing screws.

(3) Remove the lubricating cam pad and replace with a new one. The pad is held in contact with the cam by a spring which must only be set up $\frac{1}{4}$ of a turn.

(4) Lubricate the contact breaker lever pins with an approved H.M.P. grease. To do this it will be necessary to slacken the restoring spring nuts and screws and to remove the spring circlips and washers holding the levers on the pins. The levers can then be removed.

(5) Remove any oil or grease from the surface of the contact points with petrol.

(6) On reassembly, set the contact breaker gaps to 0·012 in. In order to avoid a false setting, this measurement must be taken at the centre of the points and not across the width of the points.

Care should be taken to see that all washers are replaced in the correct order and that the restoring spring screws and lock nuts are retightened. See that the gauze windows are quite clean.

Clean the inside of the distributor block and examine the carbon and spring of the distributor rotor. The carbon must not rotate in the spring.

Finally replace the distributor rotor and secure in position by the two screws, followed by the distributor block and screen.

BEVEL GEARBOX

A bevel gear-box is provided in the fighting compartment for the purpose of driving the dynamo and turret pump (*see* Fig. 168). It also carries the starter motor by which the engine is started.

MAINTENANCE.

Check WEEKLY that all nuts are tight and that the split pins are in position in the coupling bolts. Examine casing for excessive oil leaks, and if present, check condition of oil seals. Do not remove these unless absolutely necessary.

LUBRICATION.

Top up with engine oil EVERY 250 MILES. To do this remove the filler plug and by means of a syringe, fill up to the level of the plug.

VEHICLE HISTORY AND SPECIFICATION

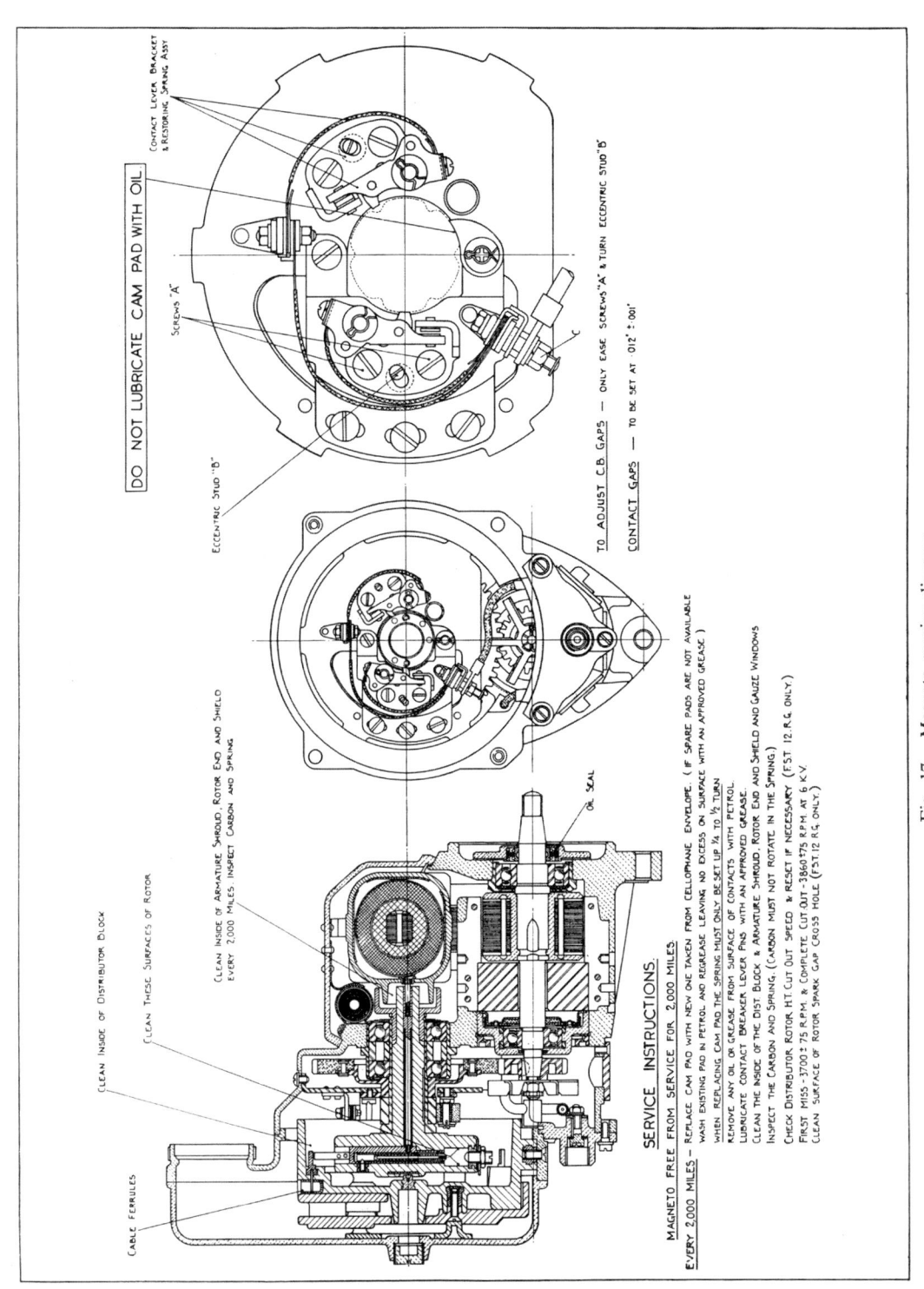

Fig. 17.—Magneto service diagram.

CROMWELL TANK

(5) A steering brake for each track. By applying one of the steering brakes the driver brings the necessary gear train into action. This acts through the epicyclic gears and differential so that either track is speeded up or slowed down, as required. The steering gear train becomes a reverse gear by locking the secondary gear shaft, so that the vehicle can be driven backwards.

LUBRICATION.

The gearbox should be filled with gear oil to the high-level mark on the dipstick (*see* Fig. 18). The capacity is approximately 5 gallons. The easiest place for filling is the round cover shown in Fig. 19. First clean away any dirt around this cover, remove the setscrew nearest the lifting eye and slacken off the other one. Then lift and swing aside the cover. Take care not to drop the setscrew or washer into the gearbox.

Check the level WEEKLY and top up when necessary. Drain and flush the gearbox and refill to dipstick mark EVERY 1,000 MILES. Remember to check for oil leakage by examining the outside of the gearbox before draining.

MAINTENANCE.

Apart from lubrication, the only maintenance required is on the brake system. For this information refer to Chapter IV A.

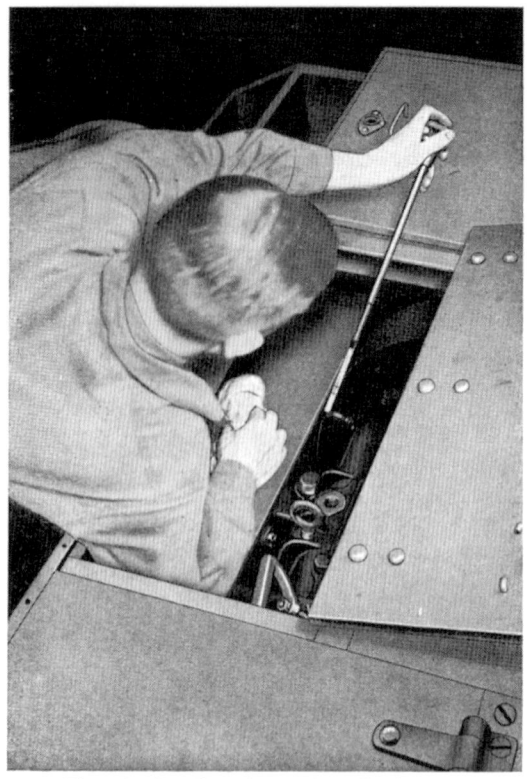

Fig. 18.—Reading the gearbox dipstick.

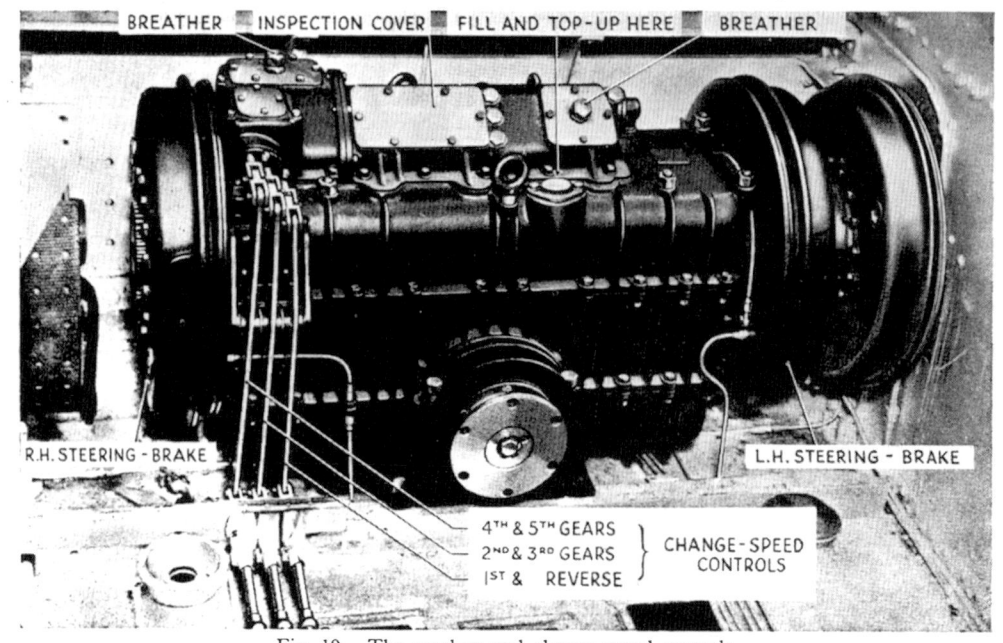

Fig. 19.—The gearbox and change-speed controls.

VEHICLE HISTORY AND SPECIFICATION

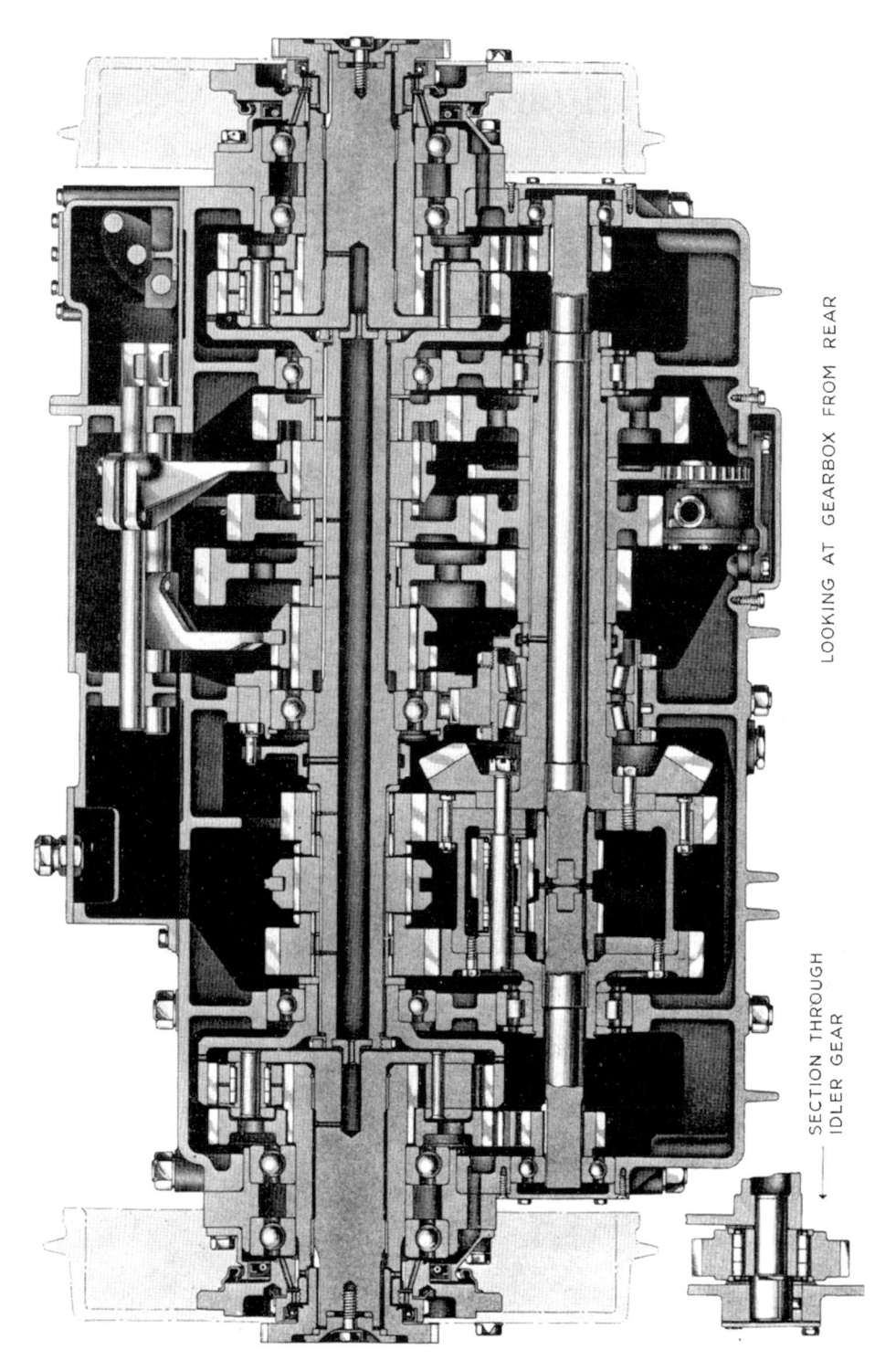

Fig. 171.—Section through gearbox.

LOOKING AT GEARBOX FROM REAR

SECTION THROUGH IDLER GEAR

CROMWELL TANK

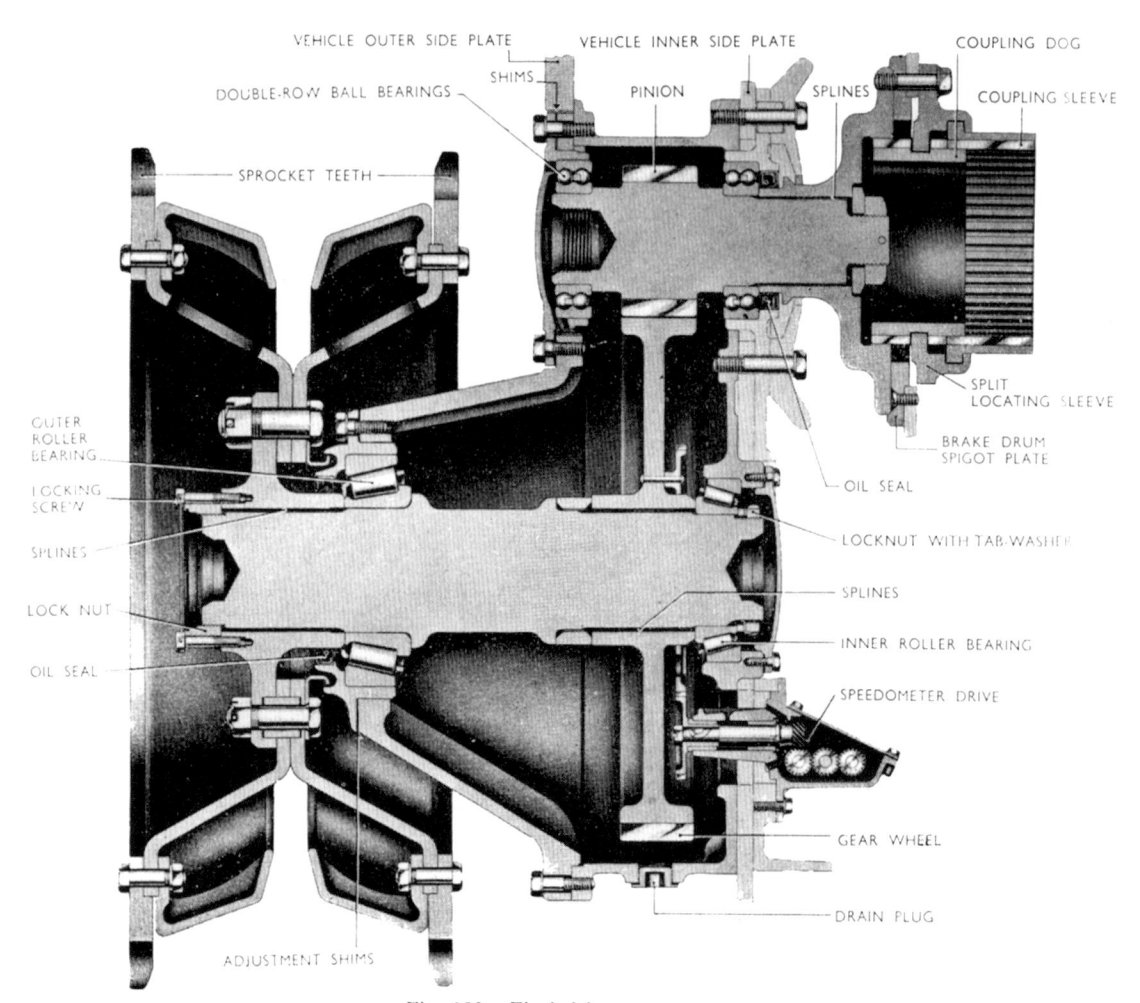

Fig. 182.—Final drive arrangement.

THE FINAL DRIVE

A reduction gear is provided between the gearbox output shafts and the driving sprockets by means of spur gears located in a housing secured between the inner and outer hull plates on each side of the vehicle.

The speedometers for the driver and commander are both driven from the left-hand sprocket shaft (*see* Fig. 182).

LUBRICATION.

An oil filler is provided in each final drive housing (*see* Fig. 20), and this must be filled with oil to the level of the filler.

Check level EVERY 250 MILES and top up when necessary. If oil overflows when cap is removed it is an indication that water has entered the final drive, in which case it must be drained. Drain the housings EVERY 1,000 MILES by means of the plug in the base of the housing and refill with one gallon of oil (*see* Fig. 20).

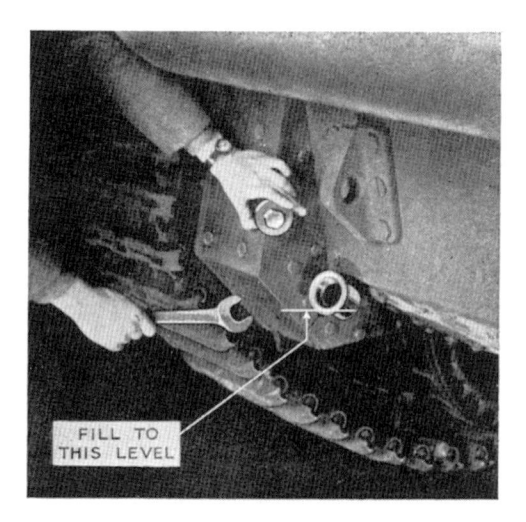

Fig. 20.—Final oil drive filler.

Fig. 21.—Final drive sprocket.

MAINTENANCE.

No running adjustments are required. Check all nuts (particularly on the sprockets) EVERY 250 MILES.

Excessive oil leakage indicates a faulty oil seal (*see* Fig. 182), which should be examined and replaced if necessary.

To do this, break the track near the sprocket as explained in Part 4 of this Chapter. Remove locking screw and washer. Unscrew the lock nut with the special spanner provided and remove the sprocket.

Examine the oil seal, and if it appears perfect leave it alone. If it is damaged, lift it out and fit a new seal. Reassemble in the reverse order, and *be careful not to damage the oil seal* when sliding the sprocket on to its driving shaft splines.

TRACKS AND TENSIONERS

TRACKS.

The tracks are driven by sprocket wheels at the rear of the vehicle, the latter having double teeth which engage the manganesed-steel links of the track.

CROMWELL TANK

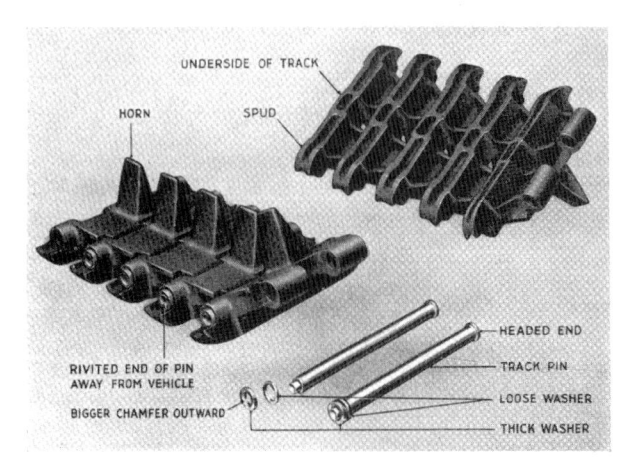

Fig. 22.—Sections of track.

A new track consists of 125 links, but it is necessary to add one spare link, making a total of 126, for the initial "running in" period. This is only a matter of a few miles' running, after which the spare link can be removed and each track will then number 125 links until such time as it becomes necessary to remove another link, due to normal wear, in order to keep the track correctly tensioned. This may occur several times, at varying intervals, during the life of a track.

Each link (see Fig. 22) has a tread or "spud" to engage the ground and a positioning lug or "horn" is formed on the inner face to centre the track on the driving sprockets, the road wheels and the track tensioner wheels.

The links are hinged together by hardened-steel pins. A head is formed at the inner end of these pins, while their outer ends are reduced in diameter to take a thick washer over which the end of the pin is riveted. This thick washer must be fitted on the pin, small chamfer first, so that the pin end can be riveted over into the large chamfer (see Fig. 22). A loose washer is interposed between the thick washer and the link. This construction is clearly shown in Fig. 22.

The head of the pin is always placed *towards* the vehicle so that the riveting can be done on *the outside*, away from the vehicle. It is most important that the track be fitted in the manner shown in Fig. 23, that is, with the *spuds trailing as they pass round the sprockets*.

MAINTENANCE.

Do not lubricate the tracks at all, but keep them as clean as possible. Examine tracks DAILY for loose pins.

Replacing a Track Pin.—When the track has been working under arduous conditions, it is occasionally found that the thick washers (see Fig. 22) become loose or even drop off, so that the pin will commence to work out. A new pin can be fitted in the following manner, without removing the track, and the job is most easily done between the rear road wheel and the driving sprocket.

The pin which is to be replaced will generally be part-way out of its hole. Insert an old discarded pin into the hole and knock the pin right out. This leaves the track held in position by the old pin which is being used as a tool. Insert a new pin and proceed to knock out the "tool" pin in the opposite direction, that is, away from the vehicle. When this operation is complete, fit the loose washer and then the thick washer and rivet the pin over as in Fig. 24. Use as little force as possible

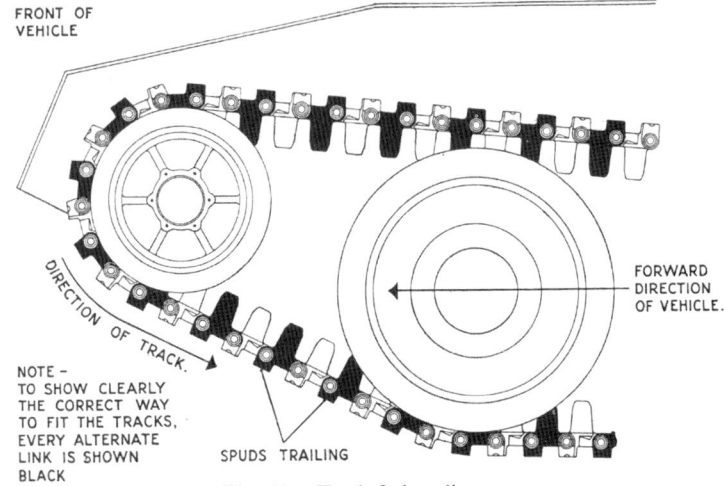

Fig. 23.—Track-fitting diagram.

when hammering the new pin home, or otherwise the reduced diameter end will be burred and it will be difficult to fit the two washers.

To remove a Track.—Under certain circumstances it may be necessary to remove a track so that new links can be fitted. To do this, first run the vehicle on to firm level ground, if practicable. Slacken the track in the manner described under "Adjustment of Track Tension" (page 40), and with the gear lever in neutral and foot-brake off, rotate the sprocket by means of a crowbar so that the bottom of the track is slack between the sprocket and the rear road wheel.

Knock out a link pin by placing a drift against it at the riveted end, and hitting the drift sharply with a heavy hammer. Then rotate the sprocket in the opposite direction so as to disengage that portion of the track which is around it.

With the crew positioned between each road wheel at the side of the vehicle, drag the top run of the track over the idler wheel and lay it on the ground in front of the vehicle.

Replace the damaged links, driving out the link pins as described above. Insert new pins by riveting over as shown in Fig. 24. Take care to support the pin head as shown in B, Fig. 24, when riveting the pin end.

To replace a Track.—With the track repaired and the crew arranged alongside the vehicle as before, drag the top run of the track over the idler wheel and along the road wheels. Attach a wire rope to the top run rear link and weave the rope in and out of the sprocket teeth. Again using the crowbar, rotate the sprocket so that the track is pulled over the sprocket teeth and meets the other end of the track.

Support both link ends and replace the pin. Fit the two washers and rivet over the end of the pin as shown in Fig. 24. Finally, adjust the track tension as described on page 40.

A broken track can be repaired and replaced in this way provided it is not completely shed.

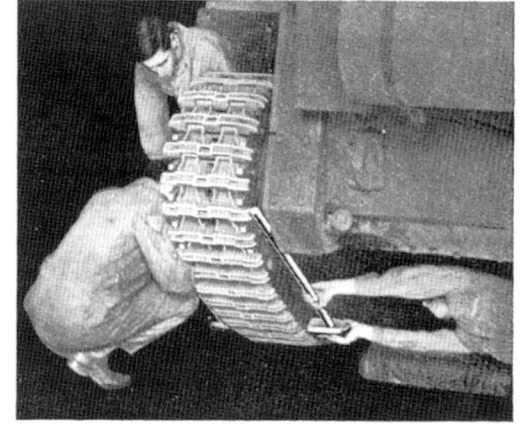

A   Fig. 24.—Riveting a track pin.   B

To fit a new Track.—Proceed in the manner described under "To remove a Track", until the old track is on the ground with the top run pointing forward.

Place the new track, which must be exactly the same length, in line with the rear of the old track, i.e. pointing rearward. Both tracks should then form a single line, the new one being a continuation of the old one.

The vehicle must now be driven in reverse gear so that the new track is under the road wheels with the larger section lying forward.

As only one track is fitted, it will be necessary to lock the free sprocket before the vehicle will move. To do this, pull the steering lever on the *same* side as the fitted track. Then use the clutch to drive the vehicle backwards.

Drive the vehicle very slowly until the road wheels are over the new track. Then complete the operation as described under "To replace a Track".

CROMWELL TANK

Note.—Where possible, it is quicker to procure a tow from another vehicle, as it will be appreciated that the method described above is, of necessity, rather slow.

Should a track be shed, it must be repaired and refitted as described above, i.e., the track should be placed on the ground behind the vehicle and in direct line with the road wheels.

TRACK TENSIONER

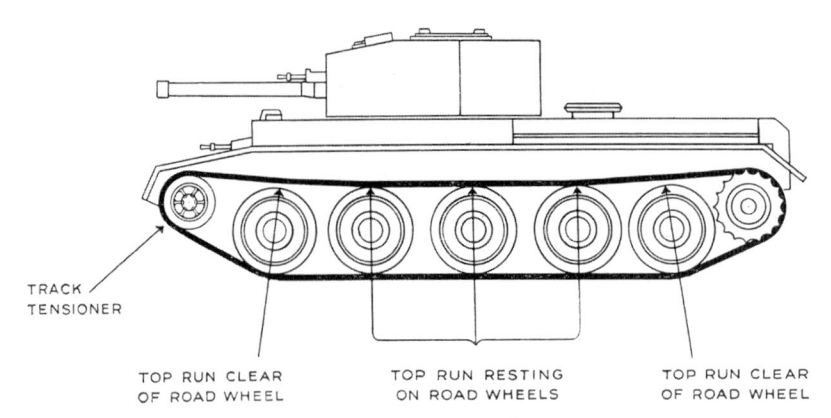

TOP RUN CLEAR OF ROAD WHEEL

TOP RUN RESTING ON ROAD WHEELS

TOP RUN CLEAR OF ROAD WHEEL

Fig. 25.—Track correctly adjusted.

TENSIONERS.

The track must always be properly tensioned as shown in Fig. 25, and to check this the vehicle should be run on to flat ground. The top run of the track should be clear of the front and rear road wheels, but should rest lightly on the three centre wheels.

Adjustment of each track is provided for by tensioners fitted at the front of the vehicle. Each tensioner (*see* Fig. 183) consists of a rubber-tyred wheel running on ball and roller bearings mounted on an eccentric axle. This axle is pivoted in a fixed housing bolted between the inner and outer hull plates of the vehicle.

The tensioners (*see* Fig. 183) are fitted with a ratchet wheel (1) and a pawl arm (3) by which the ratchet wheel is locked in position. The pawl arm is itself secured by the lock-nut (5). Two slots are provided for insertion of the end of the adjusting lever which is carried on the right-hand side of the engine compartment roof.

Adjustment of Track Tension.—To disengage the ratchet wheel, first unscrew the lock-nut (5) so as to release the spring-loaded pawl arm. Then insert the end of the adjusting lever into one of the two slots and lift upwards to tighten the track. There is no danger of the tensioner slipping backwards and so slackening the track as the pawl arm (3) is spring-loaded into engagement with the ratchet wheel (1) and will "click" round over it.

Check to see that the correct tension has been achieved as shown in Fig. 25, and then tighten up the lock-nut (5).

MAINTENANCE.

The tensioners are grease lubricated and should be greased EVERY 250 MILES through the nipples incorporated in the idler wheel hubs. The eccentric axles must also be greased EVERY 250 MILES, the two grease nipples being located on the right-hand side of the front gunner's compartment, the grease being forced along piping to each eccentric axle at points (8), (Fig. 183).

SUSPENSION

Each of the ten road wheels is independently sprung. This is done by arranging that the wheels revolve on pivoted axle-arms. The movement of each axle-arm is controlled by a spring suspension unit. On the front, second, fourth and fifth pairs of wheels, two-way shock-absorbers are fitted. Both the springs and shock-absorbers are protected by the hull outer side plates, leaving only the road wheels and tracks exposed.

Rubber buffers are fitted on the vehicle frame to prevent undue strain on the suspension due to extreme shocks which may be experienced when travelling over very rough ground. It will therefore be seen that the suspension system consists of four main parts:—

(1) Road springs.
(2) Hydraulic shock absorbers.
(3) Pivoting axle arms.
(4) Road wheels.

ROAD SPRINGS.

A full description of these is given in Chapter III B.

Lubrication.—The road spring casings are packed with grease on assembly and no attention is required between workshop overhaul periods.

Maintenance.—The ground clearance of the vehicle, that is, the distance from the *level ground* to the underside of the floor plate, is approximately 16 in. This should be checked EVERY 500 MILES.

If the ground clearance varies considerably from the figure of 16 in., broken springs should be suspected. For instance, if one side of the vehicle has a clearance of only 12 in., examine for spring breakages on that side. *Always test on level ground.*

When travelling over rough ground, broken road springs can sometimes be detected by an occasional thump, which is caused by an axle-arm being flung up against its rubber buffer when the wheel passes over an obstacle, there being very little resistance on a unit with broken springs.

A quick check on broken springs can be made by levering each wheel upwards separately. If one wheel has less than average resistance a closer examination should be carried out.

Adjustment.—No adjustment is necessary as the springs are set to length on assembly.

HYDRAULIC SHOCK ABSORBERS.

The object in fitting these units is to assist the road springs to absorb the shocks, and so secure a more comfortable ride. They are fitted on the front, second, fourth and fifth pairs of wheels, and are illustrated by Figs. 186 and 188.

As will be seen, the cylinder is divided into two parts by the displacement head; the upper part (to the right of the head) acts as a reserve tank and fluid enters the working chamber (to the left of the head) through ball valves.

When mounted on the vehicle, the shock absorber oscillates with its companion road spring. This causes the fluid to be displaced within the absorber cylinder, so damping the rough riding. (*See* Chapter III B for description of this mechanism.)

Maintenance.—Servicing is necessary EVERY 500 MILES. Take care not to allow particles of grit to enter the shock absorbers. Carefully clean the area surrounding the filler plug, and then remove the plug. Use a *clean* long-nosed oil can to inject *clean* oil into the filling hole until the casing is full. Do not permit the fluid to wash around the hole when filling, as this will allow dirt to become mixed with it.

Replace the filler plug, at the same time fitting, if possible, a new filler plug washer. The shock absorber is now overfilled, but the surplus oil is ejected from the relief valve when the vehicle moves off and the suspension starts to operate. This loss of fluid is quite normal and should not be confused with leaking.

PIVOTING AXLE ARMS.

These members form the connection between the road wheels and the vehicle. One arm of each member pivots in the corresponding hull cross tube, while the other arm is an axle for the road wheel. (*See* Chapter III B for full description.)

Lubrication.—The arm of each member pivoted in the hull cross tube is automatically pressure lubricated from pumps in the front gunner's compartment (*see* Fig. 227). Leakage from the bearings is controlled by a sealing ring fitted between the axle-arm and the inner side plate.

Maintenance.—The axle arms must be inspected EVERY 250 MILES for oil leakage. If any occurs, examine the sealing rings and if necessary replace them. EVERY 250 MILES check level of suspension tube lubrication reservoir (in driver's compartment) and top up as required.

ROAD WHEELS.

Each road wheel unit consists of a pair of disc wheels bolted to a common hub which is mounted on roller bearings and revolves on the short projecting axle shaft of the axle arm member (*see* Fig. 187).

Solid rubber tyres are moulded to the rims of the wheels and these absorb shock between the track links and the wheels and also help to reduce noise.

Dirt and water are excluded from the bearings by a hub cap at the outer end of each hub and a seal at the inner end. The hubs are packed with grease on assembly.

Lubrication.—The road wheel hubs must be greased EVERY 250 MILES through the nipples on the hubs (*see* Fig. 26).

Maintenance.—EVERY 250 MILES check all wheel nuts for tightness. Always do this in a definite sequence such as is suggested in Fig. 26. Note that all road wheel nuts on the *right-hand* side of the vehicle have *right-hand* threads and therefore tighten *clockwise*, while the nuts on the *left-hand* side of the vehicle have *left-hand* threads and tighten *anti-clockwise*.

While checking the wheel nuts, test the hub-cap set-screws and seal retaining screws, to make sure they are all quite tight.

Fig. 26.—Road wheel—showing correct sequence for tightening nuts.

VEHICLE HISTORY AND SPECIFICATION

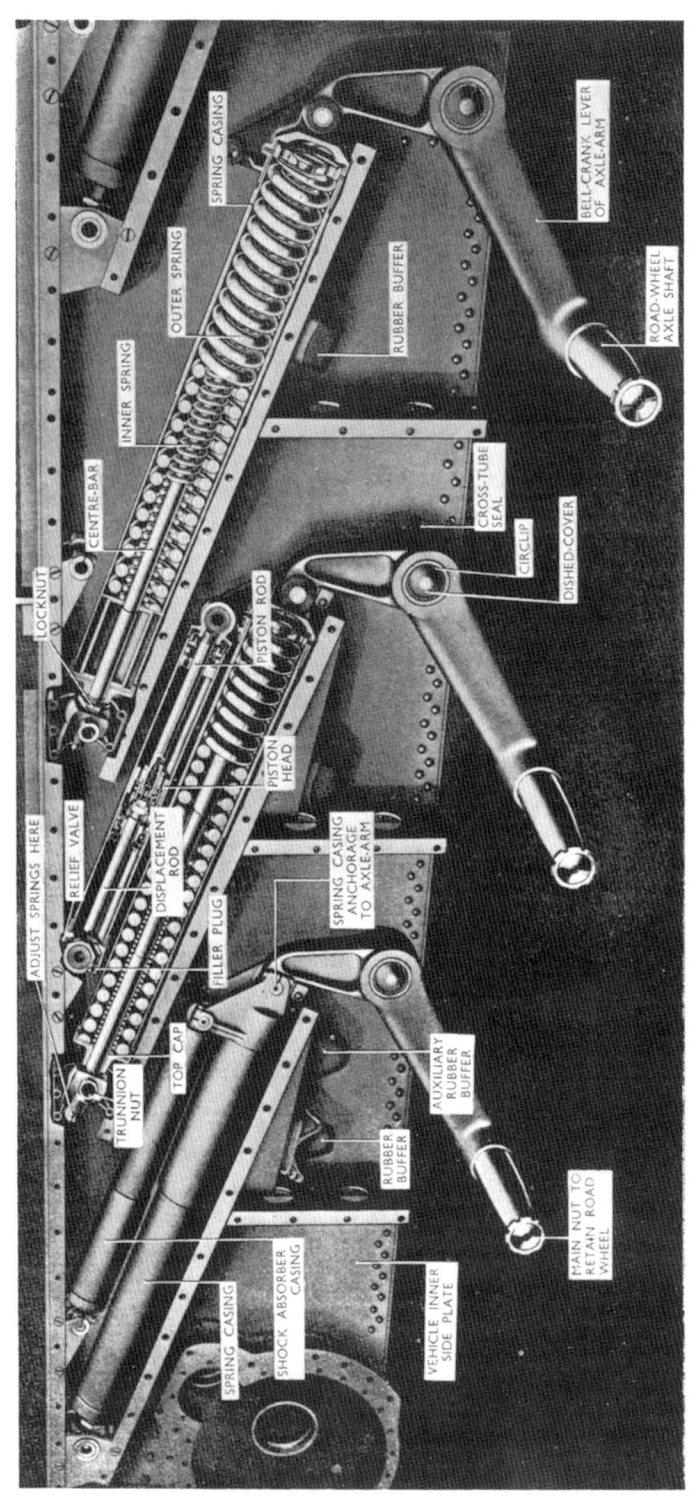

Fig. 186.—Suspension, showing road-spring and shock-absorber assembly in section.

Fig. 27.—Steering and track brakes.

STEERING BRAKES AND TRACK BRAKES

There are two sets of brakes:—**THE STEERING BRAKES** which are attached to the gearbox, and **THE TRACK BRAKES** which are anchored to the hull sides (*see* Fig. 27). Both are generally similar in design and are hydraulically operated and totally enclosed as protection against oil and dirt. The reserve tank for the hydraulic fluid is on the right-hand side of the driver's compartment.

STEERING BRAKES.

The steering brakes are applied by hand levers in the driver's compartment. The *left-hand* lever controls the *right-hand* brake and the *right-hand* lever controls the *left-hand* brake. These levers should be applied smoothly and gently. Harsh application gives erratic steering, particularly when travelling at high speeds on the road.

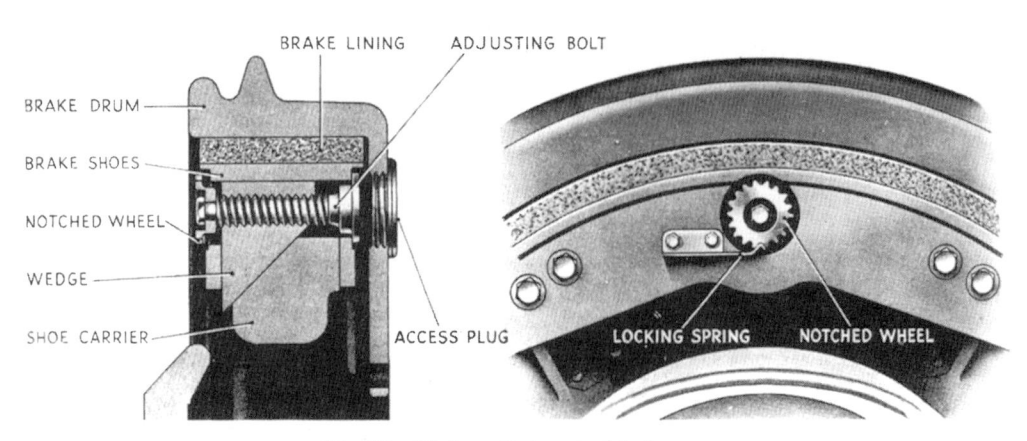

Fig. 28.—Wedge adjustment of brakes.

When driving on the lower gears, the sharper the turn the greater the effort required to operate the steering levers.

Do not apply the steering controls when the vehicle is stationary and the engine running, even when the gear lever is in neutral, unless a pivot turn is needed. If a pivot turn to the left is required pull the left-hand lever. The left-hand track then moves backwards while the right-hand track moves forwards, so that the vehicle turns to the left about its own centre. Pulling the right-hand lever has the opposite effect and the vehicle pivots to the right. Therefore *take care* when touching either steering lever while the engine is running and the vehicle is stationary.

Skid turns are only possible when reverse gear is engaged, when pulling the right-hand lever locks the left-hand track and vice versa (*see* "Driving Instructions", page 8).

TRACK BRAKES.

The track brakes are used for slowing down the vehicle or bringing it to rest and are operated by the foot pedal in the driver's compartment.

When "parking" the vehicle press the foot pedal hard down, at the same time *pushing* the ratchet control knob until the ratchet teeth engage the pedal. The pedal will then stay down and the brake ON. To release the brake press hard on the foot pedal, and if the ratchet does not spring out of engagement *pull* the knob to disengage it.

LUBRICATION (ALL BRAKES).

No lubrication is necessary. Efficient steering and braking depends upon friction, so keep the brake drums and shoes absolutely clean. No oil or grease should be permitted on these surfaces under any circumstances. Lubricant on the linings reduces the friction and therefore the steering and stopping power of the brakes.

MAINTENANCE (ALL BRAKES).

Check the fluid level in the reserve tank WEEKLY and top up if necessary. Keep an eye on the indicator-rod and always top up when this falls to its lowest position. Pour in fluid until the indicator stops rising; the tank is then full. The capacity of the reserve tank is about 2 pints, while the hydraulic system altogether holds approximately 6 pints of fluid. *The necessity for frequent topping-up indicates a leak in the system, which must be traced and rectified.*

Test both steering and track brakes DAILY. They should respond to the controls immediately. If there is excessive travel on either steering lever or the foot pedal, adjust the brake shoes as described below, but if after having adjusted them correctly there is a definite spongy feeling, bleed the appropriate hydraulic system.

Adjustment.—Correct adjustment of all brakes is most essential. In order to compensate for wear between the brake shoes and the drums a wedge adjustment is provided. These wedges slide in inclined slots in the shoe-carriers and push the shoes outwards towards the drums when the adjuster bolt is rotated.

Fig. 28 shows the method of adjustment. The wedge is pulled along the slot by the adjusting bolt, so forcing the shoe outwards from the shoe-carrier. A wheel is fitted on a square section of the bolt and retained by a self-locking nut. This wheel has external notches which are engaged by a locking spring, so that the bolt cannot turn until required to do so for adjustment. When adjustment of the brake shoes is necessary, unscrew the access plugs in the side of the brake drum—two plugs on each drum. Rotate the drum until the adjusting bolt is visible through the access hole. The same hexagon-headed key is used to release these plugs as is used to make the actual adjustment, there being a different size hexagon at each end of the key.

Steering Brakes.—With the brake OFF (that is, steering lever fully forward) turn the adjusting bolt in the direction of the arrow marked on the rim of the drum until the shoe presses hard on the brake drum. Then repeat this operation for the other shoe of the same brake. Next pull the steering lever to the ON position two or three times (right-hand lever for left-hand brake and left-hand lever for right-hand brake). This ensures that both shoes are centralized in the drum. Take brake OFF (lever forward) and retighten both adjusting bolts. At this stage there is no clearance between the shoes and drum.

As the adjusting bolt is rotated, the locking spring is moved up and down by the notches on the wheel, and these notches are used as a means of checking the shoe clearance. From the "no clearance" position given

Fig. 29.—Adjusting the track brakes.

above, turn the bolt backwards *six or seven notches* and the brakes are correctly adjusted. Replace the access plugs in the brake drum.

Track Brakes.—To adjust these, the procedure is with one exception the same as for the steering brakes. The only difference is that the foot brake pedal is pressed hard down two or three times to centralize the shoes, instead of pulling the steering levers.

Bleeding the Hydraulic Systems.—Bleeding (expelling air) should only be necessary when refilling after the system has been drained, or some portion of it has been disconnected. This is done by arranging an intentional "leak" and then pumping fluid through the pipe-lines until all air is expelled. The intentional "leak" is provided by bleeder nipples and there is one of these above each brake. Carry out the operation on each brake in turn.

The same operation should be carried out when dealing with the clutch withdrawal mechanism (*see* page 35) except that the clutch pedal is actuated to pump fluid through the pipe-lines. The bleeder nipple for this is on the end of the left-hand side cylinder block.

First check that the reserve tank is full, and if not top up. A short length of clean rubber tubing and a clean glass jar with a small quantity of clean fluid in it is needed for all bleeding operations.

Remove the bleeder nipple cover and push one end of the rubber tube on to the nipple and let the other end rest in the fluid in the jar (*see* Fig. 30). Unscrew the nipple one complete turn and operate the steering lever (for steering brake), the foot pedal (for track brake) or the clutch pedal (for clutch withdrawal mechanism). Do this several times, giving the lever or pedal full strokes and *keeping the end of the rubber tube under the surface of the fluid* in the jar.

Continue this until no more air bubbles are seen coming from the rubber tube in the jar, and when satisfied that all air has been expelled, tighten the bleeder nipple *before* removing the rubber tube from the fluid in the jar. Then remove the rubber tube from the nipple and replace the nipple cover.

When all the bleeding is completed, test the steering and track brakes and clutch withdrawal mechanism by running the vehicle, when instant response to the controls should be obtained.

The fluid bled from the system can be used again, but it should be filtered and allowed to stand for 24 hours to allow it to become de-aerated before being used.

The necessity for frequent bleeding indicates a faulty pipe joint or worn cylinder cups.

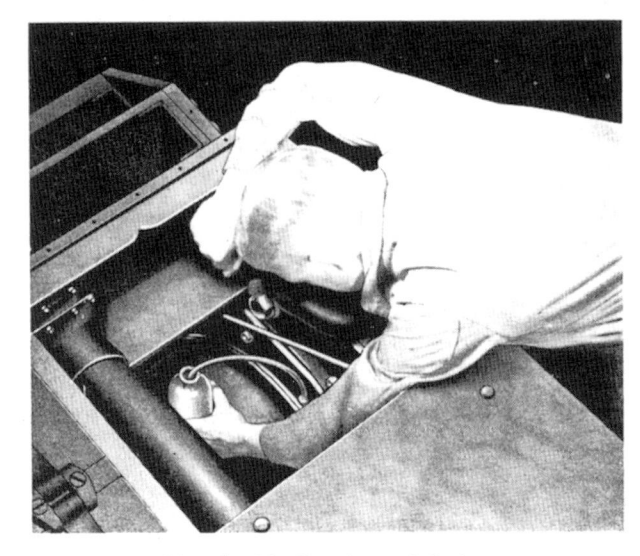

Fig. 30.—Bleeding the track brakes.

VEHICLE HISTORY AND SPECIFICATION

THE HULL

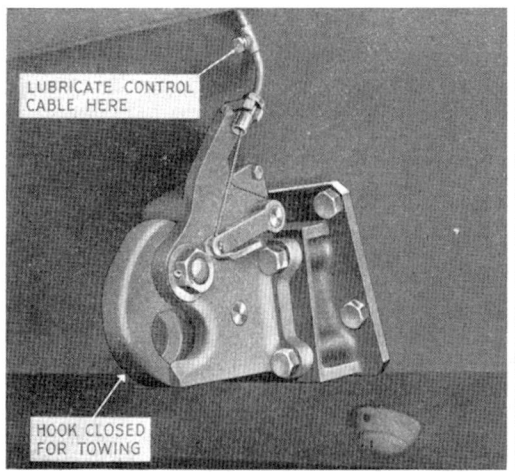

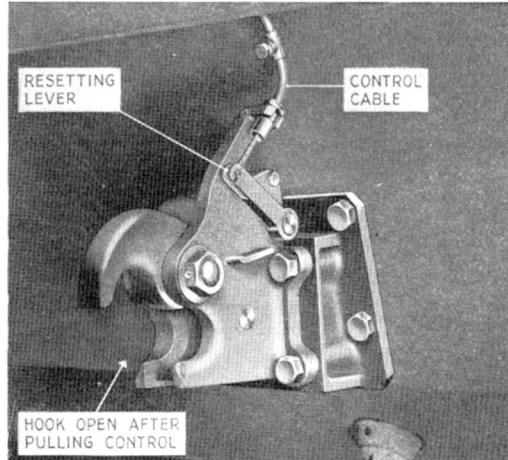

Fig. 61.—Rotatrailer towing hook.

The hull is divided into four compartments:—
(1) **The Driver's Compartment.**—This is in the right-hand part of the nose of the vehicle.
(2) **The Front Gunner's Compartment.**—In the left-hand part of the nose of the vehicle.
(3) **The Fighting Compartment.**—This is amidships, below the turret, and houses the rotating platform which bears the commander, gunner and loader-operator.

Towing eyes are provided at both the front and rear ends of the vehicle, while lifting eyes are mounted on top of the nose and also at the top of the inner sideplates at the rear of the vehicle.

A special hook for towing a Rotatrailer is fitted at the rear of the vehicle (*see* Fig. 61). This is operated by cable from a handle in the top left-hand rear corner of the fighting compartment (*see* Fig. 62). By pulling this handle the hook is opened and the trailer released. The hook can only be re-set from outside the vehicle.

DRIVER'S COMPARTMENT.

The driver's compartment houses the instrument panel, compass, steering-brake levers, track-brake pedal and all driving controls. For instructions in the use of the instruments and driving, *see* "Driving Instructions".

Access to the compartment is either by the door in the roof above the driver's seat, or should these be shut, through the doors in the turret roof and then through the hole in the bulkhead at the back of the driver's compartment.

To open driver's doors from inside the vehicle (or from outside through visor) pull the chain which runs along the leading edge of the right-hand door. This withdraws the spring-loaded fasteners and enables the driver to swing the doors upwards.

NOTE.—*Never close all doors when leaving the vehicle as they cannot be opened from outside if properly shut.* Always leave the driver's visor open, or the commander's cupola doors in such a position (i.e. with one door overlapping the other), that the driver's doors or commander's cupola can be opened from outside the vehicle.

Engine Controls.—These are three in number, are grouped on the right-hand side of the driver's compartment and are easily accessible. They comprise an accelerator hand lever, and a carburetter strangler lever. The third lever, which is disconnected on this vehicle, is for use with the "Liberty" engine for ignition timing.

(1) *Accelerator.*—This can be operated either by hand or foot. When it is necessary for the driver to operate both clutch and brake pedals at the same time, as when starting on a hill, the hand lever is used. It can be fixed in position by tightening the thumb-screw on the lever.

(2) *Strangler lever.*—This operates the valves in the strangler valve body of the induction system and is used in conjunction with the Ki-gass pump for cold starting conditions. It is spring-loaded to the "forward" or "fully open" position. (*See* "Driving Instructions".)

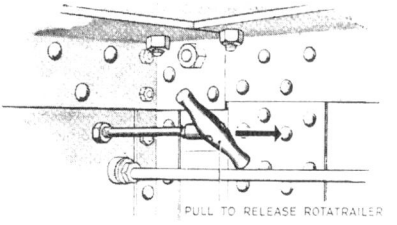

Fig. 62.—Rotatrailer hook control.

75

CROMWELL TANK

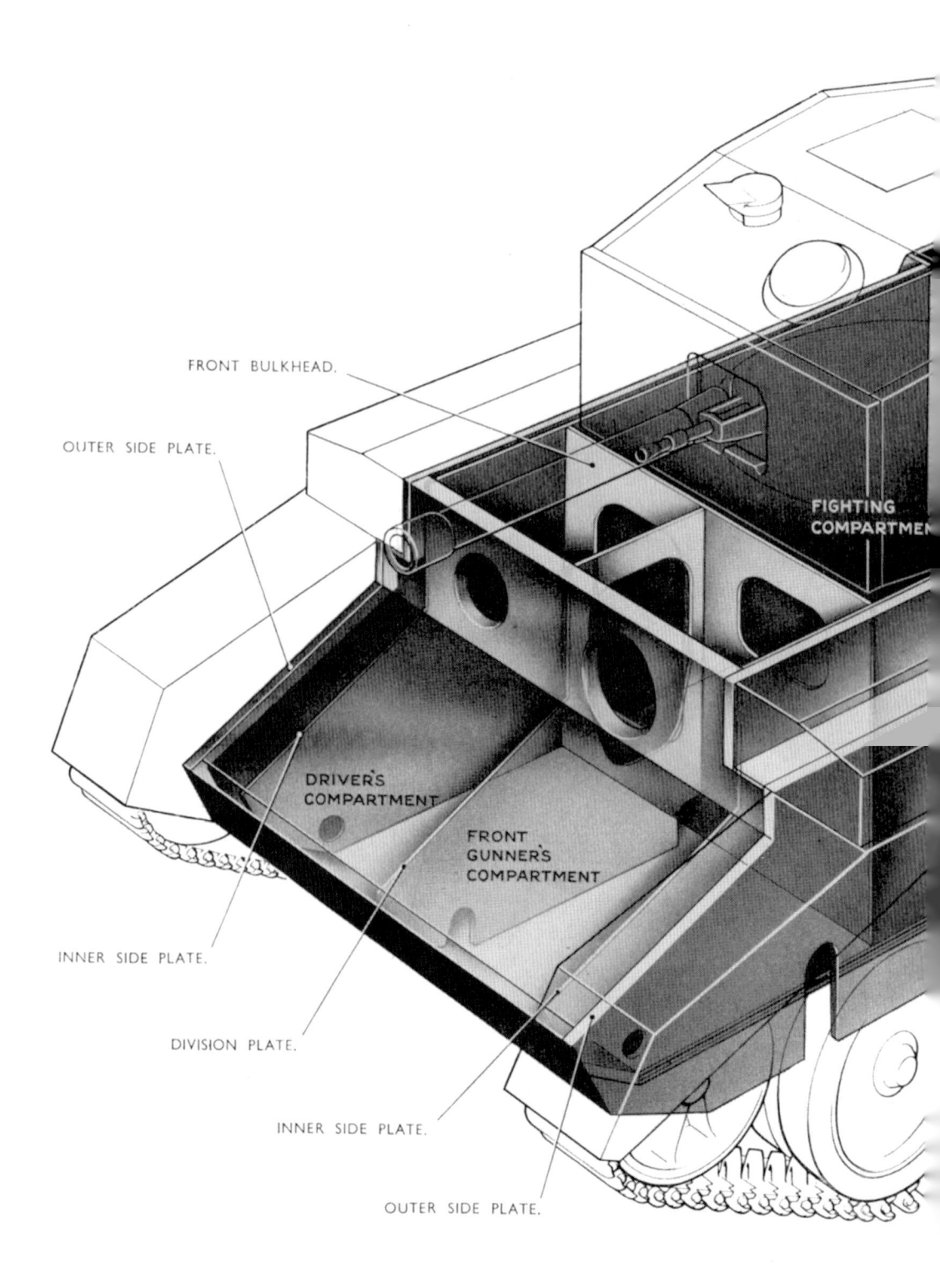

FRONT BULKHEAD.

OUTER SIDE PLATE.

FIGHTING COMPARTMENT

DRIVER'S COMPARTMENT

FRONT GUNNER'S COMPARTMENT

INNER SIDE PLATE.

DIVISION PLATE.

INNER SIDE PLATE.

OUTER SIDE PLATE.

VEHICLE HISTORY AND SPECIFICATION

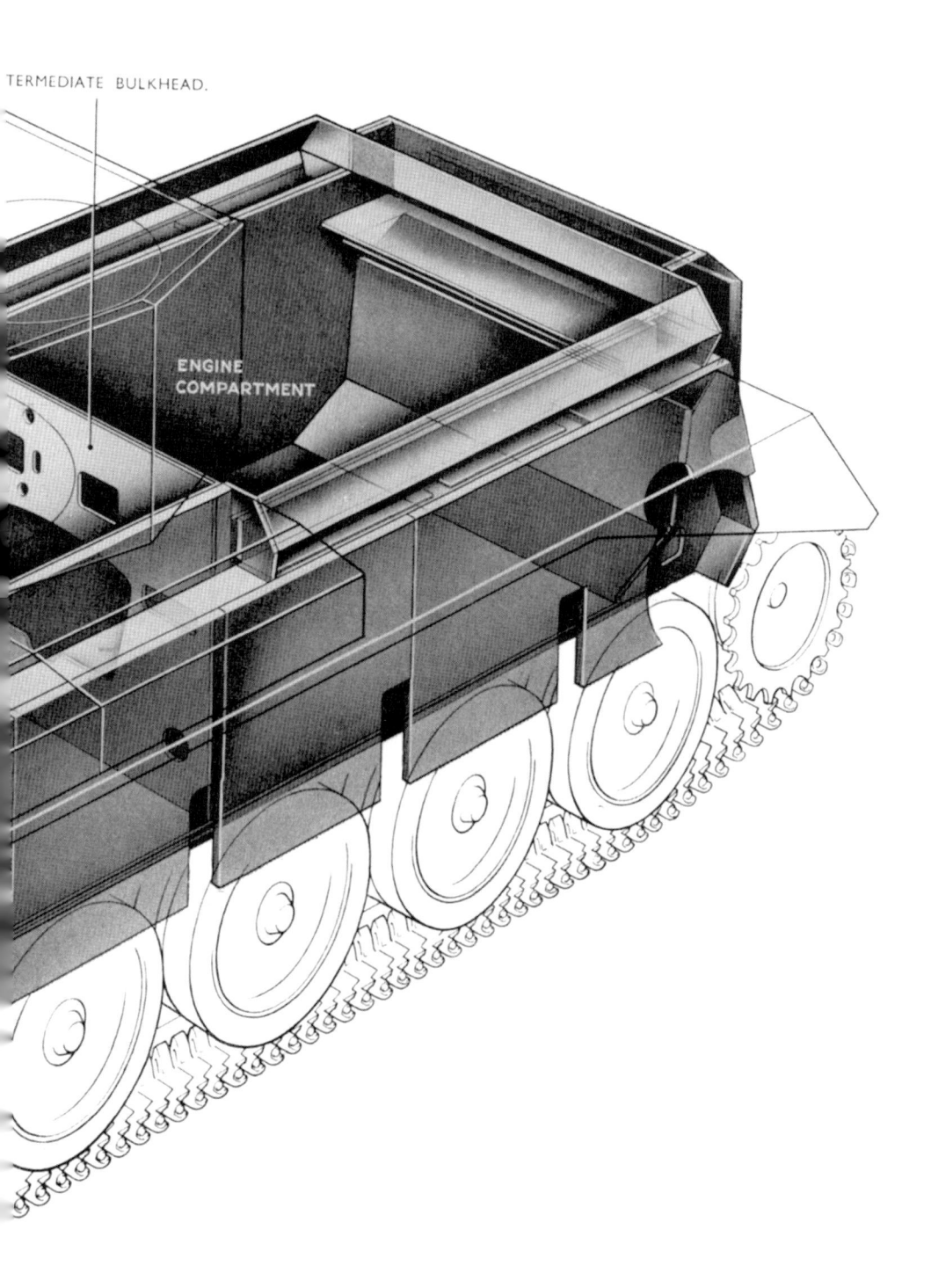

Fig. 228.—Layout of vehicle plating.   Fig. 228.

CROMWELL TANK

Vision Arrangements.—The driver is provided with a visor in the front and two periscopes in the roof. This visor is armoured and incorporates a small wicket door and a main door. The wicket door can be opened and the main door left closed; or the complete unit can be opened when the vehicle is not under fire. This gives the driver a wide range of vision. To open the complete unit, pull the spring-loaded handle outwards (*see* Fig. 3), move the main catch to the left in its slot and swing the handle also to the left. To open the wicket door only, press the operating plunger, at the same time moving the handle as before. In this case be careful not to move the main catch. The driver then has a smaller aperture to look through and is protected by a very thick glass block.

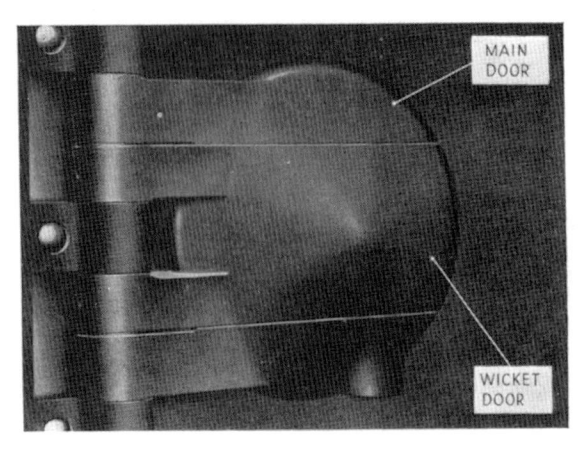

Fig. 63.—Driver's visor closed.

If this glass block is damaged, it can be removed by lifting the securing catch. Replace with a spare block and lower the catch to its original position. If this has to be done while under fire *the wicket door must be kept closed.*

The driver has two periscopes, one to the left and one to the right of the visor. They are provided with control handles and each periscope is padded so that the driver can steady his forehead against it and secure a good view. For further details, *see* Chapter VII A.

Driver's Seat.—This is mounted on slides providing adjustment fore and aft, to suit the driver's comfort. By releasing a catch at the front right-hand side, a range of movement is obtained to suit drivers of varying stature. The back rest can be lifted slightly in its sockets and then hinged backwards or forwards so as to give access to the driving compartment from the fighting compartment.

Front Sludge Drain.—On the right, in front of the driver, is the front sludge drain in the hull floor (*see* Fig. 3). This is operated from inside the vehicle only. To open the drain, lift the cam lever and swing it hard over to the right. When the lever is lifted over to the left again, the drain is closed by a spring. Keep the mechanism clean and oil the cam lever pivot when required.

Lubrication.—Keep the driver's roof doors in good working order by WEEKLY inspection and oiling when required.

The reserve tank for the hydraulic brakes is on the right-hand wall and this should be checked WEEKLY and topped up as required.

The reserve tank for the axle-arm lubrication system, also on the right-hand wall of the driver's compartment, should be topped up EVERY 250 MILES.

Fig. 64.—Driver's visor, wicket door open.

There is one nipple at the front of the change-speed box and three nipples on the change-speed rods on the floor. These should receive attention EVERY 250 MILES.

Each periscope has two nipples on the circular slide. Lubricate these EVERY 250 MILES, but do not overdo this.

The seat slides and the various controls in the compartment should be inspected and oiled if necessary EVERY 250 MILES.

VEHICLE HISTORY AND SPECIFICATION

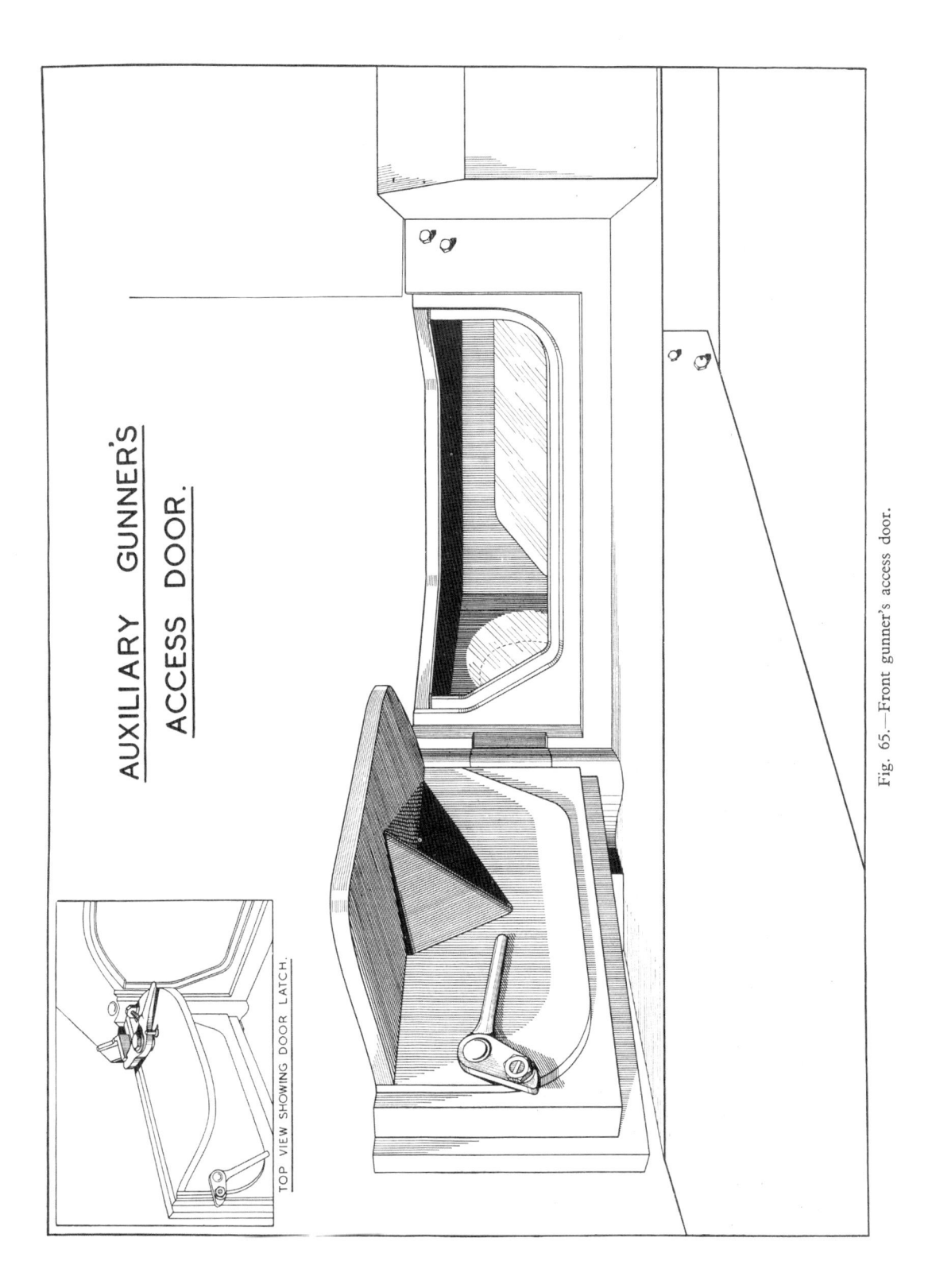

AUXILIARY GUNNER'S ACCESS DOOR.

TOP VIEW SHOWING DOOR LATCH.

Fig. 65.—Front gunner's access door.

Maintenance. — The glass block in the driver's visor and also the periscope lenses must be cleaned by wiping with a wet rag and polishing with a soft cloth. Where mud has hardened on, wet it thoroughly before removing to avoid scratching the surface of the lenses. To prevent fogging, apply a small amount of anti-dim compound No. 2 to the glass. If a lens is broken the pieces must be thoroughly brushed out with the brush provided before fitting a new one.

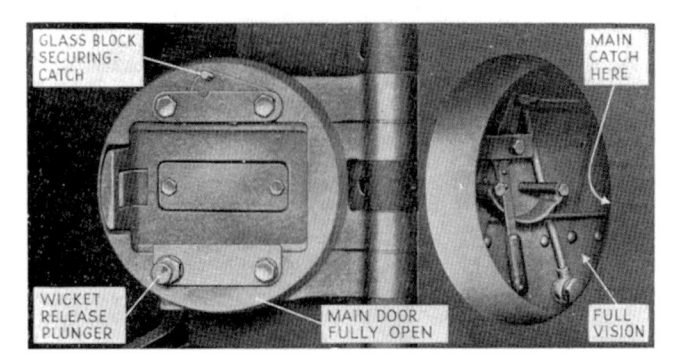

Fig. 66.—Driver's visor, fully open.

FRONT GUNNER'S COMPARTMENT.

The front gunner's compartment contains a 7·92 mm. Besa machine-gun, the CO_2 bottles for fire fighting, the axle-arm lubrication pumps, and an electrically-operated extraction fan for ventilation.

Access to this compartment is through the front gunner's side door (*see* Fig. 65) or through the doors in the turret roof in the same manner as outlined for the driver's compartment, and then through the hole provided in the division plate.

Vision Arrangements.—No periscope is provided for the front gunner, but a sighting telescope is fitted for use with the Besa machine-gun.

Pumps for Axle-Arm Lubrication System.—The cross-tubes carry the bearings for the axle-arm pivot shafts, and these bearings are lubricated by pressure pumps mounted on the floor, to the right of the front gunner's compartment. The pumps draw oil from the reserve tank on the right-hand wall of the driver's compartment, and deliver it under pressure to all the cross-tube bearings. They are automatically-operated each time the driver depresses the clutch pedal (*see* Fig. 227). As the amount of oil to be delivered to each bearing has been established by test, *do not make any alteration*.

For Seating, Lubrication and Maintenance, *see* remarks under "Driver's Compartment".

FIGHTING COMPARTMENT.

The fighting compartment extends the full interior width of the vehicle. The front bulkhead separates it from the driver's and front gunner's compartment, while the rear bulkhead forms a division between this and the engine compartment. Extending downwards into this compartment from the turret and rotating with it is the turntable which carries the commander, gunner, and loader-operator.

On the right-hand wall at the front of this compartment is the electrical control board, and below it the main switch-box. Below this, anchored to the floor, is the auxiliary charging set. The batteries are cradled on the same wall at the rear of the compartment.

In the rear corner by the left-hand wall is the recuperator for the power-traverse, and nearby the remote control fuel-tap is mounted on the rear bulkhead (*see* Fig. 127) and also the Ki-gass fuel pump and commander's speedometer.

In the centre of the rear bulkhead are the magneto emergency stop switches (*see* Fig. 49), while at either side are the air-cleaner doors. Near the floor is the bevel gearbox with the starter-motor on top, the dynamo on the right-hand side and the power traverse variable-flow pump on the left-hand side.

The operating handle for opening the rotatrailer hook is in the top rear corner above the power traverse recuperator, while the handle for jettisoning the auxiliary fuel tank (if fitted) is in the opposite top rear corner above the batteries. The base-junction for the power traverse is mounted in the centre of this compartment and a metal cover is fitted to the turntable platform to surround and protect it.

Drains.—The centre drain is slightly to the right-hand rear of the fighting compartment and must be opened when draining the power traverse system. It is reached by removing the detachable board in the turntable platform. To open the drain, push the handle downwards; to keep it open, give the handle a half-turn. The drain is closed by a spring (*see* Fig. 60).

The rear sludge drain is at the rear of the vehicle floor, but is operated by a lever in the fighting compartment—on the left-hand side of the rear bulkhead (*see* Figs. 49 and 60). To open the drain, lift up the lever. The drain is self-closing under pressure of a spring.

ENGINE COMPARTMENT.

The engine compartment extends from the fighting compartment rear bulkhead to the rear of the vehicle, covering the full interior width. Air inlet louvres are arranged along the top of each side and on the roof itself, while three outlet louvres are located at the rear.

Access Doors in Roof.—A number of hinged doors are provided in the roof in order to give access to the engine, air-cleaners, clutch, radiators, header tank, gearbox, brakes and final drive couplings. These doors are securely locked by spring-loaded tongue-type latches and are opened by the special key provided (*see* Fig. 13).

Fuel and Oil Filler Covers.—Small covers protect the fuel fillers, engine oil filler and engine oil dipstick (*see* Fig. 13). These are locked in position by a double-tongue type catch operated by the same key as above. The cover is then lifted so exposing the fuel or engine oil filler, which can be unscrewed by the same key. Should the key be mislaid it is possible to operate the catches with a pair of pliers. Both fuel and oil fillers are suitably indicated by means of the words PETROL in blue and OIL in yellow, which are painted on the inclined face of each side air-inlet louvre (*see* Parts 4 and 5, Chapter I A).

Access Covers and Drains in Floor.—Suitable covers are provided in the floor to give access to the various units in this compartment. In addition, drains are arranged where necessary to allow drainage of fuel tanks, oil tanks and gearbox. All these covers and drains are sealed against water ingress and are shown in Fig. 67.

Fording Flap.—This is provided to cover the lower air outlet louvre at the rear of the vehicle. When passing through water this flap must be closed and secured by the four operating levers. These are only accessible from the outside of the vehicle (*see* Fig. 68). The levers are so designed as to hold the fording flap secure in the open position as well as ensuring a water-tight joint when closed.

Lubrication.—The hinges and catches of the access doors, the fuel and oil filler covers, and the fording flap hinges should be kept clean and oiled when necessary.

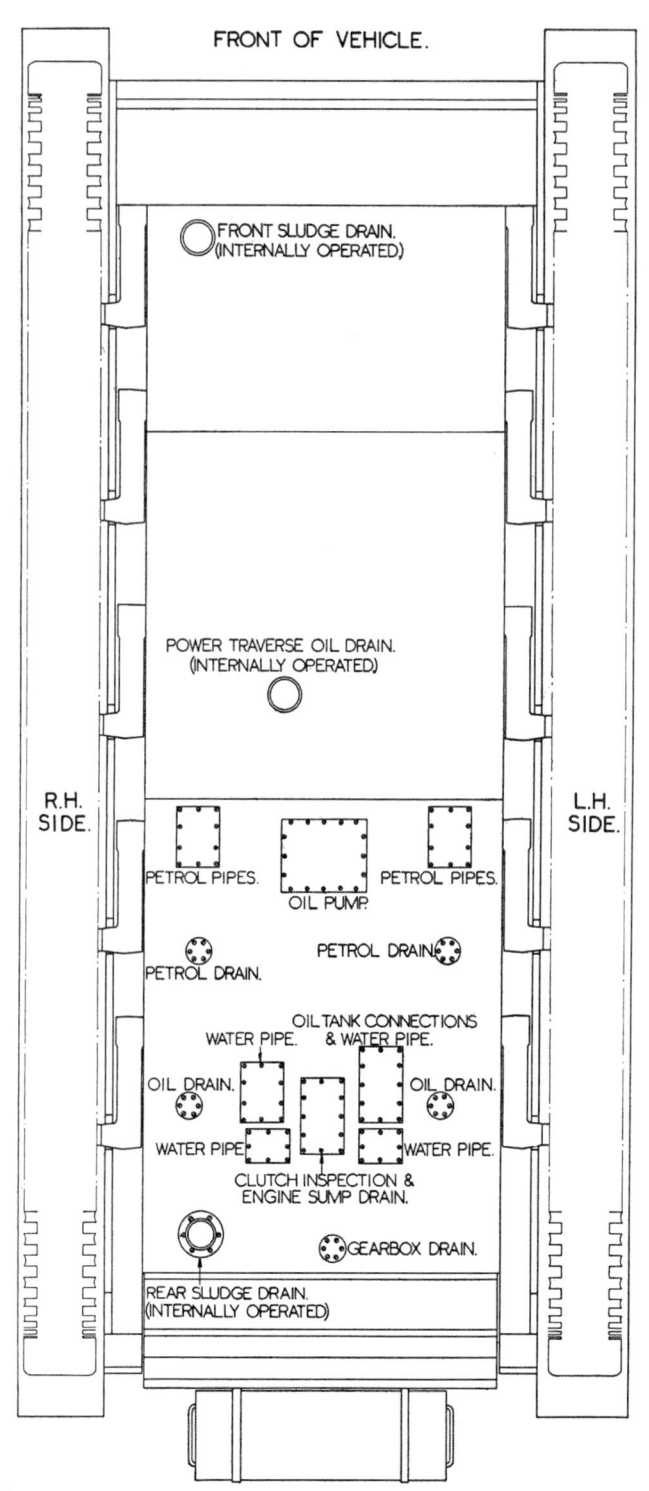

Fig. 67.—Inverted plan view of vehicle, showing drains and access plates.

VEHICLE HISTORY AND SPECIFICATION

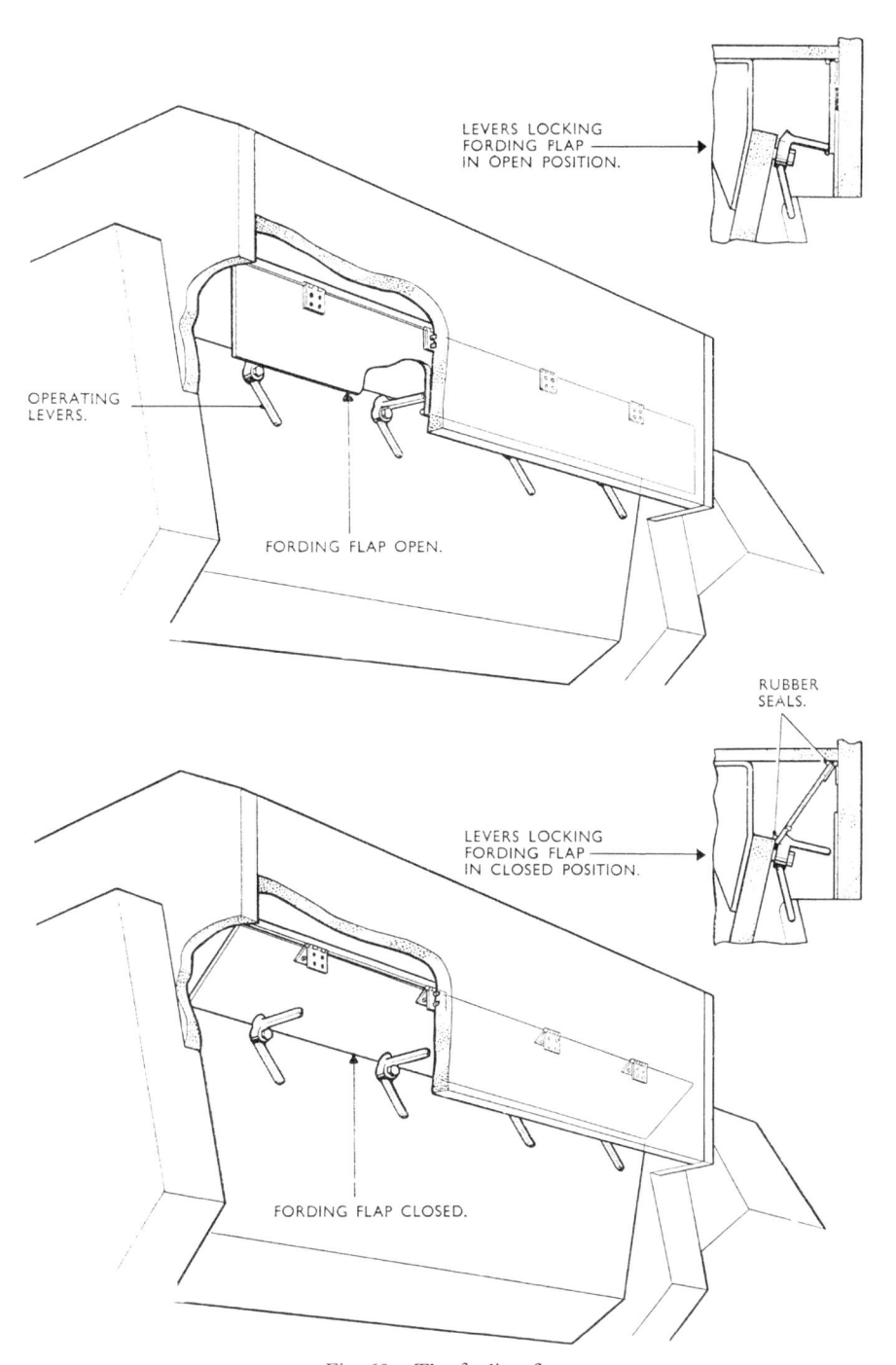

Fig. 68.—The fording flap.

THE TURRET

The turret, in which the 6-Pr. gun and 7·92 mm. Besa machine gun are co-axially mounted, is heavily armoured and can be completely rotated so that the guns can be brought to bear upon a target without having to turn the vehicle. Doors are provided in the turret roof, those on the right-hand side giving access to the loader-operator's position, while the doors in the commander's cupola on the left admit to the commander's position and gunner's seat.

Four periscopes are fitted in the roof, one for the gunner and one for the loader-operator, and two in the cupola for the commander. In addition, an electrically-operated ventilating fan is mounted in the forward part of the roof and two wireless aerials are carried on the rear part of the roof. In the right-hand forward corner of the roof a bracket is spigot-mounted. This bracket is in the form of an oblique tube and is flanged at its lower end to receive a 2-in. smoke bombthrower which is bolted to it.

Revolver ports are provided in the turret rear sides and a sighting telescope for the gunner is mounted co-axially with the guns.

TURRET ROTATION AND LOCK.

Both manual and power rotation is provided, the traversing gear being dealt with in detail in Chapter VIII B.

A travelling lock is fitted on the turret ring so that the turret can be locked solid in any desired position, and consists of a spring-loaded plunger operated by a cam-lever (*see* Fig. 69). The plunger has teeth to engage the turret ring teeth, thus ensuring a positive lock. When the turret has been traversed to the desired position, the lock must be engaged by moving the handle hard over to the left. The lock must be *completely disengaged* by releasing the handle hard over to the stop, *before* operating the power traverse —otherwise damage will occur.

Lubrication.—Inspect the travelling lock WEEKLY and lubricate if necessary, using an oil can. It should operate freely. The turret ball races are packed with grease on assembly, but should be further lubricated by means of the grease nipple provided on the left-hand side of the turret ring EVERY 500 MILES or as required.

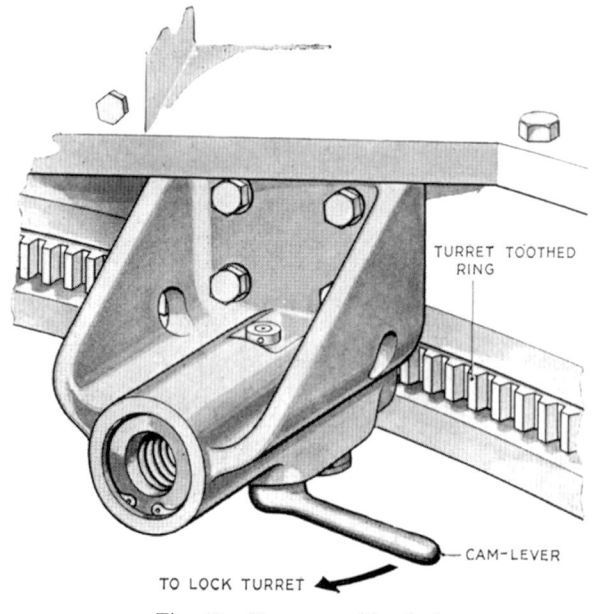

Fig. 69.—Turret travelling lock.

Maintenance.—The turret should rotate smoothly and easily. If it does not, check that the hand traverse brake is freeing properly. If not, adjust as explained in Chapter VIII A. If the hand traverse brake is not at fault and yet the turret rotates in a jerky or uneven manner, it will be necessary to lift the turret and examine the ball race tracks, which may show indentations from the balls. This is a workshop operation, and the only remedy is to fit a new race.

As speedy movement of the turret will often save lives, such indentations must be prevented at all costs, and this can be done, in a large measure, by frequently altering the direction of rotation of the turret. This is worth while remembering because, by so doing, the balls on which the turret runs are constantly moved in relation to the races, and so do not tend to make contact at the same spot when firing the guns. In addition, when travelling, the turret should be traversed slightly right or left of the dead-ahead position in order to spread the load on the ball races and, for the same reason, when the vehicle is standing, it is a good plan every week to change the direction in which the turret faces.

COMMANDER'S CUPOLA.

This is the rotating armoured cover in the turret roof, which rotates on three rollers carried on ball-bearings bolted to the cover itself. It is manually operated by two pairs of traversing handles, and can be locked in four definite positions by means of a spring-loaded bolt. A locking-handle, operating on one of the doors, permits both doors to be locked from inside. Two spring-loaded catches are provided outside the cupola to hold the doors open.

Lubrication and Maintenance.—Keep the doors, hinges, catches, bolt and locking-handle in good working order by DAILY inspection and oiling when required. Oil the three rollers and their ball-bearings very sparingly EVERY 250 MILES, and at the same time check the three bolts on which they are mounted for tightness.

LOADER'S DOORS.

These provide the alternative means of entering the turret. To open them from inside the vehicle, pull the chain which runs along the leading edge. This withdraws the spring-loaded fasteners and enables the doors to be swung upwards.

Lubrication and Maintenance.—Keep the doors in good working order by DAILY inspection and oiling when required.

REVOLVER PORTS.

Two ports are provided, one in each rear side of the turret (*see* Fig. 70). Each consists of a circular armoured door, hinged at the top in an armoured casing and opening outwards. They are locked when closed by an upright lever inside the turret which operates a spring-loaded catch at the bottom of each port. To open the port, pull the lever inwards; this releases the catch and a further pull on the lever swings the port upwards. When the lever is released, the port closes and locks itself.

Lubrication.—Test DAILY, and, if necessary, oil the door hinge (oil hole outside top), the lever pivot and spring-loaded catch.

Fig. 70.—Revolver port.

VISION ARRANGEMENTS.

Gunner's and Loader's Periscopes.—These periscopes are identical and are mounted in the turret roof. The same type of periscope is fitted in the hull roof for the driver. Each is mounted in a flange bolted to the roof plate and protected by an armoured ring with a sheet-metal top cover. The mounting allows each periscope to be rotated and tilted, and a handle is provided for controlling these movements (*see* Fig. 71).

A slide is provided for back-laying, so that vision can be obtained from either rear or front of the periscope without having to rotate it. This slide has three positions and is controlled by a spring-loaded ball and cup. In the highest position, as shown in Fig. 72, a normal view is obtained, in the middle position both main and back-laying lenses are covered, while in the lowest position the back-laying lens is brought into use. To replace damaged lenses, pull up the small release catch at the front and break the periscope as shown in Fig. 72. The lenses can then be removed and replaced.

Commander's Periscopes.—These periscopes are mounted in the commander's cupola, and are internally similar to the gunner's and loader's periscopes, with the same lenses and back-laying arrangement.

CROMWELL TANK

The top lenses, however, are protected by swivelling armoured covers, operated by levers inside the cupola. The periscopes are mounted for tilting only, any rotation required being obtainable by turning the cupola itself. Damaged lenses can be replaced in exactly the same manner as in the case of the other periscopes.

Gunner's Telescope.—A gun sighting telescope is mounted co-axially with the 6-pdr. and the Besa guns, and is described in Chapter IX B.

Lubrication and Maintenance (all periscopes).—Inspect the periscopes DAILY for good vision, cleanliness and free working. Lubricate the periscopes EVERY 250 MILES OR WEEKLY, but don't over-grease.

To clean the lenses, first remove any dirt by using a wet soft cloth gently. Then polish with a clean dry soft cloth. Where mud has hardened on, wet it thoroughly before removing it to avoid scratching the surface of the lens. Apply anti-dim No. 2 sparingly to prevent fogging. When a damaged lens has been removed, be careful to brush out *all* the broken pieces with the special brush provided before fitting a new lens.

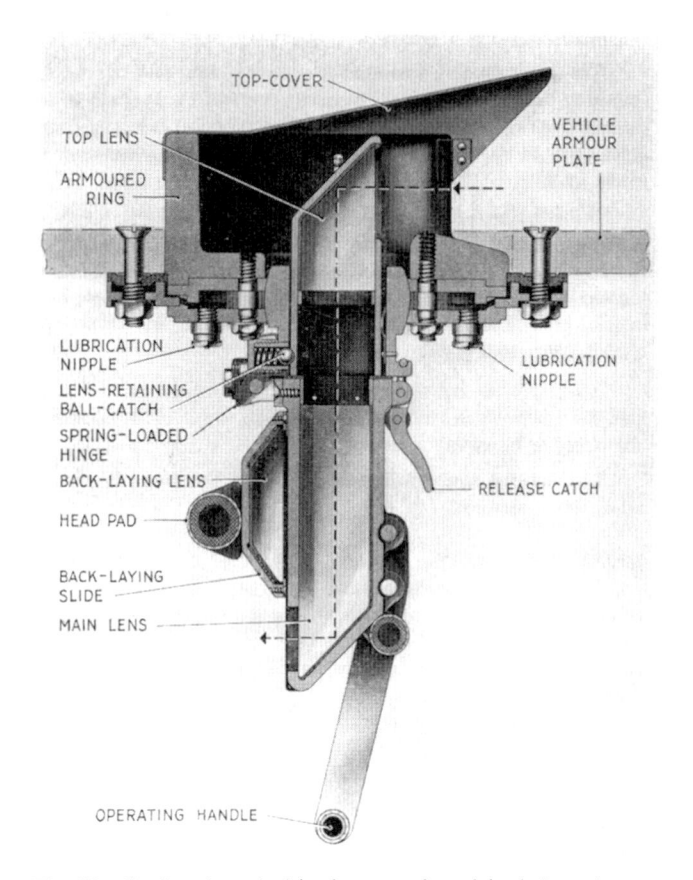

Fig. 71.—Section through driver's, gunner's and loader's periscope.

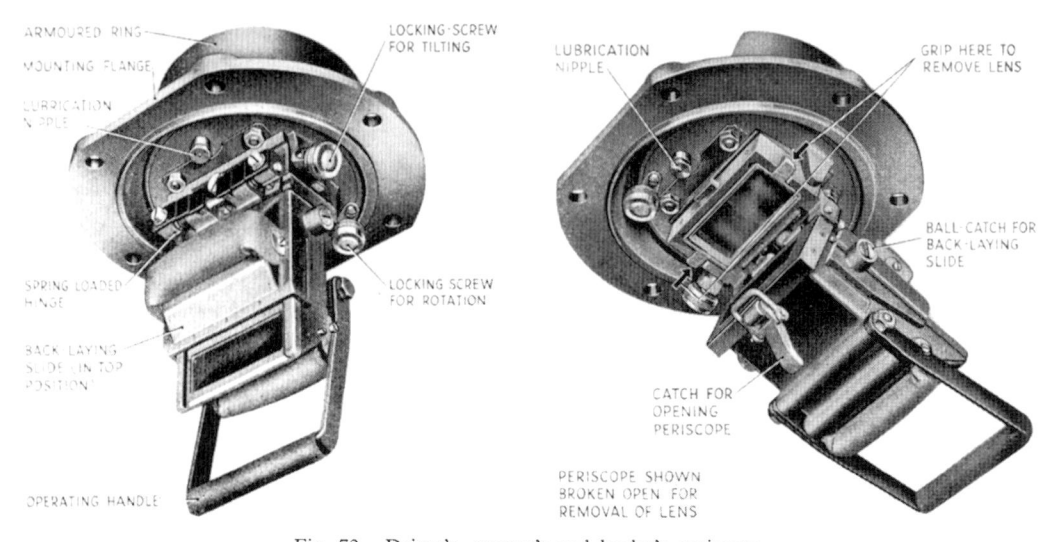

Fig. 72.—Driver's, gunner's and loader's periscope.

TURRET TURNTABLE.

Seating.—Seats are provided for the commander, gunner and loader-operator. The commander can only be seated when the cupola doors are open, but when these are closed it is necessary for him to stand on the platform. By lifting his seat slightly and pushing it over to the rear, it will serve as a back-rest.

The gunner's seat is mounted on a pedestal which is bolted to the platform. It is quickly adjustable by means of a foot-pedal. The seat pillar is spring-loaded and when the pedal is depressed a locking-plunger is disengaged and the seat can be raised or lowered as desired. When the pedal is released, the locking-plunger re-engages and the seat is locked in position.

The loader-operator's seat can be hinged over out of the way when not in use.

WIRELESS AND INTER-COMMUNICATION EQUIPMENT.

The wireless and inter-communication equipment is fully dealt with in a separate book, "Wireless Sets, No. 19, Working Instructions", obtainable from C.O.O., Donnington.

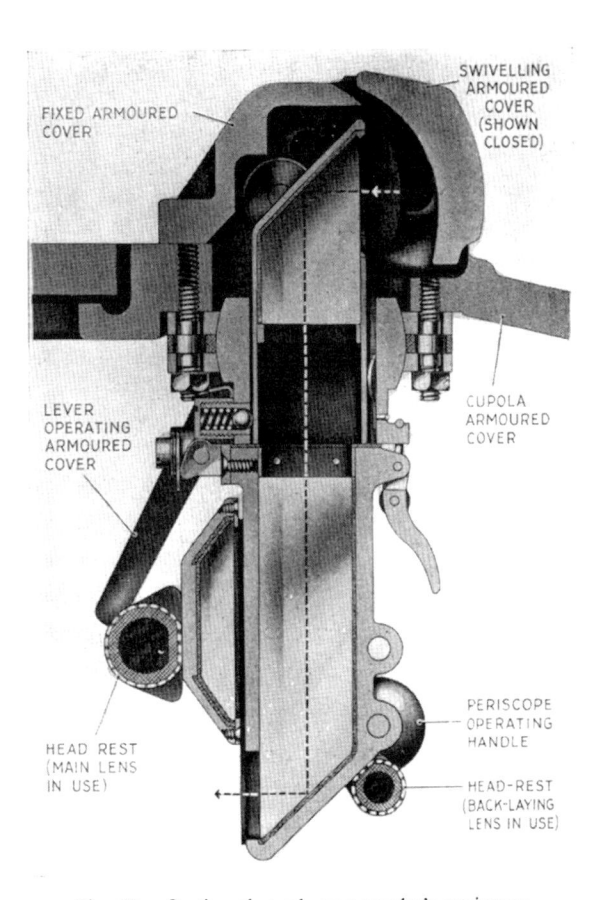

Fig. 73.—Section through commander's periscope.

Q.F., 6-PR. 7-CWT. GUN

The Q.F., 6-pr. 7 cwt. guns used in armoured fighting vehicles are adapted from anti-tank weapons to suit A.F.V. gun-mountings. The main difference is in the breech rings, which, in the ground pattern guns, are drilled and tapped for securing to the slippers, and in the A.F.V. patterns, are formed with a lug to connect to the recoil systems. The breech mechanism components are interchangeable.

PARTICULARS.

	Mk. III.	Mk. V.
Weight with breech mechanism	6 cwt. 3 qr. 5 lb.	6 cwt. 1 qr. 27½ lb.
Weight without breech mechanism	6 cwt. 0 qr. 1 lb.	5 cwt. 2 qr. 23½ lb.
Length—total	100·95 in.	116·95 in.
Length of barrel	96·2 in.	112·2 in.
Calibre	2·244 in.	2·244 in.
Rifling	24 plain section grooves.	24 plain section grooves.
Twist of rifling	1 turn in 30 calibres.	1 turn in 30 calibres.
Probable life of rifling in full rounds, Cordite W., W.M. or W.M.T.	800.	—
Probable life of rifling in full rounds, N.H.033	1,600.	—
Muzzle velocity, full charge, Cordite W., W.M., W.M.T. or N.H.033	2,675 f.p.s. (approx.).	—
Muzzle velocity, H.V.	2,800 f.p.s. (approx.).	—
Firing mechanism	Percussion.	Percussion.
Number of rounds a gun may fire before requiring examination (equivalent full charge)	180.	—

OPERATION.

To load.—Set the semi-automatic gear to S.A. fire. Open the breech, using the breech mechanism lever. Return the lever to the "breech closed" position. Insert the round, pushing it into the chamber with a sharp movement. The breech will automatically close.

To fire.—Squeeze the trigger of the remote firing control gear.

To unload.—Open the breech slowly, using the breech mechanism lever. Extract the round carefully, preventing it from falling from the breech opening with the free hand. Replace the round in the ammunition rack. Ease the firing mechanism by pressing the firing lever on the gun with the right hand and controlling the cocking handle with the left hand.

Misfire.—

ACTION BY GUNNER.	ACTION BY LOADER.
Tap the loader twice, shout "Misfire—re-cock".	Re-cock by pulling the cocking handle to the rear with two fingers of the left hand or by using the cocking lanyard. Tap the gunner once.
Squeeze the trigger.	Watch movement of the striker mechanism. If the gun fails to fire, tap the gunner twice.
WAIT FOR ONE MINUTE.	
	Open the breech slowly and examine the cap. If the cap has been struck, throw the round outside the vehicle. If not struck, replace the round in the ammunition rack and change the firing pin.

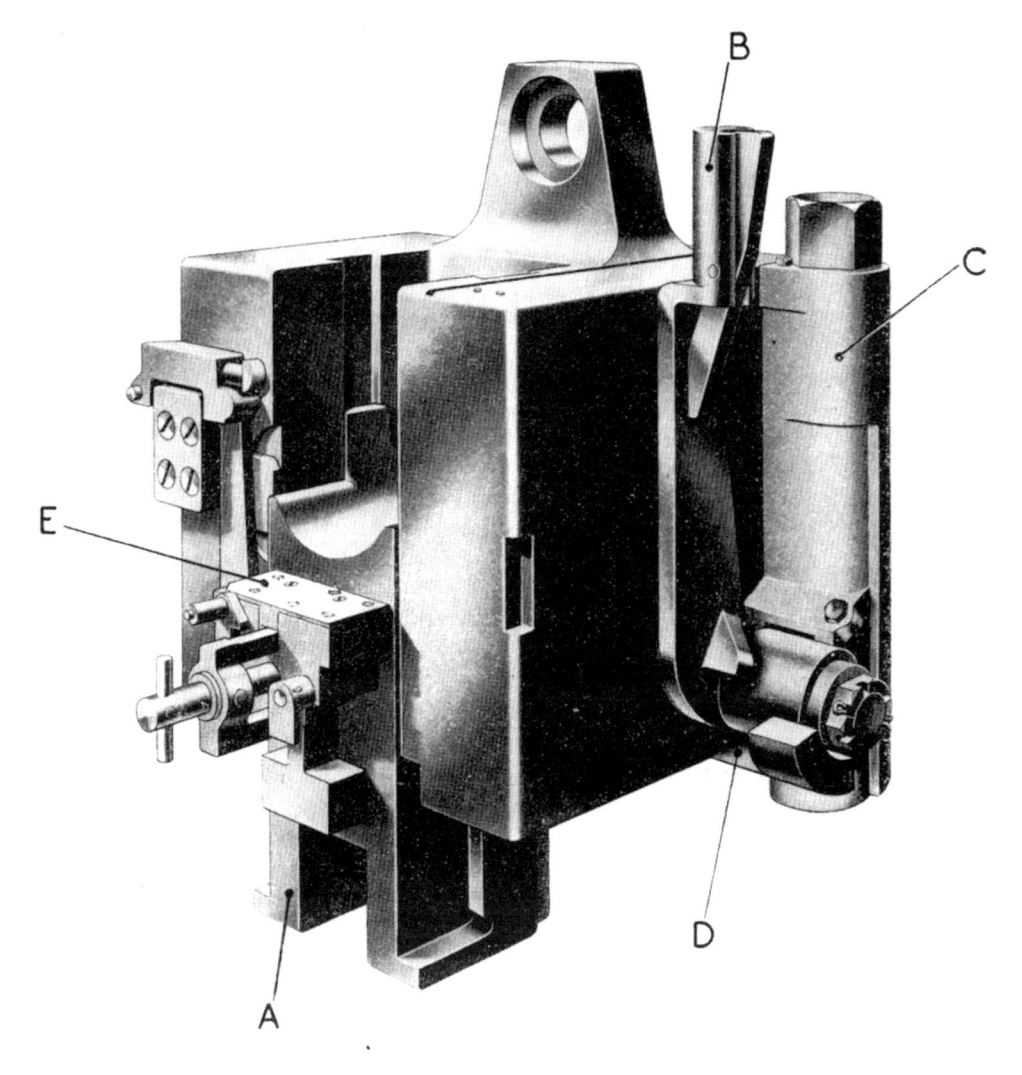

Fig. 76.—Breech mechanism—open.

A. Breech block.
B. Breech mechanism lever.
C. Spring case.
D. Rack pinion.
E. Striker case.

TO DISMANTLE THE BREECH MECHANISM (*see* Fig. 76).

(*a*) Remove the deflector and loader's shield.

(*b*) With the striker cocked and the safety catch at "SAFE", remove the striker case (E) by withdrawing the retaining catch and turning the case through an angle of 60 degrees clockwise.

(*c*) Place safety catch at "FIRE" and press sear inwards to release the striker.

(*d*) See that the gun is level and remove gun lug nut.

(*e*) Remove the actuating shaft keep pin and slotted nut, hold in position the breech block and two extractor levers, and withdraw the shaft towards the left until the breech mechanism lever (B) and rack pinion (D) can be removed. Support breech block (A) during completion of the withdrawal movement of the actuating

89

shaft, then lower breech block a little, push up and remove extractor levers and then withdraw breech block. Remove cocking link actuating pin, crank and cocking links.

TO ASSEMBLE THE BREECH MECHANISM.

(a) Assemble the breech block, with crank, striker cocking link and actuating pin. Insert the breech block a short distance into the breech ring, holding in position the two extractor levers, and place the block in the closed position, making sure that the striker cocking link is flush with the rear face of the breech block. Align the crank and extractor levers and insert the actuating shaft from the left. Place in position the breech mechanism lever and rack pinion, push home the actuating shaft and secure it with the nut and split pin.

(b) Cock the striker and insert the striker case into the breech block. Place the safety catch to "SAFE" and turn the case through an angle of 60 degrees, counter-clockwise.

(c) Open the breech and adjust the compression of the closing spring by releasing the check screw and turning the spring case cap, until the breech can be closed easily without undue slamming, with a dummy round in the breech. When the correct compression is obtained, turn the check screw to lock the spring case cap.

(d) Replace the deflector and the loader's shield, if these parts have been removed.

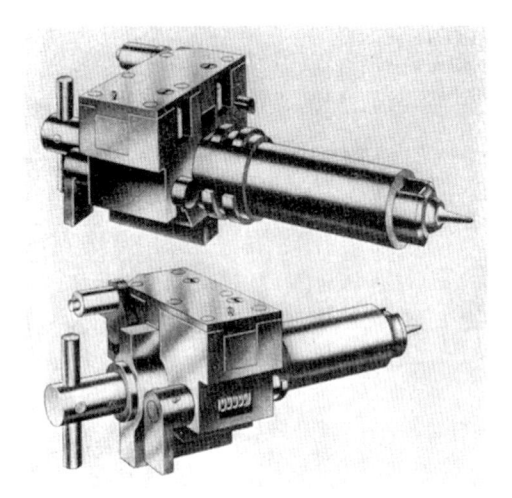

Fig. 77.—Striker case.

TO DISMANTLE THE FIRING MECHANISM.

(a) Remove the striker case from breech block and release the striker (see "To Dismantle the Breech Mechanism" (b)).

(b) Rotate the safety catch to the "FIRE" position. Grasp the cocking handle in one hand and the case in the other and press the toe of the trigger-sear to ease the main-spring.

(c) Remove the keep pin from the cocking handle and unscrew. Withdraw the cocking sleeve from the rear, and the spindle with the main-spring, from the front of the case. Remove the staple from the head of the spindle and withdraw the firing pin.

(d) Remove the safety catch retaining pin from the top of the case. Withdraw the safety catch to the rear. Take out the split pin from the spindle portion of the catch and remove the plunger and spring.

(e) Remove the split pin securing the trigger-sear spring seat and withdraw the sear and spring. Withdraw the split pins from the roller axis pins and remove the axis pins and rollers.

(f) Remove the split pin and head of the striker case retaining catch plunger and withdraw the plunger and spring from the front of the case.

TO ASSEMBLE THE FIRING MECHANISM.

(a) Insert the retaining catch plunger with the spring, in the striker case, fit on the head of the retaining catch and secure it with a split pin.

(b) Place in position the trigger-sear rollers and axis pins and secure with split pins.

(c) Insert the trigger-sear with seat and spring. The seat and spring fit in the right side of the case and are retained by a split pin.

(d) Fit the spring and plunger in the safety catch. Press the sear inwards and insert the safety catch into the striker case from the rear and set it to the "FIRE" position. Place in position the safety catch retaining pin from the top of the case.

(e) Insert the arm of the cocking sleeve in its recess to engage the slot in the trigger-sear. Press on the left end of the trigger-sear while pushing home the cocking sleeve.

(f) Fit the firing pin in the head of the striker spindle and secure it with the retaining staple. Place the main-spring in position over the spindle, insert in the front of the case and press home to engage the key in the cocking sleeve. Screw up the cocking handle and secure it with a split pin.

(g) Cock the striker and turn the safety catch to the "SAFE" position.

(h) Insert the striker case into the breech block. Set safety catch to "FIRE" and release the striker.

PROTRUSION OF THE STRIKER.

Remove the breech block from the gun (see "To Dismantle the Breech Mechanism" (e)). With the striker case assembled and the firing pin in the fired position, apply the striker protrusion gauge No. 16, to the face of the breech block. The minimum should foul and the maximum should clear the firing pin. If not correct, change the firing pin by dismantling the firing mechanism (see page 101) and removing the firing pin with the drift No. 18 inserted into the hole behind the head of the striker spindle.

EXTRACTION OF JAMMED CARTRIDGE.

If a cartridge jams in the chamber and cannot be extracted by leverage on the B.M.L., it must be removed by using the Key, Removing, Jammed Cartridges, No. 9. Remove the primer with the key, reverse the key and screw it into the primer recess. The cartridge can then be withdrawn by screwing the extracting nut on the key. Misfired rounds must be set aside for examination.

GUN, MACHINE, BESA, 7·92 MM., MARKS I, II, II★, III, III★

The 7·92 mm. Besa Machine Gun used in A.F.V.'s is an air-cooled gas-operated weapon with buffered action, ammunition being supplied by a belt holding 225 rimless cartridges. The mark is stamped on the left-hand side of the gun body.

The Mk. I gun is a converted ground pattern gun for use in A.F.V.'s.
The Mk. II gun is made as an A.F.V. weapon
The Mk. III gun has a fixed high rate of fire } See Fig. 79.
The Mk. III★ has fixed low rate of fire

The 7·92 Besa M.G. is intended for mounting in A.F.V.'s, has no ground mounting or sights, and aiming is carried out by means of a sighting telescope housed in the gun mounting.

The barrel cannot be changed unless the gun is removed from the A.F.V. mounting.

The gun can be fired dismounted provided the ejection opening is clear of the ground.

Reference numbers on the illustrations referred to in the following description of the Besa M.G. are for identification purposes, common to the Instruction Book for Armourers D.D. (E) 263.

PARTICULARS.

Approximate weight complete	48 lb. (varies according to mark).	
Approximate weight of barrel	15 lb. (varies according to mark).	
Overhaul length	3 ft. 7½ in.	
Length of barrel with flash eliminator	2 ft. 5 in.	
Rates of fire (rounds per minute):—	*High.*	*Low.*
Mk. I	750/850	450/550 ⎫
Mk. II	750/850	450/550 ⎬ Without accelerator.
Mk. II★	750/850	450/550 ⎭
Mk. III	750/850	— Fixed accelerator.
Mk. III★	—	600 No accelerator.

TO LOAD.

(a) Grasp the pistol grip with the right hand with fingers clear of the trigger and pull back the trigger guard until the cocking catch lever can be pressed down with the thumb. Slide the trigger guard forward as far as it will go and then pull it back until retained by the cocking catch. The gun is now cocked.

(b) Feed in the belt—pass the tag of the belt through the feed block from the right and pull to the left as far as it will go. The gun is now ready to fire. Tuck the end of the tag into the metal chute.

TO FIRE.

Squeeze the trigger of the remote control firing gear. Firing will continue until the trigger is released or the end of the belt is reached. If the belt is expended, the gun must be cocked again before leading in a fresh belt.

TO UNLOAD.

With the gun cocked hold back the trigger guard, pull out the cover locking pin, raise the cover and hold open by the ring suspended near the gun; remove the belt, see that the chamber is clear, lower the cover and engage the locking pin. Pull back the trigger guard, slightly depress the cocking catch lever and ease the working parts forward under control. With the trigger squeezed pull the trigger guard back, release the trigger and draw the trigger guard right back until retained by the cocking catch.

Fig. 78.—See guns are unloaded.

PRECAUTIONS.

(a) Always treat the gun as loaded until proved otherwise. Cock the gun, open the cover, and *see that the chamber is clear*.

(b) Do not fire the working parts forward when the gun is unloaded, unless absolutely necessary. Ease them forward (see "To Unload").

(c) The gas cylinder is very easily damaged. Avoid the following:—
  (i) Attempting to remove or replace the barrel when the gun is not cocked.
  (ii) When replacing the barrel, knocking the cylinder against the body of the gun.
  (iii) Firing the working parts forward with the barrel retainer disengaged.

(d) Although the parts of the gun are designed to be interchangeable, experience has shown that the components of each particular gun should be kept together and not assembled to any other gun, except in an emergency.

STRIPPING (see Fig. 79).

Do not strip the gun further than necessary. For cleaning, maintenance and examination the following procedure is adopted:—

(a) Lift off the rear baffle plate.

(b) Raise the carrying handle (46) until just clear of the lug on the right side of the body and push the barrel retainer (44) forward until clear of the slides in the body (2). Raise the carrying handle to the vertical position, lift the rear of the barrel (41) and push it forward until the guides on the barrel sleeve (40) are disengaged from the guides at the front of the body.

(c) Pull out the cover locking pin as far as it will go. Remove the cover (85).

(d) Press in the belt guide catch (if fitted) and lift the belt guide from its housing in the body.

(e) Lift the feed block from the body and slip out the feed slide.

(f) Remove the breech block (31) by lifting the rear and sliding it out backwards.

(g) Remove the accelerator (1) (if fitted) by pulling out the accelerator arm plunger from the body, turning it to the vertical position (upward for Mk. I guns and downward for Mk. II and II* guns) and lifting the accelerator from its seating in the body.

(h) Ease the working parts forward (see "To Unload").

P

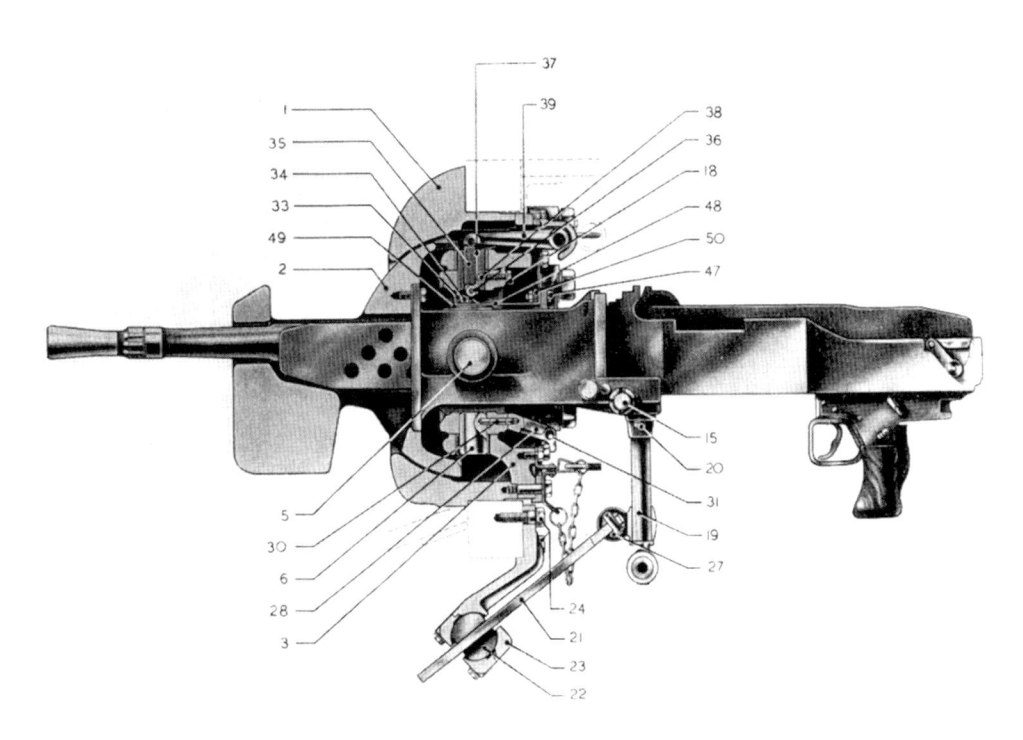

Fig. 298.—Machine-gun mounting No. 20—side section.

1. Mantlet.	22. Clamp.	35. Push rod.
2. M.G. cradle.	23. Socket.	36. Roller.
3. Inner mantlet.	24. Socket securing bolts.	37. Keyway.
5. Trunnion pins.	27. Ball and socket joint.	38. Guide pin.
6. Trunnion pins.	28. Bracket.	39. Lever.
15. Recoil bolt.	30. Dowel.	47. Adjusting bolts.
18. Locking bolts.	31. Ball end seat.	48. Cam location plate.
19. Arm.	33. Cam.	49. Rivets.
20. Arm securing bolts.	34. Cam securing bolts.	50. Shims.
21. Slide bar.		

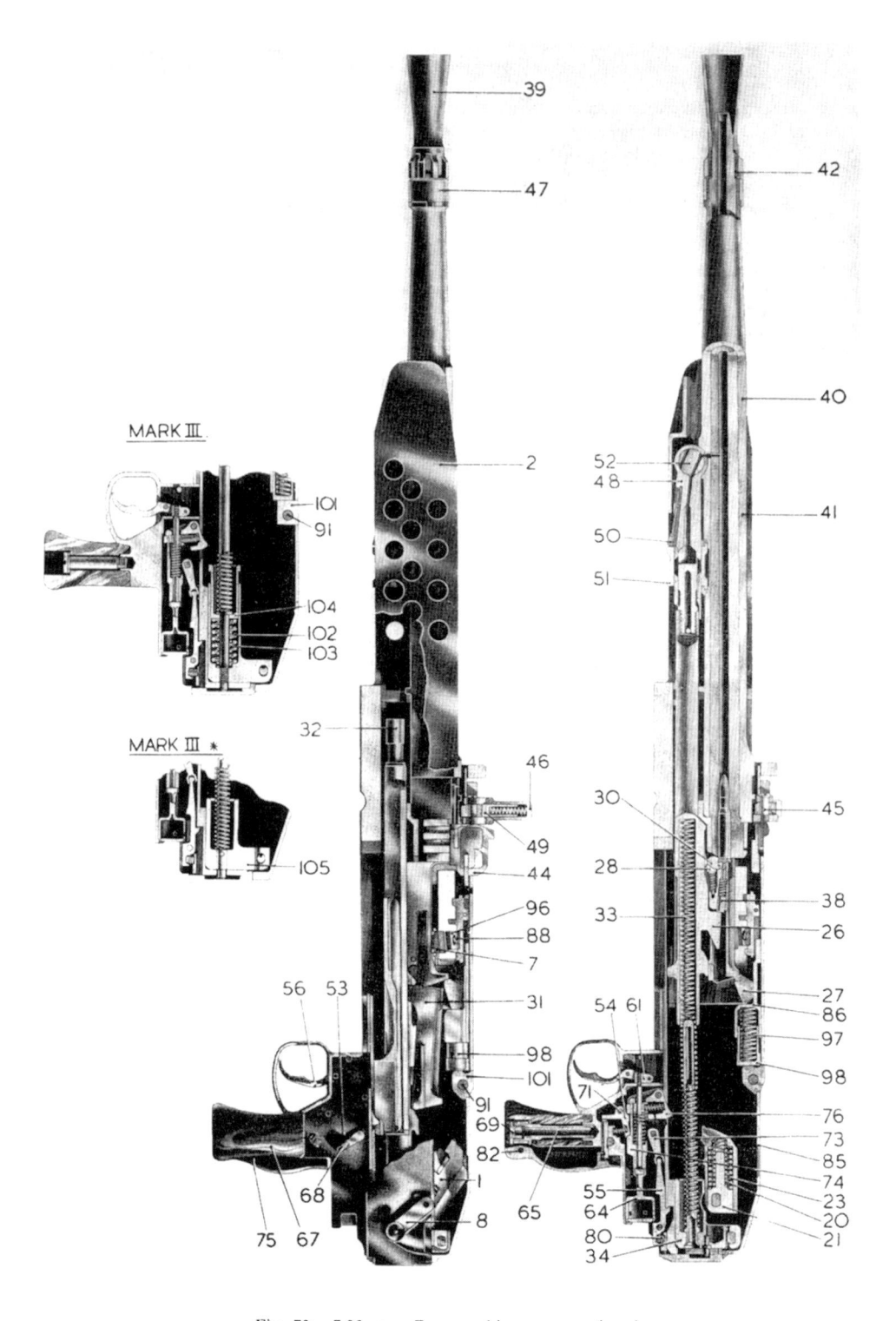

Fig. 79.—7·92 mm. Besa machine-gun—sectioned.

(i) Press the return spring guide block (34) forward (1 in. approx.) and with a lift, remove the return spring guide and return spring (33) from the body.

(j) With one hand on the piston extension and the other at the rear end of the barrel extension (27), lift out the piston (32) and barrel extension. Slide the piston out of the barrel extension.

(k) Lift out the feed lever.

(l) Raise the trigger guard catch. Grasp the pistol grip, squeeze the trigger (56), draw the trigger guard to the rear as far as it will go, release the trigger and again draw the trigger guard to the rear until it comes away from the gun.

(m) Return the barrel. With a punch or the point of a bullet, depress the gas cylinder sleeve spring (50) and, using the spanner end of the combination tool or an adjustable spanner, rotate the gas cylinder sleeve (51) until it is free of its housing in the barrel. Swing the rear end of the gas cylinder (48) away from the barrel sleeve (40) until the gas cylinder becomes detached from the barrel sleeve. Tap the gas regulator (52) out of the cylinder with a copper hammer or brass drift. Slip off the gas cylinder sleeve (51) and spring.

(n) Turn the breech block (31) upside down, lift the front end of the extractor stay (28) until it is disengaged from the extractor (30) and remove it, together with its spring. Lift out the extractor.

(o) Finally, turn the breech block upright, press the firing pin retainer downward with a punch or the point of a bullet. The spring will force the firing pin (38) out.

ASSEMBLING.

(a) Assemble the spring to the firing pin (38), and with the retainer still down, press the pin and spring into the breech block (31), taking care that the slot in the pin is facing the retainer. Push home the retainer.

(b) Turn the breech block upside down and slide the extractor (30) into its guides. Assemble the spring to the extractor stay (28) and place them in the breech block, rear end first, with the projection uppermost. Press in the front end of the stay until it is retained.

(c) Replace the gas cylinder sleeve spring in the gas cylinder (48). Slip on the gas cylinder sleeve (51), with the interruptions on the opposite side to the spring. Depress the spring and push down the sleeve so that it holds the spring depressed. Insert the gas regulator (52) into the cylinder. Engage the flange on the gas cylinder in its housing in the barrel sleeve (40) and swing the cylinder to the rear until it lies along the barrel. With the combination tool or a spanner, rotate the gas cylinder sleeve until it engages in its housing in the barrel sleeve.

(d) Raise the trigger guard catch and engage the flanges of the trigger guard with the guides in the body; with the cocking catch thumb-piece depressed, slide forward the trigger guard, keeping the fingers clear of the trigger (56). Release the cocking catch thumb-piece and drop the trigger guard catch. Pull the trigger guard back until the cocking catch (55) engages with the body.

(e) Replace the feed lever and swing its upper arm out to the right.

(f) Slide the upper flanges of the piston extension (26) into the lower groove of the barrel extension (27). With the piston in the forward position, lower the piston and barrel extension into the body.

Fig. 79 (facing)

1. Accelerator casing.	44. Barrel retainer.	71. Safety catch pin.
2. Body.	45. Carrying handle screw.	73. Cocking catch lever.
7. Feed pawl.	46. Carrying handle.	74. Sear tripper.
8. Accelerator crank arm.	47. Distance piece for (39).	75. Safety catch lever.
20. Inner accelerator spring.	48. Gas cylinder.	76. Sear.
21. Accelerator spring guide.	49. Plunger for (46).	80. Cocking catch spring.
23. Outer accelerator spring.	50. Spring sleeve for (48).	82. Pin for (75).
26. Piston extension.	51. Sleeve for (48).	85. Body cover.
27. Barrel extension.	52. Gas regulator.	86. Front recoil spring casing.
28. Extractor stay.	53. Trigger guard body.	88. Retaining pawl spring.
30. Extractor.	54. Safety catch.	91. Reaction block pin.
31. Breech block.	55. Cocking catch.	96. Retaining pawl.
32. Piston stem.	56. Trigger.	97. Recoil spring.
33. Return spring.	61. Trigger connector.	98. Rear recoil spring casing.
34. Return spring guide.	64. Trigger shaft.	101. Reaction block.
38. Firing pin.	65. Pistol grip tube.	102. } Buffer springs.
39. Flash eliminator.	67. Pistol grip.	103.
40. Barrel sleeve.	68. Thumbpiece for (55).	104. Accelerator sleeve.
41. Barrel.	69. Tube plug for (67).	105. Spring guide block.
42. Locking washer for (39).		

(g) Assemble the return spring (33) over the return spring guide (34). Grasp the top of the return spring guide block with the right hand and insert the free end of the spring into the piston extension (26). With the left hand supporting the spring, force the return spring guide forward until the guide rod enters the body and then press the guide downwards and release. See that it is correctly positioned.

(h) Cock the gun (see page 103), keeping one hand pressed down on the barrel extension.

(i) Replace the accelerator (1) (if fitted) and engage the plunger.

(j) Replace the breech block (31), making sure that it is properly settled down on to the piston extension (26).

(k) Slip the feed slide into the feed block and position the left edge of the slide itself in line with the left edge of the feed block. Lower the feed block into the body and ensure that the stud on the slide is engaged in the slot of the feed arm.

(l) Replace the belt guide in the body and press it downwards until the catch (if fitted) engages.

(m) Engage the cover (85) with the trunnions on the body, close it and push in the cover locking pin.

(n) Take hold of the barrel carrying handle (46) and raise the rear end of the barrel. Keeping the gas cylinder (48) clear of the body (2), engage the guides on the barrel sleeve (40) with the guides at the front of the body, pull the barrel to the rear and lower the breech end into the barrel extension (27). Push the carrying handle over to the right so that it rests on the ramp; knock back the handle with the hand and push it down into the locked position.

(o) Replace the rear baffle plate.

(p) Ease the working parts forward (see "To Unload", page 103).

(q) Test the gun for correct assembly by cocking and easing the working parts forward again.

STRIPPING IN ACTION.

When the gun is mounted, the barrel, piston, barrel extension, feed lever and gas cylinder cannot be removed.

The following parts can be removed if replacement or repair is required in action:—

In each case the cover must be opened first.

Breech Block and Components.—With the gun cocked. See "Stripping" (f), (n) and (o).

Return Spring and Guide.—With the working parts eased forward, after removal of the accelerator (if fitted). See "Stripping" (g) and (i).

Belt Guide.—By pressing in the catch (if fitted) and lifting out.

Feed Block and Feed Slide.—By lifting out, after removal of the belt guide.

Accelerator (if fitted). See "Stripping" (g).

Trigger Guard.—See "Stripping" (l).

Feed and Retaining Pawl Springs.—These can be replaced in emergency by manipulation, using a small screwdriver.

STOPPAGES.

Breakages are rare with the Besa machine-gun. Correct handling, attention to maintenance and periodical examination are essential to ensure freedom from stoppages, most of which are due to faulty handling, careless preparation or lack of inspection.

It is essential to protect the gun and ammunition from rain, dust, and extreme cold, and efforts should be made to avoid overheating.

It is advisable to "run-in" new guns during training to bring to light any defects which can be remedied before battle.

Parts of a gun found reliable should not be exchanged with other guns, except in an emergency.

Stoppages fall within the following groups, and will be dealt with in subsequent sections:—

(a) Misfires and related stoppages.
(b) Stoppages due to the cartridge not being driven clear of the belt.
(c) Extraction and ejection stoppages.
(d) Feed stoppages.

Each stoppage has "indications" by which it may be diagnosed. Many stoppages give the same indication and must be distinguished by elimination. Many stoppages have associated stoppages which give an indication as to the cause. "Immediate Action" (I.A.) is the action carried out by the gunner to make the gun fire again in the least possible time, and should be almost instinctive.

PRECAUTIONS WHEN CLEARING STOPPAGES.

Serious damage to guns and injuries to gunners will result upon careless handling when loading or clearing stoppages, and the following precautions should be observed:—

(a) Keep the fingers clear of the trigger when cocking.
(b) Always cock the gun or hold back the working parts by the trigger guard; open the cover and do not release the trigger guard until engaged by the cocking catch.
(c) When cocking, once the action of drawing back the working parts has been commenced, they must not be allowed to slip forward even if they cannot be drawn right back. Carelessness in this action will result in a double feed, with a possibility of a round in the breech being fired by a round in the belt when the cover is raised, and usually results in a bullet lodged in the bore.
(d) If a lodged bullet is suspected the bore must be cleared before firing to prevent the barrel being bulged and the breech block fractured.
(e) Do not support the cover with the head, but suspend the cover from the roof of the vehicle by the ring provided.
(f) Clear the chamber as soon as possible, as an overheated gun will give a "cook-off" with the same results as in (c).
(g) Never fire the working parts forward even if the gun is clear unless the cover is closed and locked.
(h) When removing the belt, ensure that the exit guide—if not fitted with a retaining catch—is not drawn out of place.
(i) When replacing the belt in the gun see that the first round is in line with the chamber.

Any unusual or persistent stoppages should be reported and the gun handed in to an armourer, together with defective parts and samples of fired and unfired ammunition and belts. A statement should be made of the circumstances, and particulars on the ammunition boxes should be quoted.

THE 2-IN. BOMBTHROWER, MARK IA*

(*See* Figs. 80 and 81)

A two-inch bombthrower is fitted to fire smoke-emitting bombs from inside the A.F.V. Alignment for aiming is obtained by swinging the turret on to the target, using the turret sighting vane as a sight. Range for aiming is obtained by adjusting a gas regulator valve fixed to the side of the bombthrower. Maximum range, 150 yards.

There are two types of bomb, the type being clearly marked on the body.

The bomb smokes an area of about 33/40 sq. yds. in still air.

REMEMBER:—
(1) To aim UP WIND and let the smoke drift to the target.
(2) That a HIGH WIND will move and DISPERSE smoke quickly.
(3) To RELOAD.
(4) The bombthrower must always be in the CLOSED POSITION, except when actually loading or unloading.

LUBRICATION AND MAINTENANCE.

All working parts should be kept thoroughly cleaned and oiled and free from burrs. Before new lubricants are applied, the old should be removed to prevent grit being retained. After lubrication, *operate the mechanism.*

Lubricants:—
(1) Mineral jelly.—Generally.
(2) C.70 (or M.160) oil.—All bright parts.
(3) Grade 2 kerosene *oil.*—For removing the above.

No parts will be burnished.
Keep the bombthrower free from rust and the bores slightly oiled.
Remove fittings frequently to check operation, but don't use unnecessary force.
Only ARTIFICERS should remove BURRS.
Report any flaw or crack at once.
Before firing—clean and dry the bore.
After firing—wash the bore in hot water (if available), and oil when cool.
Paraffin can be used on very dirty bores, and if no water is available.
Do NOT use SODA in any form to clean the bore.
All spare parts should be tested for interchangeability as soon as possible after receipt.

TOOLS CARRIED IN THE A.F.V.

6-PR. GUN.
  BRUSH, SPONGE, No. 3, MK. I, WITH ROPE, LANYARD AND LEAD BALL, for cleaning the bore.
  CAP, SPONGE, No. 6, MK. I.
  CAN, OIL, LUBRICATING, ½-PINT WESCO WITH FLEXIBLE SPOUT.
  LANYARD, COCKING, No. 4, MK. I.
  PLIERS, FLAT NOSE, 6 IN.
  SPANNER, ADJUSTING, 11 IN.
  TOMMY, ACTUATING SHAFT, for breech mechanism.
  SPANNER, TUBULAR BOX, D.E. WHIT. $\frac{5}{16}$ IN. × $\frac{3}{8}$ IN.
  TOMMY BAR, ¼ IN. × 5 IN.
  IMPLEMENT, AMMUNITION.
  KEY, REMOVING JAMMED Q.F. CARTRIDGES, No. 9.
  KEY, No. 7, MK. II.
  DRIFT, No. 18.
  GAUGE, STRIKER, PROTRUSION, No. 16, MK. I.
  STAPLE, RETAINING, FIRING PIN, MK. I.
  SPANNER, No. 675, MK. I.
  SPANNER, GLAND NUT.

2-IN. BOMBTHROWER.
  BRUSH, CLEANING BORE.
  WRENCH, BREECH MECHANISM, No. 359, MK. I, for positioning the firing hole bush.
  WRENCH, BREECH MECHANISM, No. 360, MK. I, for removing the rear barrel sleeve.
  TONGS, EXTRACTOR, for removing misfired bombs from rear barrel.

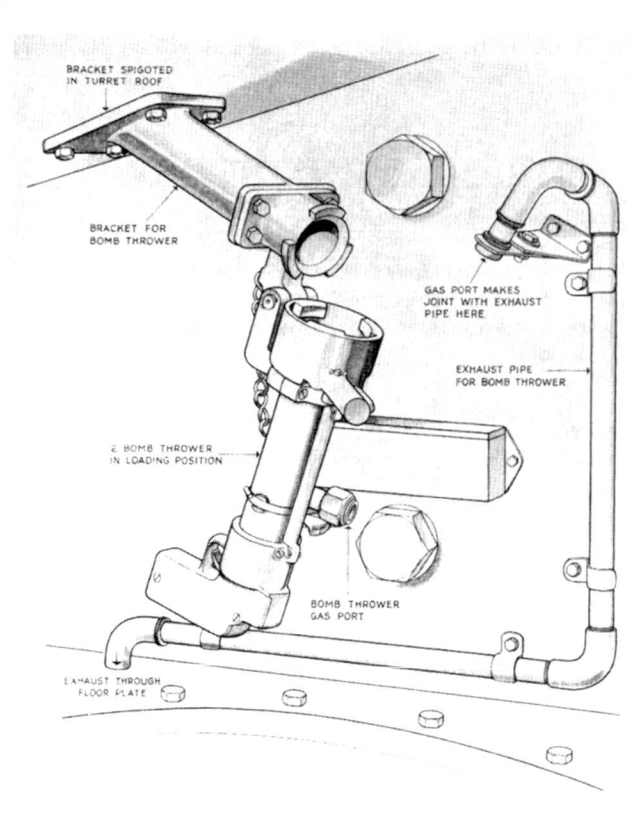

Fig. 80.—Bombthrower—loading position.

7·92 MM. BESA M.G.

PLUG, CLEARING, BESA 7·92 MM. M.G., MK. I (*see* Fig. 82)
PLUG, CLEARING, BESA 7·92 MM. M.G., MK. II (*see* Fig. 83) } For removing separated cases from the chamber.

TOOL, COMBINATION, BESA 7·92 MM. M.G., MK. I (*see* Fig. 84), for removing gas cylinder sleeve and flash eliminator, and as a grip on the carrying handle, when removing a hot barrel. The spanner end provides a copper hammer and the handle end accommodates two plain and two forked screwdrivers.

TOOL, COMBINATION, BESA 7·92 MM. M.G., MK. II (*see* Fig. 85), simplified version of the Mk. I with the screwdrivers and hammer omitted.

ROD, CLEANING, ·303 IN. M.G., MK. II B or V, for cleaning and oiling the bore, and for removing "hard extractions".

BRUSH, ROD, CLEANING, CYLINDER, BESA 7·92 MM. M.G., MK. I, for cleaning the gas cylinder.

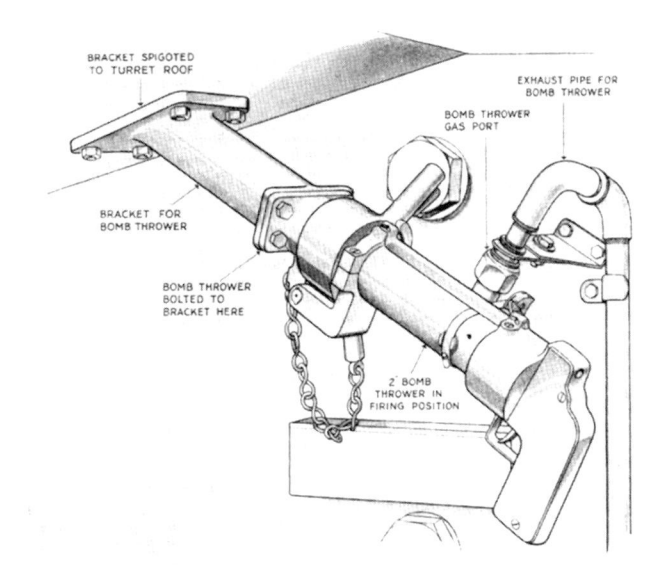

Fig. 81.—Bombthrower—firing position.

MOP, ROD, CLEANING, CYLINDER, BREN ·303 IN. M.G., MK. I, for wiping out and oiling the gas cylinder. It should be covered with flannelette, when used.

BOTTLE, OIL, MK. IV or V, for carrying graphited grease RD.1179.

BOX, SMALL PARTS, M.G., No. 4, MK. I, for carriage of small spares for the gun.

AMMUNITION

MARKINGS ON Q.F. 6-PR. 7-CWT. AMMUNITION.

(a) General.

(i) Ammunition issued to the Service is marked to facilitate indentification and to ensure segregation in store and transport. Markings also ensure that the correct types are used and assist in tracing defects in design and manufacture.

(ii) Care should be taken in handling ammunition, to avoid damage to the markings.

(iii) Q.F. fixed ammunition is batched for the purpose of recording the components used in the make-up of the cartridge, and ammunition of the same batch should give consistent shooting. Each batch contains a propellant charge of one lot only, i.e. it was all made at the same place and time, but the fuses may be of more than one lot.

(iv) Batches are distinguished by consecutive numbers, preceded by the appropriate letter, e.g. "Batch E.1" denotes the first batch of shell ammunition. When it is found necessary to use more than one lot of fuses in a batch, it is divided into sub-patches, as follows:—"Batch E.1"—containing rounds with first lot of fuses; "Batch E.1—A"—containing rounds with second lot of fuses; "Batch E.1—B"—containing rounds with third lot of fuses.

(v) Batches will be stored separately and will be so arranged as to avoid dividing a batch or sub-batch.

(vi) A label is affixed to the inside of each box giving particulars of the components contained in the ammunition. When it is necessary to replace original components by those of other lot numbers, the letter "X" will be appended to the batch or sub-batch numbers on the box. It will also be stencilled on the side of the cartridge case when the fuse is changed. The letter "X" denotes that the box contains components other than those originally packed.

(vii) If possible, ammunition will be repacked in the boxes from which it was removed. Failing this, the batch or sub-batch number on the box must be amended.

Fig. 87.—Don't be careless with ammunition.

VEHICLE HISTORY AND SPECIFICATION

(b) **Cartridges.**

    (i) Stamped on the base:—
        Calibre of gun.
        Mark of empty case. Letter "S" added if the primer hole has been rebushed.
        Manufacturer's initials or trade mark.

        ⟨S⟩ if the case has been scleroscope tested.

        The letter "C" followed by an "F" for every time the case has been filled.
        The letter "F" barred out thus "F̶" for every time the case has been filled but not fired.
        BLACK if containing a blank charge and existing markings no longer applicable, barred out.

    (ii) Stencilled on the side:—
        Batch letter, number and sub-batch letter.
        "U" denotes practice projectile with reduced charge.

        Propellant code letter in a rectangle:—

    |O| indicates W, W.M. or W.M.T. cordite.
    |E| indicates N.H. powders (nitro-cellulose).

        H.V. and $1\frac{1}{2}$ inch band in front of the rim if a high-velocity round.

    (iii) Stencilled on side of blank charges:—
        BLANK. Mark of cartridge. Weight, size and forms of powder. Initials or monogram of filling firm. Date of filling (month and year).

    (iv) Stencilled on the base:—
        "AP" when the cartridge is fitted with an armour-piercing shot.
        "PRAC" when the cartridge is fitted with a practice projectile.
        The symbol "T" in red if a tracer is fitted.
        "R" when the cartridge has a reduced charge.

(c) **Primers.**

    (i) Stamped on:—
        Number and mark of primer.
        Manufacturer's initials or trade mark.
        Date of manufacture of empty primer.
        Lot number.
        Initials or monogram of filling factory.
        Date of filling (month and year).

    (ii) After repair:—
        Contractor's initials or trade mark and date.
        Letter "M" denoting repair and refilling.

(d) **Projectiles.**

    (i) Stamped on:—
        Steel maker's code letters and cast number.
        Calibre and mark.
        C.S. if cast steel. B.S. if bar steel.
        Manufacturer's initials or trade mark.
        Lot number of empty projectiles.

    (ii) Painting:—
        A.P. shot are painted black.
        Practice projectiles are painted black.

(iii) Stencilling round the head:—
A red ring denotes that the projectile is filled wholly or partially with an explosive.
Two white rings round the nose denote A.P.

(iv) Stencilling round the body:—
Yellow band denotes practice projectile.

(v) Additional markings:—
Design number of method of filling.
Initials or monogram of filling factory or station.
Date of filling (month and year).
A white tip denotes shot.

(e) Fuses.

Stamped on:—
Number and mark of fuse.
Manufacturer's initials or trade mark.
Date of manufacture (month and year).
Initials or monogram of filling factory or station.
Date of filling (month and year).
Lot number of filling (the letter "Z" denotes a detonator filled with lead azide).

(f) Tracers.

(i) Stamped on:—
Number and mark of tracer.
Manufacturer's initials or trade mark.
Date of manufacture (month and year).
Initials or monogram of filling factory or station.
Date of filling (month and year).

(ii) Painting:—
Black band near base denotes filled.

(g) Packages.

Q.F. 6-pr. ammunition is issued in boxes C.263 or C.264, holding 4 or 6 cartridges respectively, each round in a container.

Markings indicating the contents are placed on the top and sides of boxes where they can be seen when properly stacked.

(i) Painting:—
Wooden boxes are stained vandyke-brown; steel boxes painted Service colour.

(ii) Stencilling on top:—
Number of cartridges in box.
Calibre of gun.
Nature of projectile.
Batch letter, number and sub-batch letter.

(iii) Stencilling on side:—
Calibre of gun.
Batch letter, number and sub-batch letter.
O.D. when the box has been oil dressed.

(iv) Labels:—
Packer's label and a label giving particulars of batched ammunition affixed to the underside of the lid
Two station labels affixed over the junction of the lid and box.
Government explosive and classification label on the side of the box.

VEHICLE HISTORY AND SPECIFICATION

Cartridge, Q.F., 6-pr., 7 cwt.	Case empty.	Primer, percussion.	Charge.	Tinfoil.	Tracer.	Projectile.	Fuse.
Armour-piercing shot, Mk. IT, foil	Mk. I	No. 15, Mk. II	1 lb. 13 oz. 8 dr. W.T. or W.M.T. Cordite	1 dr.	Internal	Shot, A.P., Mk. IT, IIT, IIIT or IVT	—
Armour-piercing shot, Mk. IIIT, foil	,,	,,	2 lb. 5 oz. 6 dr. N.H. 033	,,	,,	Shot, A.P., Mk. IT, IIT, IIIT or IVT	—
Armour-piercing shot, Mk. IIIT, foil	,,	,,	1 lb. 13 oz. 8 dr. W.T. or W.M.T. Cordite	,,	,,	Shot, A.P., Mk. VT, VIT or VIIT	—
Armour-piercing shot, Mk. IVT, foil	,,	,,	2 lb. 5 oz. 6 dr. N.H. 033	,,	,,	Shot, A.P., Mk. VT, VIT or VIIT	—
H.V. armour-piercing shot, Mk. IT, foil	,,	,,	2 lb. 7 oz. N.H. 033	,,	,,	Shot, A.P., Mk. IT, IIT, IIIT or IVT	—
H.V. armour-piercing shot, Mk. IIIT, foil	,,	,,	2 lb. 7 oz. N.H. 033	,,	,,	Shot, A.P., Mk. VT, VIT or VIIT	—
Armour-piercing shot, with cap, Mk. IT, foil	,,	,,	1 lb. 13 oz. 8 dr. W.T. or W.M.T. Cordite	,,	,,	Shot, A.P., with cap, Mk. VIIIT	—
Armour-piercing shot, with cap, Mk. IIIT, foil	,,	,,	2 lb. 5 oz. 6 dr. N.H. 033	,,	,,	Shot, A.P., with cap, Mk. VIIIT	—
Practice, Mk. IT, foil	,,	,,	2 lb. 5 oz. 6 dr. N.H. 033	,,	,,	Shot, practice, Mk. IT or IIT	—
Practice, Mk. IIIT, foil	,,	,,	1 lb. 13 oz. 8 dr. W.T. or W.M.T. Cordite	,,	,,	Shot, practice, Mk. IT or IIT	—
Practice, Mk. IIIT, foil	,,	,,	2 lb. 5 oz. 6 dr. N.H. 033	,,	,,	Shot, practice, Mk. IIIT, IVT, VT or VIT	—
Practice, Mk. IVT, foil	,,	,,	1 lb. 13 oz. 8 dr. W.T. or W.M.T. Cordite	,,	,,	Shot, practice, Mk. IIIT, IVT or VT	—
Practice shot, flat-headed, Mk. IT, foil	,,	,,	Reduced charge, 1 lb. 1 oz. 6 dr. W.M. 061 Cordite	,,	,,	Shot, practice, flat-headed, Mk. IT, IIT, IIIT or IVT	—
Practice shot, flat-headed, Mk. IIIT, foil	,,	,,	Reduced charge, 1 lb. 5 oz. N.H. 025	,,	,,	Shot, practice, flat-headed, Mk. IT, IIT, IIIT or IVT	—
H.E. shell, Mk. I, foil	Mk. IM	,,	2 lb. 5 oz. 6 dr. N.H. 033	,,	,,	H.E., 6-pr., Mk. VII	Percussion, D.A. No. 244
H.E. shell, Mk. IIT, foil	,,	,,	2 lb. 5 oz. 6 dr. N.H. 033	,,	Shell No. 13	H.E., 6-pr., Mk. XT	Percussion, D.A. No. 244
Blank	,,	No. 20	15 oz. blank L.G, G.12 or R.F.G.2	—	—	—	—
A.P.C., P.C.	—	—	—	—	Internal	Shot, A.P.C, B.C., Mk. XT	—

7·92 MM. BESA AMMUNITION.

The 7·92 mm. M.G. takes a rimless cartridge comprising case, cap, charge and bullet.

The base of the cartridge is stamped with the mark, contractor's initials or recognised trade mark, and the last two figures of the year of manufacture. The annulus is coloured to indicate the character of the cartridge.

The following marks of cartridges are issued:—
    Cartridge S.A. Besa 7·92 mm.   Mk. I.Z and Mk. II.Z annulus coloured purple.
    Cartridge S.A. armour-piercing 7·92 mm.   Mk. I.Z and Mk. II.Z annulus coloured green.
    Cartridge S.A. tracer 7·92 mm.   Mk. I.Z and Mk. II.Z annulus coloured red.
    Cartridge S.A. incendiary 7·92 mm.   Mk. I annulus coloured blue.
    Blank drill and dummy cartridges are available.

The cartridges are carried in belts holding 225 rounds, the filled belts being stored in wooden boxes holding two tinned-plate boxes or liners from which the gun is fed direct. Each liner holds two belts which may be loaded, with ball, ball and tracer, A.P., or incendiary or a combination in definite proportions.

The boxes and liners are labelled to state the contents.

2-IN. BOMBTHROWER AMMUNITION.

The ammunition for the 2-in. bombthrower consists of two types of cartridge:—
    Cartridge, 2-in. Bombthrower (18 grain ballistite), Mk. I;
    Cartridge, 2-in. Bombthrower (42 grain G.20);

and two types of smoke bomb:—
    Bomb, Smoke, 2-in. Bombthrower, Mk. I and II;
    Bomb, Smoke, Bursting, 2-in. Bombthrower, Mk. III.

Both cartridges and bombs have the usual markings, as have also the boxes and packages. The boxes hold eighteen rounds in packages of six and are painted green to denote smoke ammunition. The smoke bombs are also painted green, a red band denoting that they are filled and a white band if they contain white phosphorus.

The Mk. II smoke bomb differs from the Mk. I in that a short delay occurs in the emission of smoke. The Mk. III contains as a smoke composition white phosphorus and is assembled with a D.A. percussion fuse covered with a safety cap, which must be removed before firing.

CARE AND PRESERVATION OF AMMUNITION.

Ammunition is not foolproof—be careful of it. Keep it away from water, rain, damp, direct sunshine and gas, whether it is stored in the vehicle or in packages. Try to avoid extreme heat or cold. Ordinary temperatures will not affect ammunition.

Load or unload ammunition in dry weather, or under cover. Loads in open vehicles should be covered by tarpaulin. See that the "B" echelon ammunition is properly sheeted. If the ammunition package has been exposed to wet in transit, make sure there is no water inside. If so, dry the contents of the package and carefully repack.

Don't throw packages about.

Always stack ammunition under cover, and provide for a free circulation of air. If possible stack ammunition packages on battens. Keep them 12 in. clear of walls, and leave passages of at least 18 in. between stacks. Maximum height of stacks allowed is 12 ft. Try to keep one end of each package visible.

On receipt of ammunition, examine all labels carefully to see that the ammunition is suitable and sort it into kinds if there are several in the consignment. Look for broken seals, open any boxes which appear to have been tampered with, and ensure that the contents correspond with the labels and are still serviceable.

Ready-use ammunition.—The amount of ammunition unpacked from boxes must be governed by the stowage room in the vehicle. Ammunition must not be unpacked unless necessary, and the opening of sealed liners containing M.G. ammunition should be deferred until the last possible moment, as the liners cannot be resealed.

Ammunition stowed in a vehicle must be inspected weekly and before action, by the crew commander. If possible, ammunition ready for use, should be "turned over" by expenditure. Do not oil ammunition as this leads to the accumulation of dust.

The clip, No. 36 Q.F., protecting the primer in the cartridge case, *must be kept in position* until the round is required.

Inspection of ammunition.—Every round must be inspected before using. When time permits, rounds should be gauged by being offered into the breech, but *the striker case must first be removed* from the breech block.

The *projectile* must be clean and free from dust or grit. It must be secured tightly in the cartridge case and the driving band must be undamaged. If H.E. shell, the fuse must be tight and no signs of exudation of the shell filling be visible.

The *cartridge case* must be clean, have no cracks or serious dents. Short cracks at the mouth up to ¼ in. may be disregarded, cracks elsewhere necessitate rejection. The rim must be undamaged, and the primer must be flush with the base and screwed tightly home; if sunken or projecting it must be rejected.

Damaged ammunition.—Damaged or faulty ammunition should be returned immediately in its original boxes, care being taken to see that the labels are not missing, as these are the means of tracing faulty batches to their source. If ammunition has to be returned in boxes other than the originals, the labels must be altered to correspond with the contents. Reports of faulty ammunition must always be accompanied by an extract from the box labels giving the batch dates of the cartridges.

Ammunition salvage.—Fired cases, spent belts, felt strips and packing pieces, empty liners and boxes are all required as salvage and must be returned whenever circumstances permit. Live rounds must be separated from empty cases. If conditions do not permit sorting, the boxes of empties should be conspicuously labelled to indicate that live rounds are present.

Don't—Hammer or tap packing cases containing ammunition.
Tamper with a round.
Use live rounds for drill purposes.
Have rusty rounds.

SIGHTING TELESCOPES

TESTING AND ADJUSTING.

Upon the correct adjustment of sights depends the effectiveness of fire and the frequent testing of sights is of great importance.

Sights should be tested after removal and re-insertion in the mounting before firing and especially after firing or travelling, when shocks and vibration may have disturbed the telescope.

(a) To test 6-Pr. Gun.

Select a well-defined object, approximately 1,000 yards distant, on which to lay the gun. Fix fine wires horizontally and vertically across the front face of the muzzle of the 6-pr. gun in the four axis lines marked. It will be necessary to remove the muzzle weight if fitted. Remove the striker case. Align the bore of the gun on the distant object, using the intersection of the cross-wires as a foresight and the hole in the firing hole bush as a backsight and lock the mounting in position. To obtain accurate alignment the eye should be drawn back as far as possible from the firing pin hole without losing sight of the aiming mark. Re-check the alignment several times and ensure that the gun has not moved. If the sights are correct, the intersection of the vertical cross-line in the telescope and the zero line should be on the same spot of the distant object as the gun. The short horizontal line above the intersection of the cross-lines indicates zero. If there is an error, adjustment will be necessary.

(b) M.G.

Remove the breech block and accelerator (if fitted) from the M.G. (*see* "Stripping", page 103) so as to give a view through the bore of the barrel and the sight hole at the rear of the body. If the mounting is correct the gun should lie on the same point of aim as the 6-pr. gun. If deviation is present it should be reported to a gun fitter immediately.

R

(c) **To adjust the Telescope.**
Slacken the four adjusting screws. The diaphragm on which the range scales are marked can be moved vertically by pressing the top or bottom adjusting screw, and horizontally by pressing the right or left screw. Tighten the screws when adjustment is correct.

(d) **Precautions.**
(i) It is essential that the sights be taken exactly in the centre of the bore of the gun. Considerable error will arise if the eye is not in the line of the axis.

(ii) Movement of the gun after alignment and prior to the completion of the test will negative the result. Such movement may be produced by movement of the tank as a whole, jolting of the gun or rocking or rotation of the turret in any way. The gun and telescope must be aligned by the same man and the tests must be rechecked.

(e) **Testing the Parallax.**
(i) Telescopes should be tested periodically for parallax. Align the telescope on a well-defined object approximately 500 yards distant. Move the head vertically and horizontally while looking through the telescope.

(ii) If the telescope is correctly adjusted, there will be no apparent movement of the cross-wires. If the cross-wires appear to move with the head, adjustment is needed and the telescope will be sent for repair.

No. 20 MOUNTING.

The method of testing is similar to that described for the co-axial mounting and consists of laying the M.G. on a distant object. The line of sight through the intersection of the vertical cross-line in the telescope and the zero line should be on the same spot of the distant object as the gun. If not, the telescope must be collimated by shortening or lengthening the compression link below the M.G. cradle for obtaining lateral adjustment and by tightening or slackening the adjusting screw at the left of the telescope housing for obtaining vertical adjustment. After adjustment the lock nuts of the compression link and of the adjusting screw must be screwed home.

The No. 35 telescope fitted to the No. 20 mounting is removable, for cleaning or renewing the head, by operating the locking bolt to release the telescope clamp. The telescope can then be withdrawn downwards from its mounting.

CARE AND PRESERVATION.

A telescope when issued is in correct optical adjustment, watertight, and with the cells secured by fixing screws. It must not be taken apart unless necessary, and then only by a qualified artificer, after which it must be carefully tested and adjusted.

All metal parts are to be kept clean with a soft cloth. If very dirty, turpentine or paraffin may be used on the cloth, but abrasives such as emery or bath-brick are not to be used.

The telescope holder must be carefully protected. Any burrs or damage to the bearing surfaces will throw the telescope out of alignment.

The object glass and eye lens should be cleaned periodically with a piece of dry, clean linen, used only for that purpose.

Telescopes should be kept in a dry place.

The rubber eye guards should not be exposed to extreme temperatures, contact with oil or grease, or prolonged contact with petrol. Should oil or grease come in contact, it should be removed and the eye guard washed in clean *warm* soapy water. Rinse in clear water. Spare eye guards should be stored in french chalk, in such a way that they are not distorted.

If vision through a telescope is impaired by mist, rain or dust, the eye lens should be cleaned and anti-dim applied as lightly as possible. If this is not satisfactory, remove the telescope from the mounting bracket, clean the object glass protector and apply anti-dim.

If, after fire, the vision is impaired, it is probable that the object glass protector has been damaged by splash. Change the protector; spares are carried in the A.F.V. (*see* Fig. 88).

A greasy wad plugged into the aperture in the mantlet will give protection to the telescope, in dusty or sandy conditions and when not in actual use.

INSTALLING AND REMOVING BESA M.G.

TO INSTALL (*see* Fig. 289).

Slacken the clamping strip retaining bolt (E) with the spanner attached to the mounting and turn the recoil bolt (G) until the flat on its diameter is uppermost. Push forward the trigger guard body, slide the gun into the cradle and secure it by turning the recoil bolt. Bring the trigger guard body to the rear and lock the gun by tightening down the clamping strip. Keep the spanner in the clip provided, when not in use.

To connect the remote control firing gear, pull out the plunger and push the slide into the guide on the right side of the gun. Release the plunger, which will locate the slide, and tighten the securing screw.

To remove the gun, reverse the procedure.

DISABLEMENT OF GUNS.

To prevent the enemy using the guns, armament must be disabled by removing certain parts or damaging the guns permanently.

The first method enables the guns to be brought into action again if the opportunity is offered, but, where more than one gun is being disabled, the same parts must be removed from each to prevent the assembling of a complete gun from parts of another.

Essential parts to be removed.—The telescopes, striker case and spares of the 6-pr. gun. The breech block and spares box of the M.G.

Permanent damage to the guns.—Load the gun and place a heavy metal object, e.g. hammerhead or crowbar, down the bore with stones and earth. Drain the buffer and fire the gun from a distance.

The M.G. must, whenever possible, be removed from its mounting together with spares and ammunition, so that the crew can fight a dismounted action. If this is impossible, all working parts and spares will be removed and the gun damaged with a hammer or crowbar.

Optical instruments must always be taken when a vehicle is abandoned, as they are difficult to replace.

6-PR. AND BESA M.G. CO-AXIAL MOUNTING

The main armament is fitted in the mounting, 6-pr. and Besa Medium M.G., No. 2, Mk. II. The nomenclature, showing which Mark and the serial number of the mounting is given on an inscription plate attached to the top of the 6-pr. cradle, and should always be quoted in any written reference to the mounting.

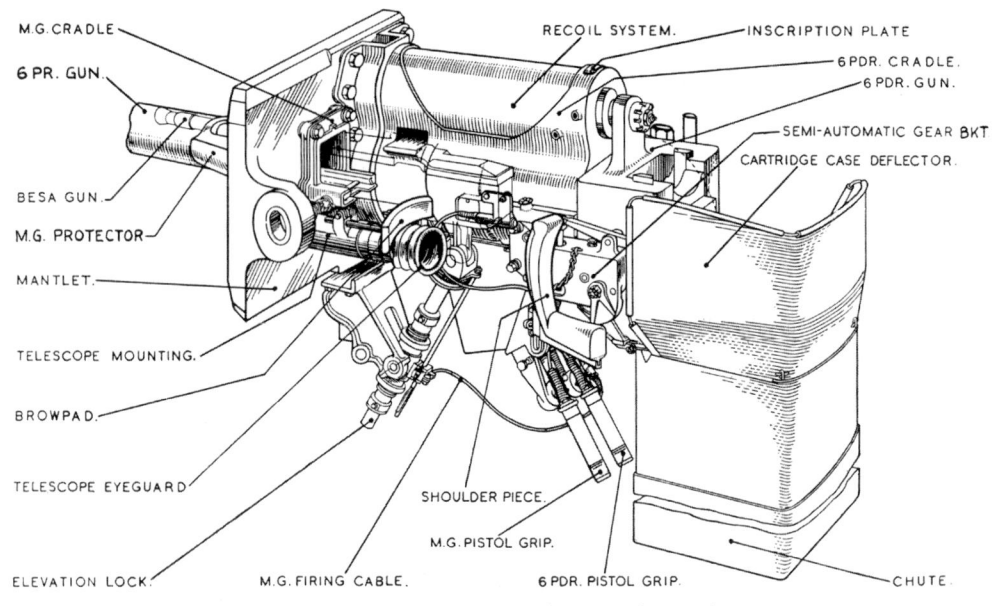

Fig. 88.—General arrangement of guns and mountings.

The mountings are of the free elevation type, i.e. elevated or depressed by pressure exerted by the gunner on a shoulder piece, aided by pushing or pulling on the pistol grip. A spiro type elevation lock is fitted. The remote control firing gears are cable operated, and adjustable at the gun attachment ends. The action of the semi-automatic gear is similar to that on other tank gun mountings, but the cam, instead of being supported by a flange on the bracket, seats on the deflector bracket arm. The telescope used is the Telescope, Sighting, No. 39, Mk. I. An alternative telescope which may be fitted is the No. 33, Mk. II S.

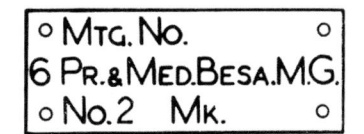

Fig. 89.—Inscription plate.

ADJUSTMENTS.

Firing gears.—Always test the firing gear of each gun before firing. It will often be found that the cables have stretched or that the attachments have worked loose. Do not adjust unless necessary.

6-PR. GUN.

The firing lever on the mounting should just bear against the firing lever on the gun. If bearing too heavily, it may cause the gun to fire as the breech block closes.

To test.—See that the gun is unloaded, cock the firing mechanism and press the trigger. If the gun fails to fire, adjustment is necessary.

To adjust.—Cock the firing mechanism, loosen the lock nuts on the cable at the firing lever end and adjust the length of cable. Do not interfere with the nut at the pistol grip end. If necessary, adjust the stop screw of the firing lever to restrain further movement after actuating the firing lever on the gun. Tighten the lock nut securely and test.

7·92 MM. BESA M.G.

The operating arm of the remote firing gear should just bear against the trigger shaft, when the trigger guard body is to the rear. If bearing too heavily, the cocking catch may not function or "runaway" firing of the gun may be caused.

To test.—See that the gun is unloaded, correctly mounted and the safety catch set at "OFF". Cock the gun and press the trigger. If the gun cannot be cocked or fired, adjustment is necessary.

Fig. 90.—Don't order wrong spares.

To adjust.—Slacken the connector lock nut of the remote control firing gear and adjust until the operating arm is just bearing on the trigger shaft. Tighten the lock nut securely and test.

The pistol grips can be rotated to suit the gunner, by releasing the clamping bolts.

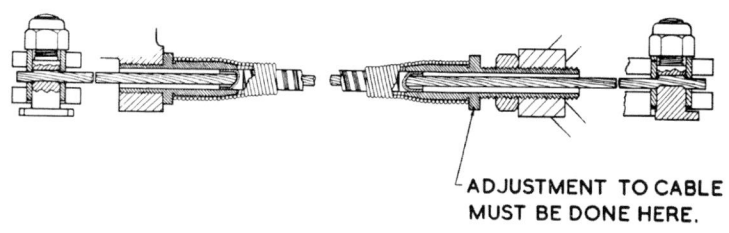

The shoulder piece can be adjusted vertically or horizontally, to suit the gunner, by loosening the securing nuts and sliding it in the direction required. Ensure that the nuts are tightened after adjusting.

Fig. 91.—Spiro lock cable.

The browpad must be adjusted to give the gunner an unrestricted view through the telescope. The arm of the browpad is clamped to allow adjustment of the distance from the eye-piece. The browpad itself can be moved to suit the forehead by slackening the wing nut securing it. If the shape of the browpad does not suit the individual user, easy improvisation can be made by the use of packing inserted under the pad or cover.

Testing for backlash.—Traverse the gun on any target with the gun pulled over to the right by men on the hull. Then push the gun to the left as far as possible.

If the movement as sighted through the telescope is more than two-thirds of a graticule, then backlash is excessive and an examination of the various parts likely to cause backlash must be made. Report "excessive backlash" to the gun fitter.

Note.—Backlash should be tested on both "Hand" and "Power" traverse.

Spiro lock (*see* Figs. 294 and 295).—Adjustments of the firing gear control bracket, including the micro adjuster of the spiro lock, may be carried out by the gunner, but those to the spirals of the lock must be effected by the unit artificer. The position of the rod (B) when correctly fitted is such that the screw (D) projects about $\frac{3}{4}$ inch through the boss on the firing gear control bracket and the bridge-piece of the rocking arm (E) should clear the connecting rod by $\frac{1}{4}$ inch with the gun locked. Adjustment is possible by means of the knurled screw (C) and the screw (D), both of which should be tightly locked after adjustment.

The cable (W) must not be adjusted by the anchor bolts holding the inner cables at each end, but by means of the cable adjuster (HH) where it is connected to the firing gear control bracket.

Adjustment of the spiro lock micro adjuster, should it be necessary, is effected by lengthening or shortening the effective length of the connecting link of the link and lever mechanism. Tighten the lock nuts after adjustment.

LUBRICATION.

The most important reason for oiling the lock is to prevent rust. The general purpose oil used for lubrication is too viscous and must not be used. The oil is retained in the lock for a considerable time, so frequent oiling is unnecessary. To oil the lock, remove the upper plug from the rear of the centre bracket and inject a few drops of *buffer oil*; remove the top cover from its upper fixing and smear the slide bar with *buffer oil*; replace the plug and cover. Elevate and depress the gun several times to distribute the oil.

The recoil system is dependent for efficient working on (i) correct filling, (ii) strength of the springs, (iii) the packings in the glands. Careful observation should be kept on the system. The liquid used is "Oil, mineral, hydraulic buffer", generally referred to as "Service buffer oil". On active service, should this be unobtainable, any thin lubricating oil may be used. If nothing more suitable can be obtained, use water.

In no circumstances use fuel oils such as petrol, or illuminating oils such as paraffin or kerosene.

Alternative liquid may cause damage to the buffer and every effort should, therefore, be made to obtain the correct oil as soon as possible to replace it.

Only clean liquid may be used. Before any is put into the buffer it should be strained, as it is of utmost importance that the oil should be clean and free of foreign matter. Oil emptied from buffers must not be re-used except in an emergency.

Fig. 92.—Don't use highly inflammable oils.

To fill the buffer (*see* Fig. 288).—
  (1) Ensure that the gun is in the fully run-out position.
  (2) Depress the gun as far as possible, i.e. to approximately 9 degrees.
  (3) Remove filler plug (U).
  (4) Open the run-out adjusting valve (Y) a few turns noting the original setting.
  (5) Pour the buffer oil in slowly through the filler hole with the oil can until no more can be inserted. The buffer holds 1½ pints.
  (6) Replace the filler plug and elevate and depress the gun several times, finally returning the gun to the maximum depression.
  (7) Remove the filler plug and top up with buffer oil. (It is advantageous to run the vehicle on to sloping ground, so that the total depression can be increased to 20 degrees.)
  (8) Withdraw ⅛ gill of oil (approximately two dessertspoonfuls), increasing to the minimum quantity which will give satisfactory run-out. The quantity withdrawn must not exceed ⅜ of a gill (approximately 4½ dessertspoonfuls).
  (9) Replace the filler plug.
  (10) Close adjustment valve to original setting.

To empty the buffer.—Lay the gun at the horizontal position. Remove the filler plug (U). Remove the drain plug and catch the oil in a suitable clean receptacle. A trough to carry the oil clear of the gun can easily be improvised if necessary. When the flow ceases, elevate the gun and allow the buffer to drain.

Stuffing boxes are fitted to prevent leakage round the piston rod and run-out adjusting valve. Only when a leak occurs should an adjustment be made.

The buffer piston rod gland nut (*see* Fig. 288 (P)) is locked by a catch which must be disengaged before the gland can be tightened. Dismantle any plates, etc., in the turret to gain access to the aperture at front of the cradle. A hole is provided in the cradle to insert a tommy bar for lifting the catch. With the "C" spanner provided, tighten the gland nut until the catch will engage in the next notch. Re-examine for leakage and tighten further if necessary. Make certain that the locking catch re-engages the gland.

If the leakage cannot be stopped by tightening the gland, an auxiliary packing must be inserted. Use the Tool, Artillery, No. 229, for removing the packing supporting ring. The packing used is interposed hemp and lead wire. Be sure the gland is locked after adjusting.

If a leakage should occur at the adjusting valve stuffing box, check the setting of the valve (*see* Fig. 288 (Y)) by closing it first. Open it about two or three turns, slacken the gland lock nut and tighten the gland. Tighten lock nut. Reset the valve to its original position. The approximate setting for the valve should be a quarter-turn open. Greased hemp packing is used in this stuffing box.

The recuperator springs can be simply tested by elevating the gun to its fullest extent. If the gun is not held in the run-out position the springs are weak and must be changed. Changing necessitates removing the cradle from the mantlet, and should only be undertaken by workshops. When tightening the nut securing the buffer cylinder to the gun lug, slacken back one-eighth of a turn from fully tightened position before securing tab.

The following are the more common faults likely to be experienced in action, the possible causes, and remedies.

Fault	*Cause*	*Remedy*
Recoil, violent or excessive.	Insufficient liquid in buffer	Fill buffer.
Run-out violent	Loss of liquid in buffer	Fill buffer.
	Adjusting valve open too much	Adjust valve.
Run-out sluggish	Adjusting valve closed too much	Adjust valve.
	Cradle or guideways dry	Lubricate.
Failure to run-out by short amount.	Expansion of oil due to heating when firing	With the gun at full depression, slacken the filling plug and release oil and air until gun runs up. Retighten plug.
Failure to run-out by large amount.	Adjusting valve closed	Adjust valve.
	Obstruction in cradle guideways	Remove obstruction.
	Cradle or guideways dry	Lubricate.

MACHINE GUN, No. 20, MOUNTING

The M.G. mounting is of the gimbal type and is situated forward in the vehicle, on the left of the driver. The inner mantlet and cradle in which the M.G. is mounted moves on trunnions both vertically or horizontally in an outer mantlet. The vertical trunnions give a traverse, left or right, of $22\frac{1}{2}$ degrees, and the horizontal ones an elevation or depression of $12\frac{1}{2}$ degrees. The No. 35 Mk. I sighting telescope is fitted on the left of the mounting, and is moved by parallel link and lever motion actuated from the gimbal ring and cradle, to correspond with the direction of fire. A split spherical joint, held in a bracket bolted to the hull, when tightened by a handwheel, clamps a slide bar to lock the mounting in position. Aim is controlled by pressure on a handle attached to the underside of the cradle and the firing grip of the M.G. The M.G. is fired by finger pressure on the trigger.

The sighting telescope is removable from its mounting by releasing the locking bolt immediately above the eyepiece.

MAINTENANCE.

The working surfaces and mechanism must be kept free from dust and well lubricated, particular attention being paid to the bearing surface of the link and lever mechanism by means of which motion of the M.G. is imparted to the sighting telescope. Special attention must be given to the table at the left side of the telescope mounting, as dust or dirt thereon may cause the slipper to give an incorrect movement to the table and affect the alignment of the sighting telescope.

Lost motion at any of the points of connection of the telescope link and lever mechanism must be eliminated, as slackness at any joint will seriously affect the correct movement of the telescope in synchronism with the M.G.

CROMWELL TANK

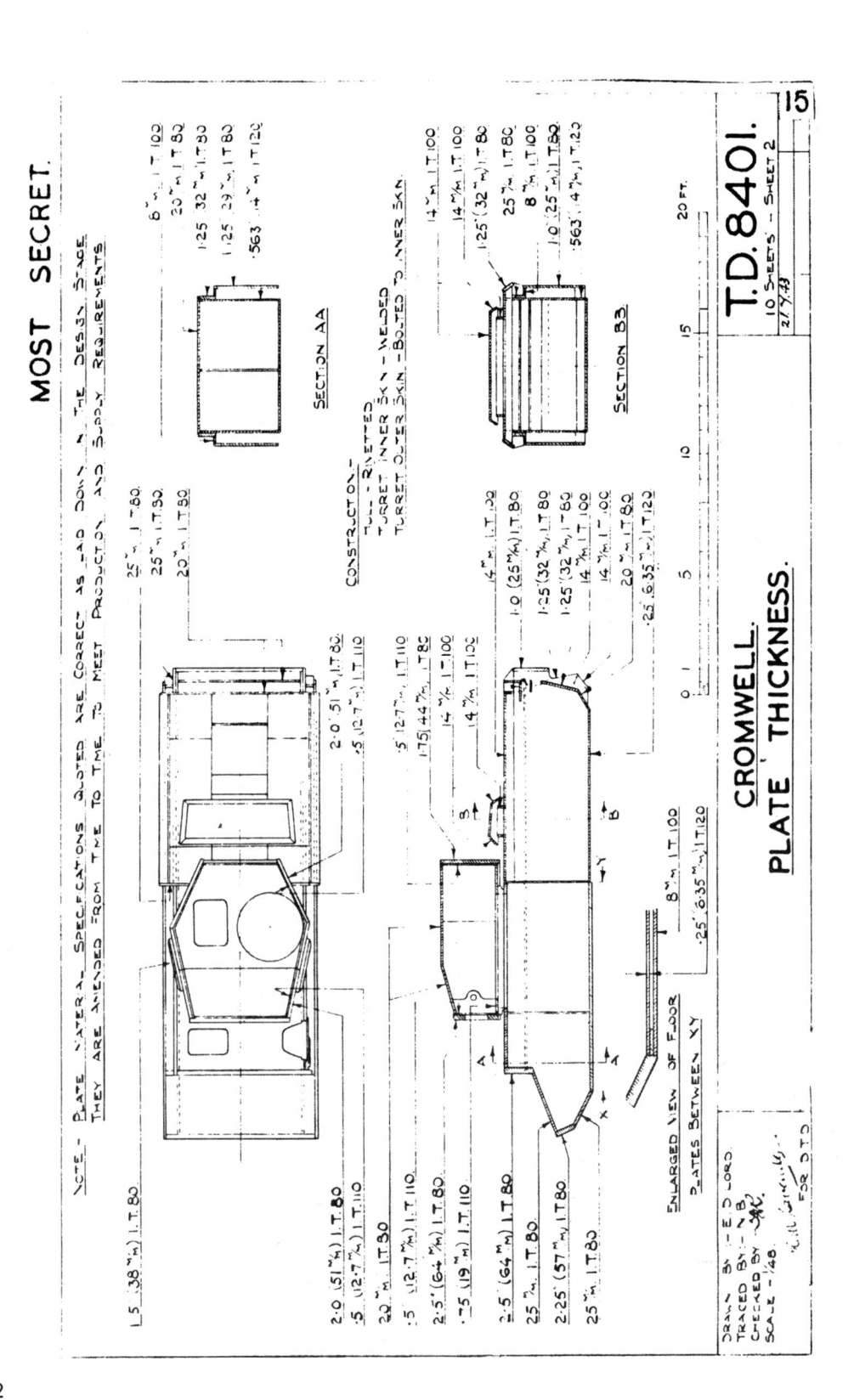

VEHICLE HISTORY AND SPECIFICATION

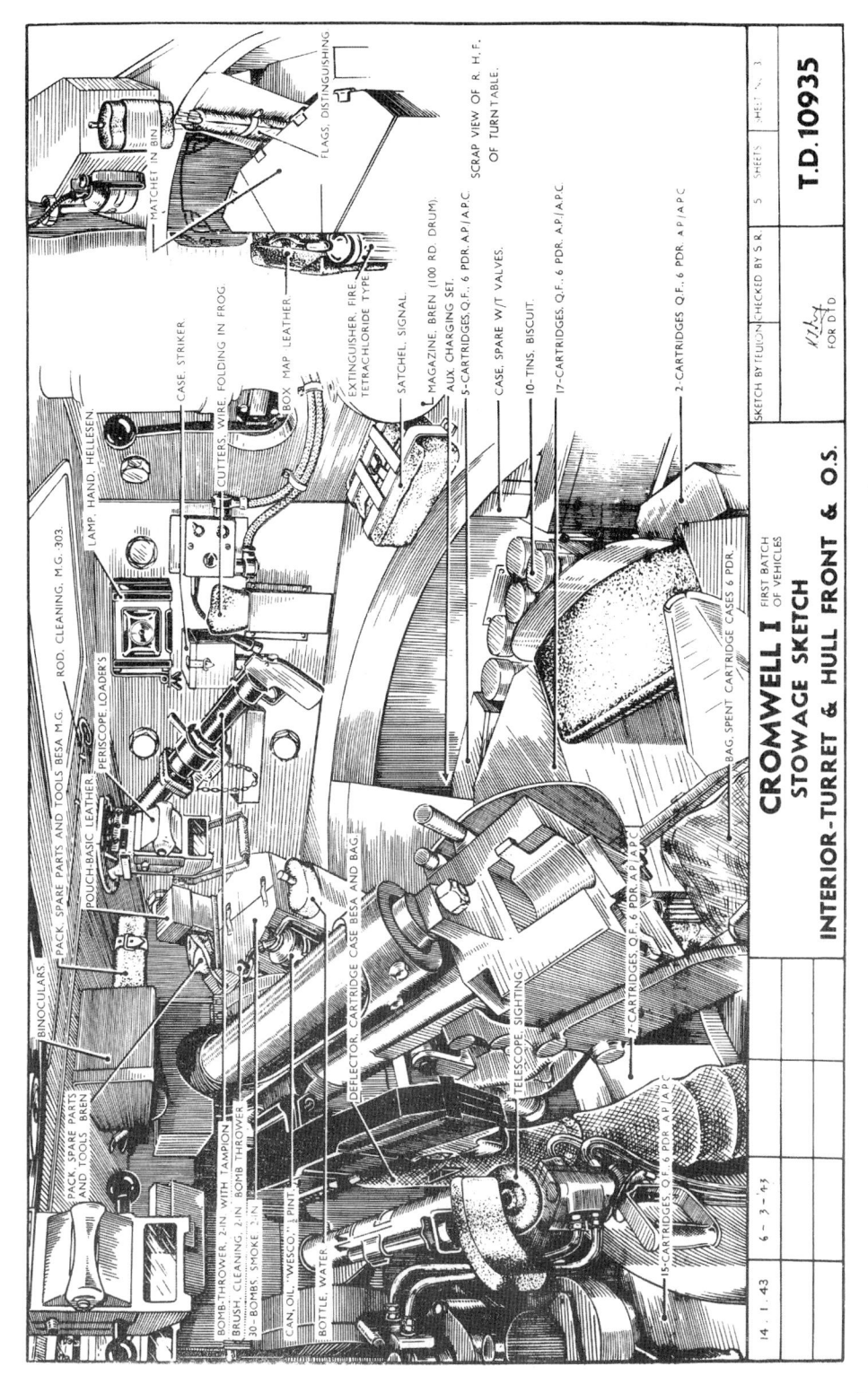

CROMWELL I FIRST BATCH OF VEHICLES
STOWAGE SKETCH
INTERIOR - TURRET & HULL FRONT & O.S.

T.D.10935

CROMWELL TANK

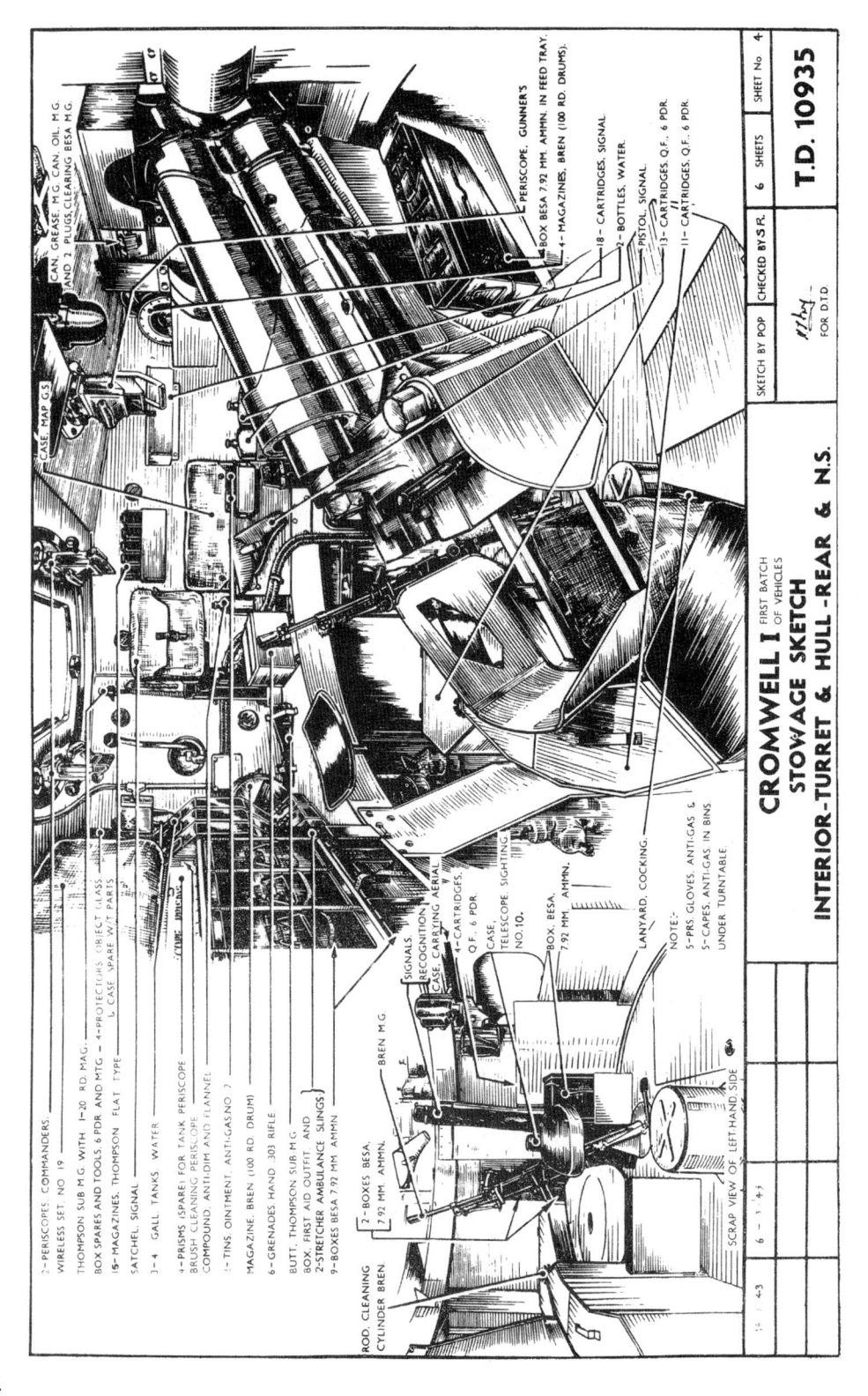

VEHICLE HISTORY AND SPECIFICATION

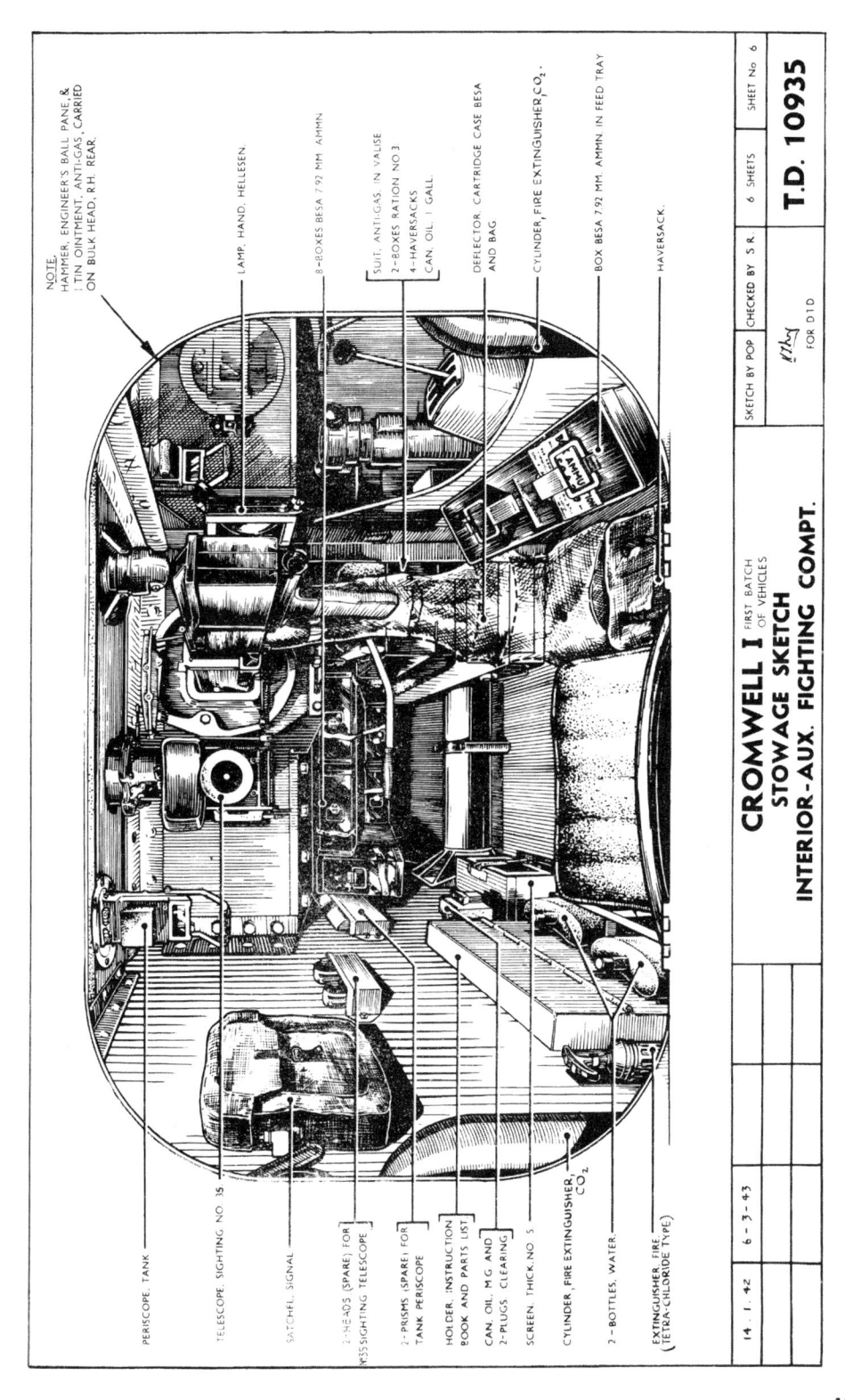

CROMWELL TANK

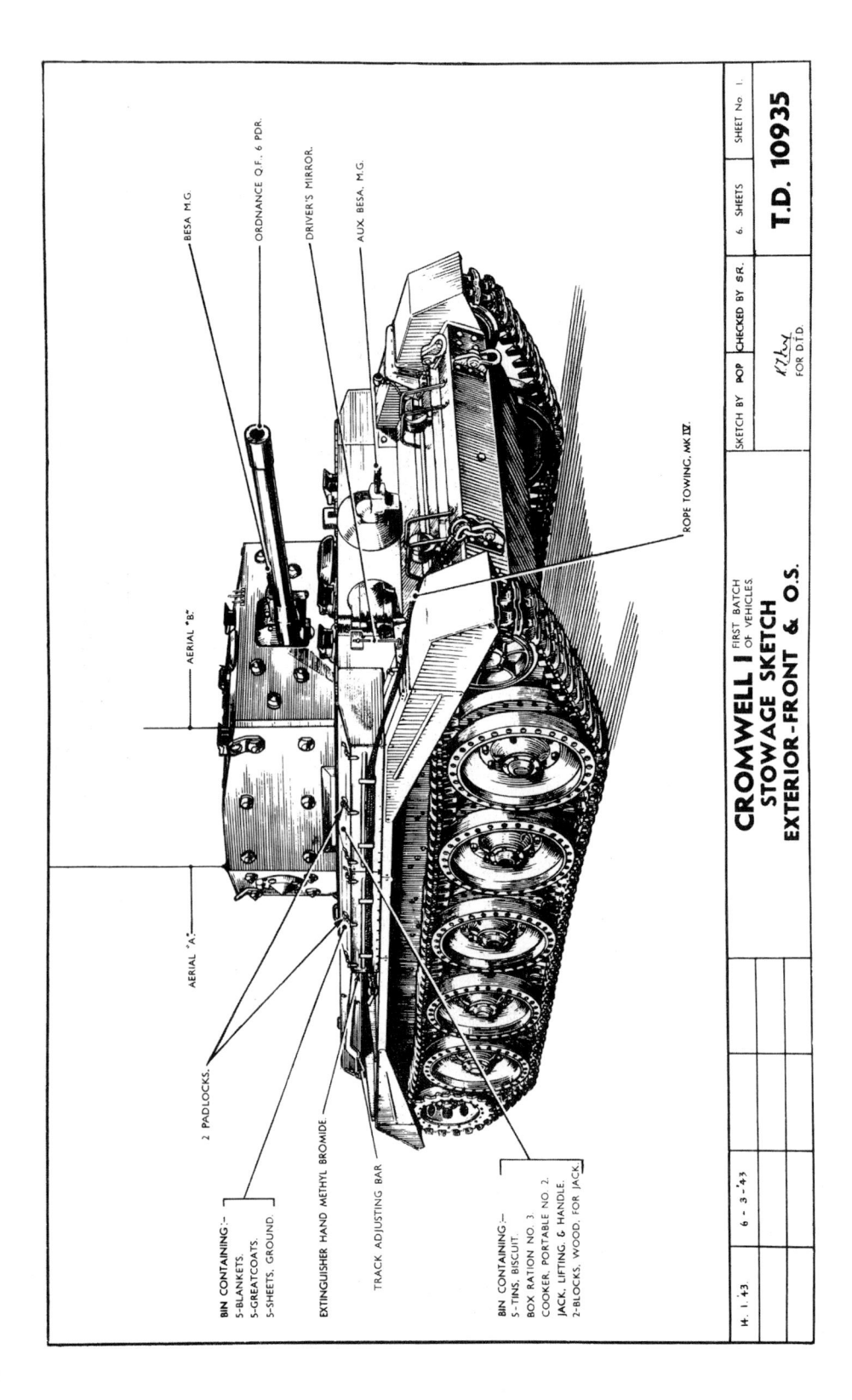

VEHICLE HISTORY AND SPECIFICATION

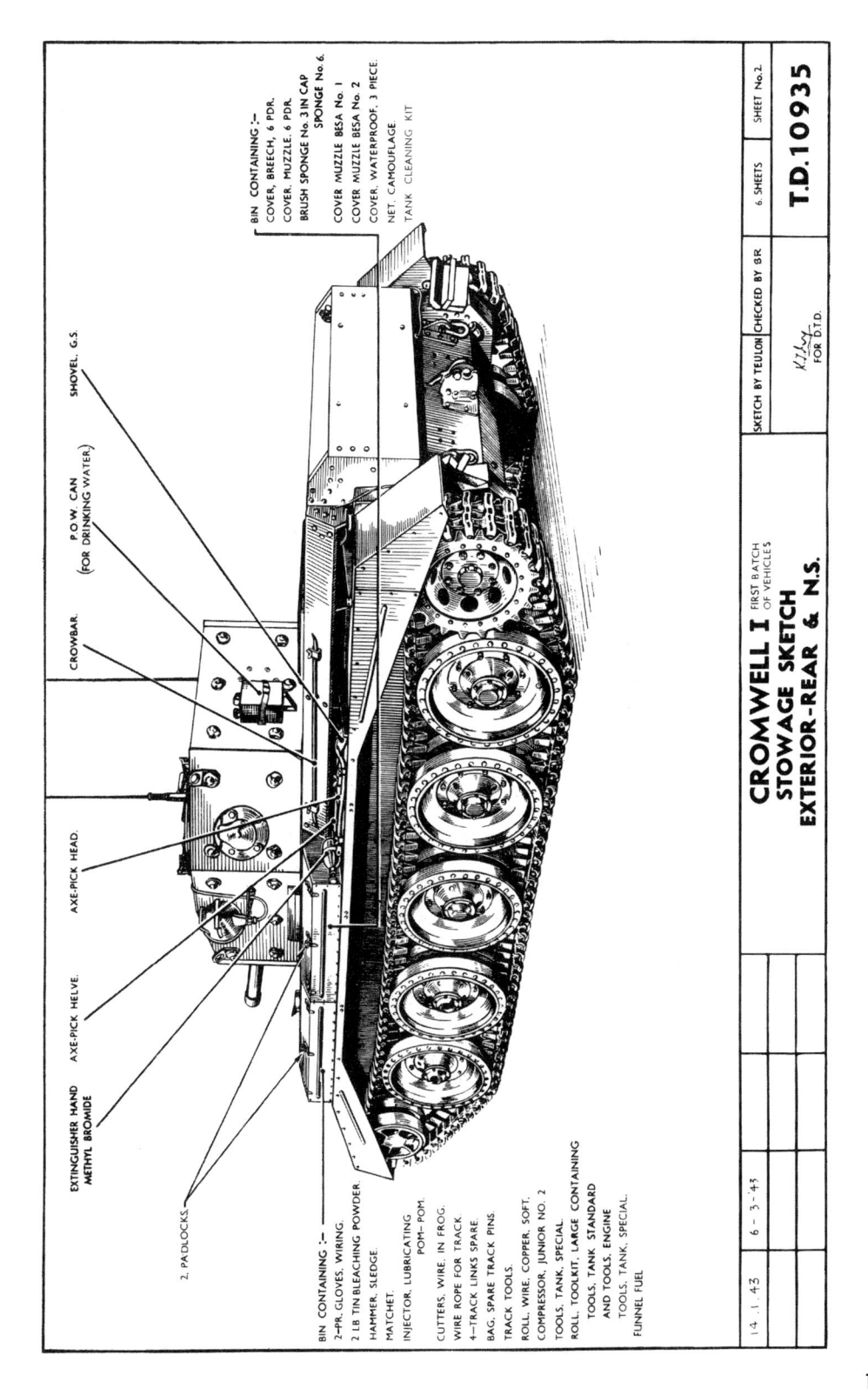

CROMWELL I FIRST BATCH OF VEHICLES
STOWAGE SKETCH
EXTERIOR – REAR & N.S.

T.D.10935 — SHEET No. 2 — 6 SHEETS

Sketch by Teulon — Checked by BR

14.1.43 / 6-3-43

Labels:
- EXTINGUISHER HAND METHYL BROMIDE
- AXE-PICK HELVE
- AXE-PICK HEAD
- CROWBAR
- P.O.W. CAN (FOR DRINKING WATER)
- SHOVEL, G.S.
- 2. PADLOCKS
- BIN CONTAINING :—
  - COVER, BREECH, 6 PDR.
  - COVER, MUZZLE. 6 PDR.
  - BRUSH SPONGE No. 3 IN CAP SPONGE No. 6.
  - COVER MUZZLE BESA No. I
  - COVER MUZZLE BESA No. 2
  - COVER, WATERPROOF, 3 PIECE.
  - NET. CAMOUFLAGE
  - TANK CLEANING KIT
- BIN CONTAINING :—
  - 2-PR. GLOVES, WIRING.
  - 2 LB TIN BLEACHING POWDER.
  - HAMMER, SLEDGE.
  - MATCHET.
  - INJECTOR, LUBRICATING POM-POM.
  - CUTTERS, WIRE. IN FROG.
  - WIRE ROPE FOR TRACK.
  - 4—TRACK LINKS SPARE
  - BAG, SPARE TRACK PINS.
  - TRACK TOOLS.
  - ROLL, WIRE, COPPER, SOFT.
  - COMPRESSOR, JUNIOR No. 2
  - TOOLS, TANK, SPECIAL.
  - ROLL. TOOLKIT. LARGE CONTAINING TOOLS, TANK STANDARD AND TOOLS. ENGINE
  - TOOLS. TANK. SPECIAL.
  - FUNNEL FUEL

CROMWELL TANK

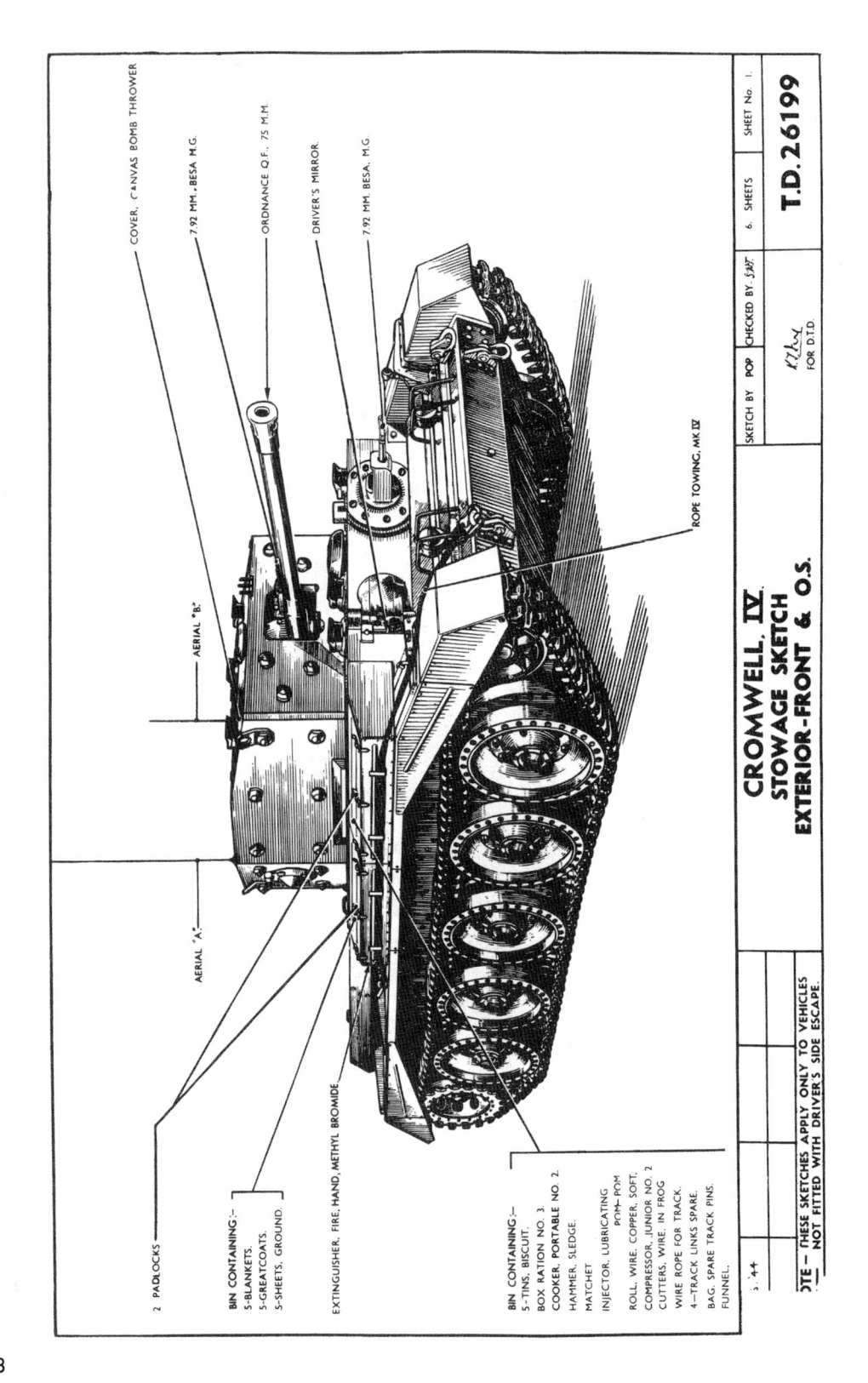

VEHICLE HISTORY AND SPECIFICATION

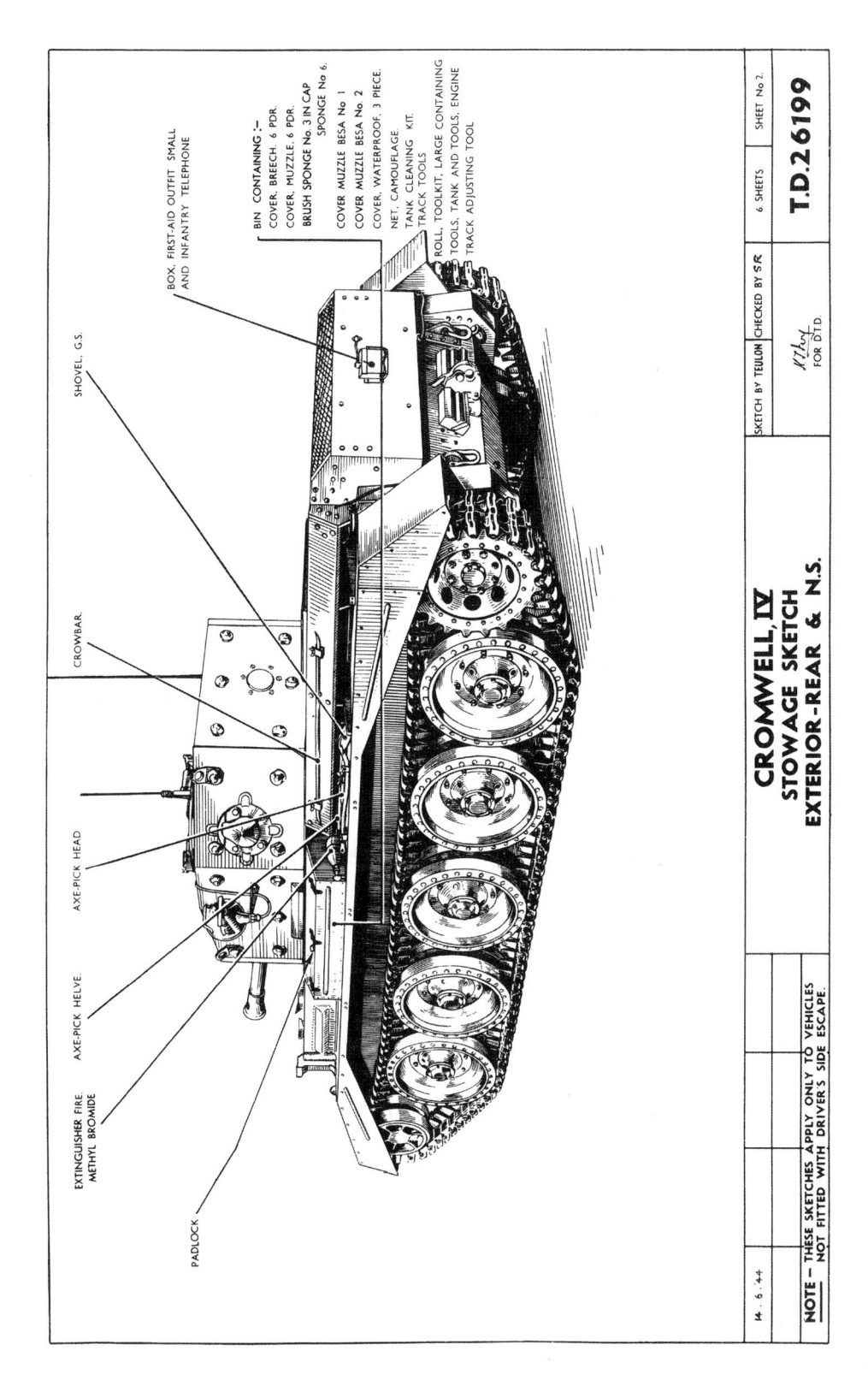

CROMWELL TANK

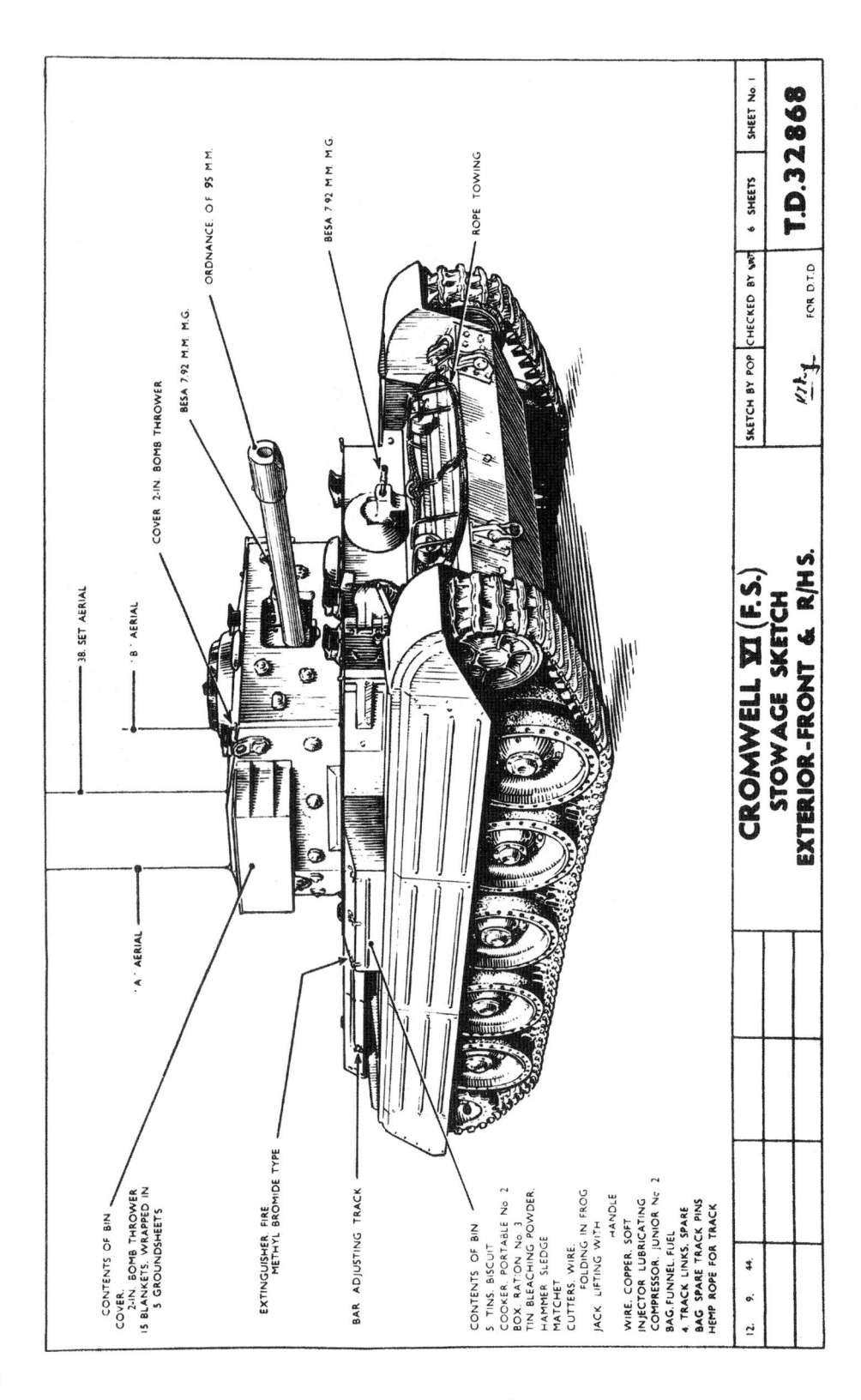

VEHICLE HISTORY AND SPECIFICATION

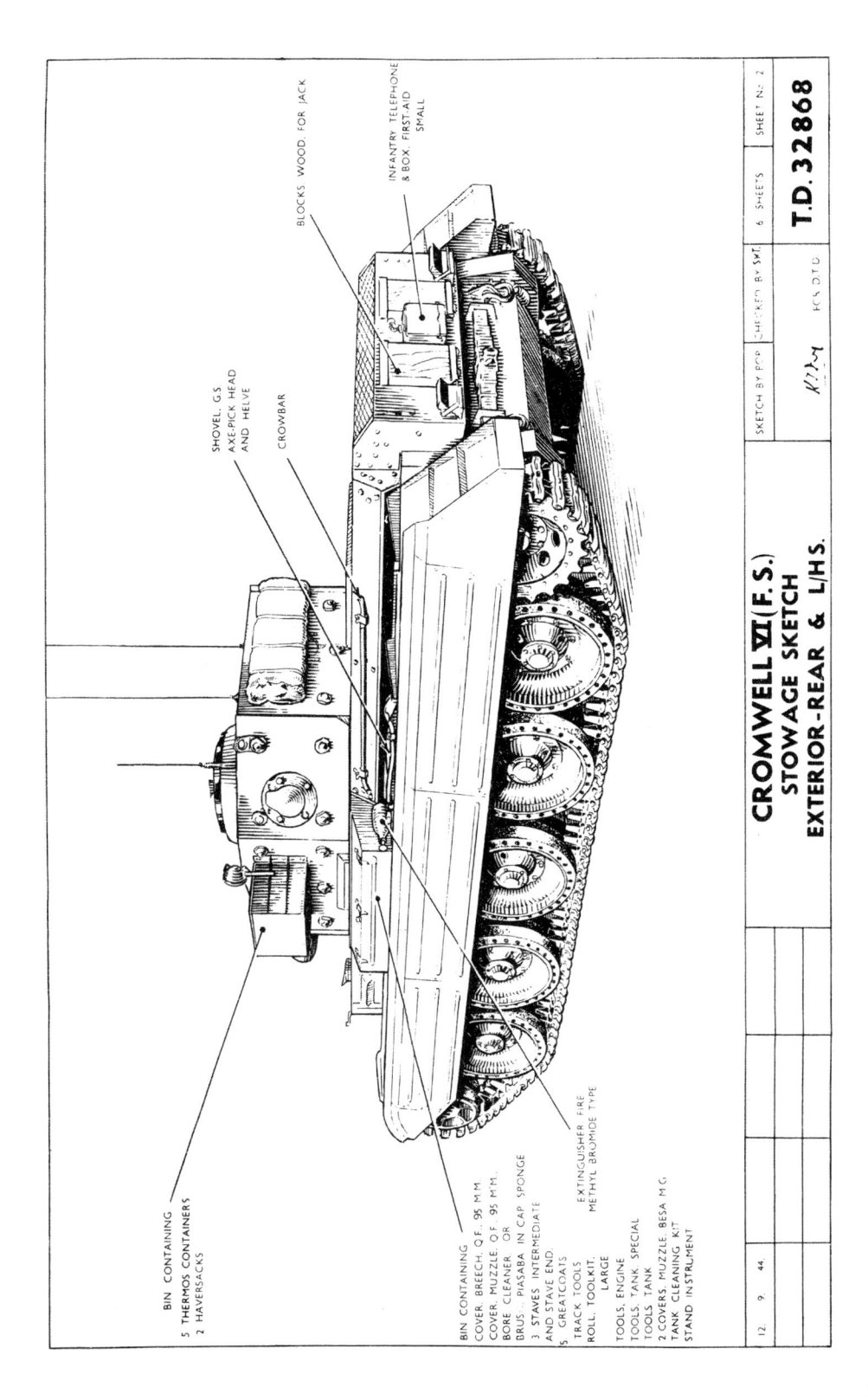

CROMWELL TANK

BC. 38071.

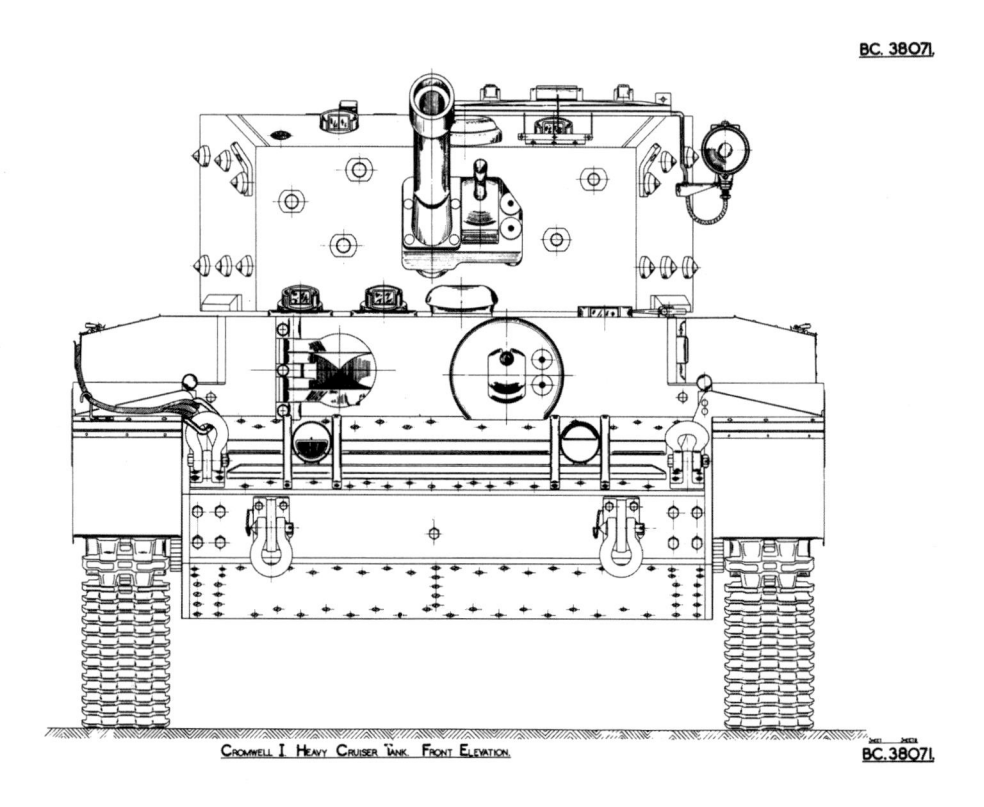

Cromwell I Heavy Cruiser Tank. Front Elevation.   BC. 38071.

BC. 38071.

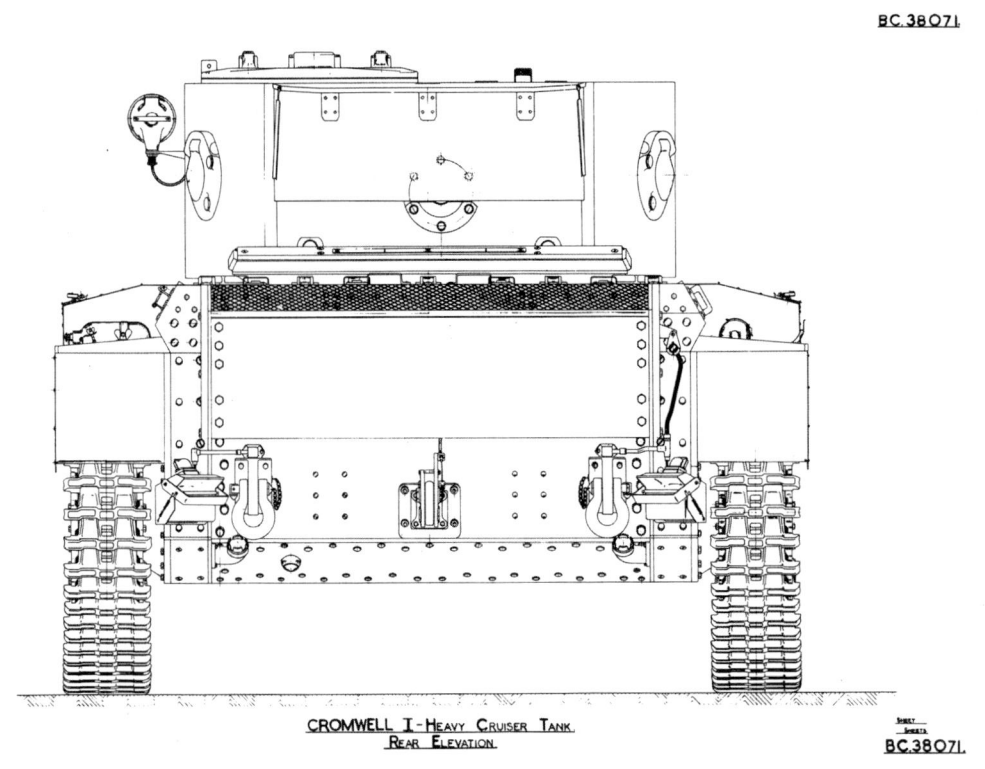

Cromwell I - Heavy Cruiser Tank. Rear Elevation.   BC. 38071.

VEHICLE HISTORY AND SPECIFICATION

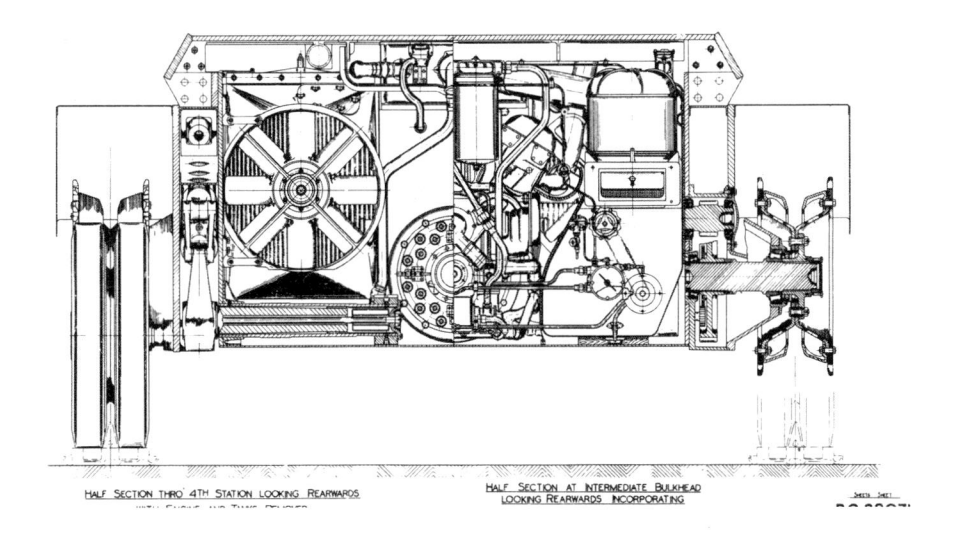

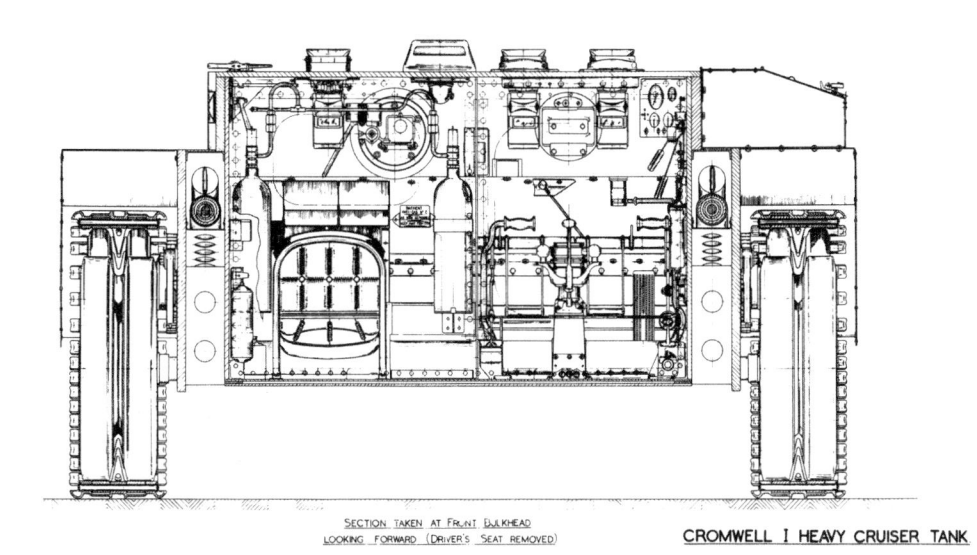

HALF SECTION THRO' 4TH STATION LOOKING REARWARDS

HALF SECTION AT INTERMEDIATE BULKHEAD LOOKING REARWARDS INCORPORATING

SECTION TAKEN AT FRONT BULKHEAD LOOKING FORWARD (DRIVER'S SEAT REMOVED)

CROMWELL I HEAVY CRUISER TANK

CROMWELL TANK

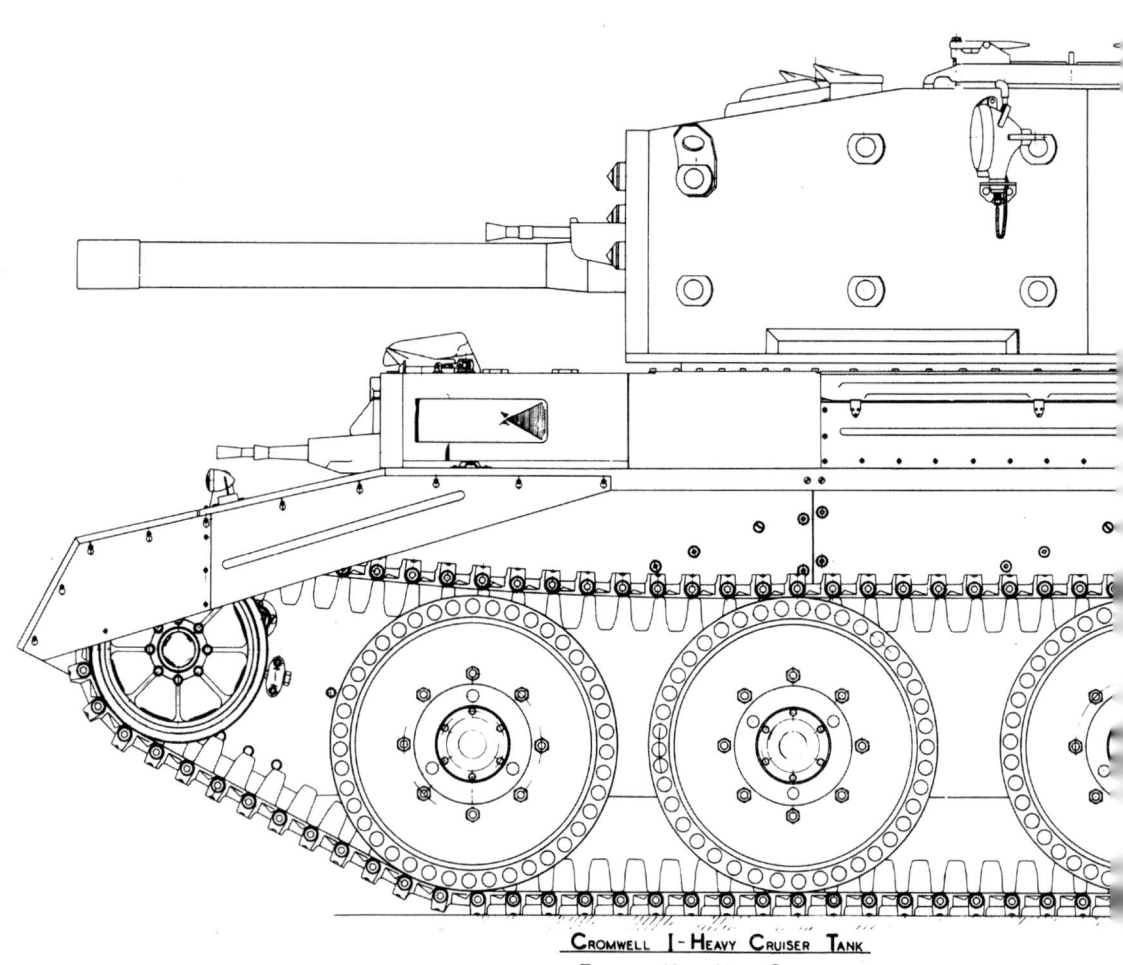

Cromwell I - Heavy Cruiser Tank
External View - Near Side

VEHICLE HISTORY AND SPECIFICATION

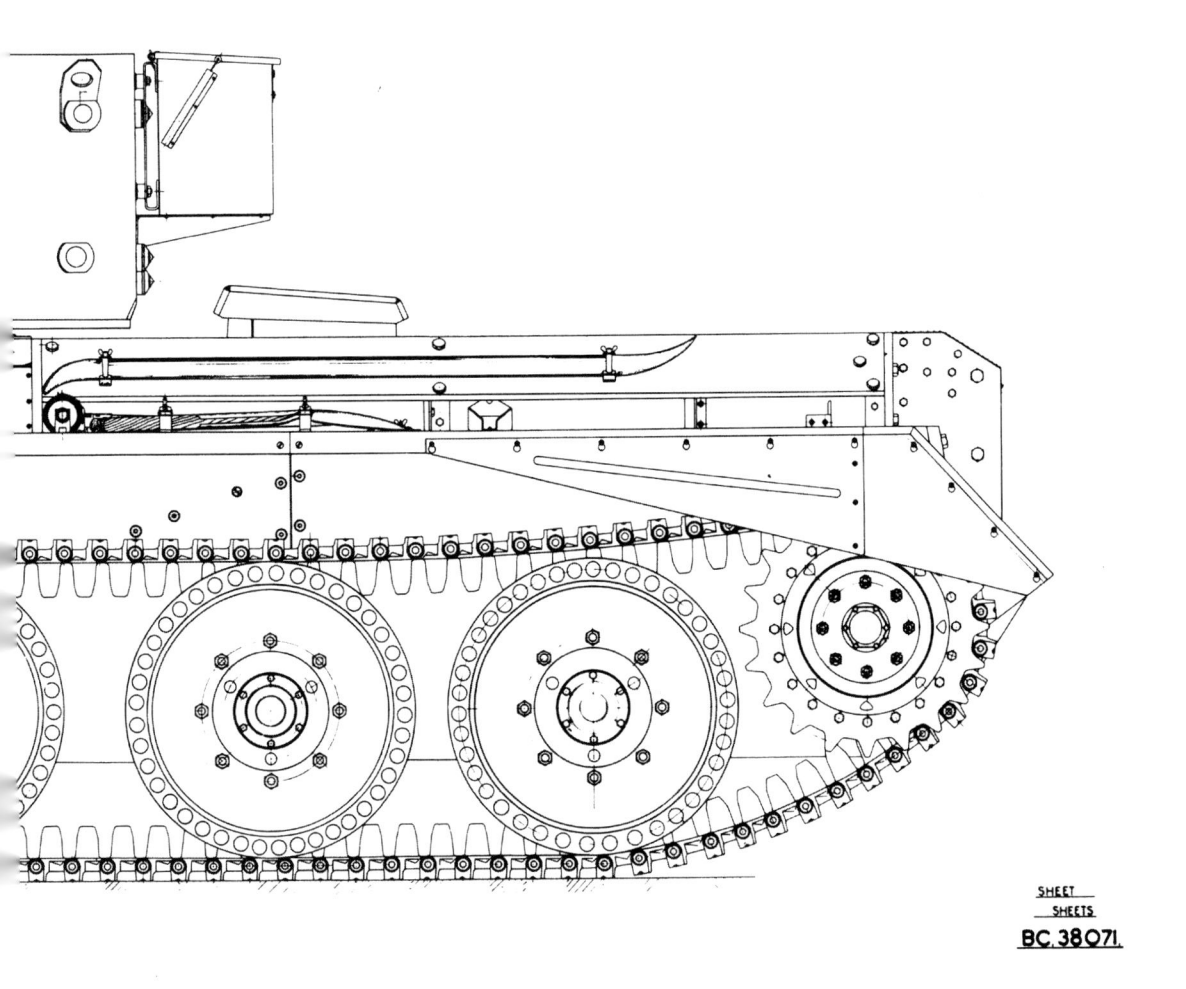

BC.38071.

CROMWELL TANK

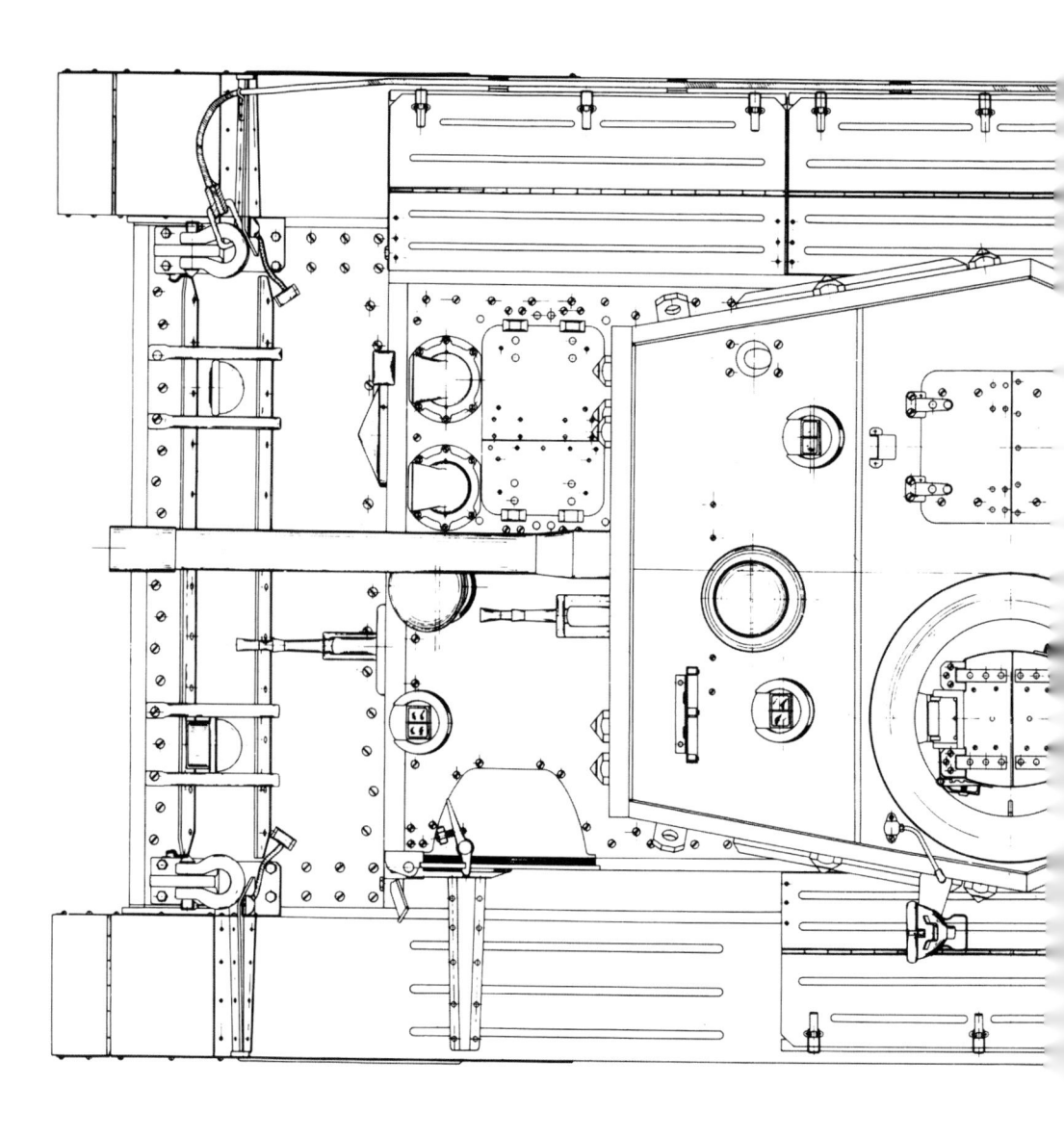

VEHICLE HISTORY AND SPECIFICATION

B.C. 38071.

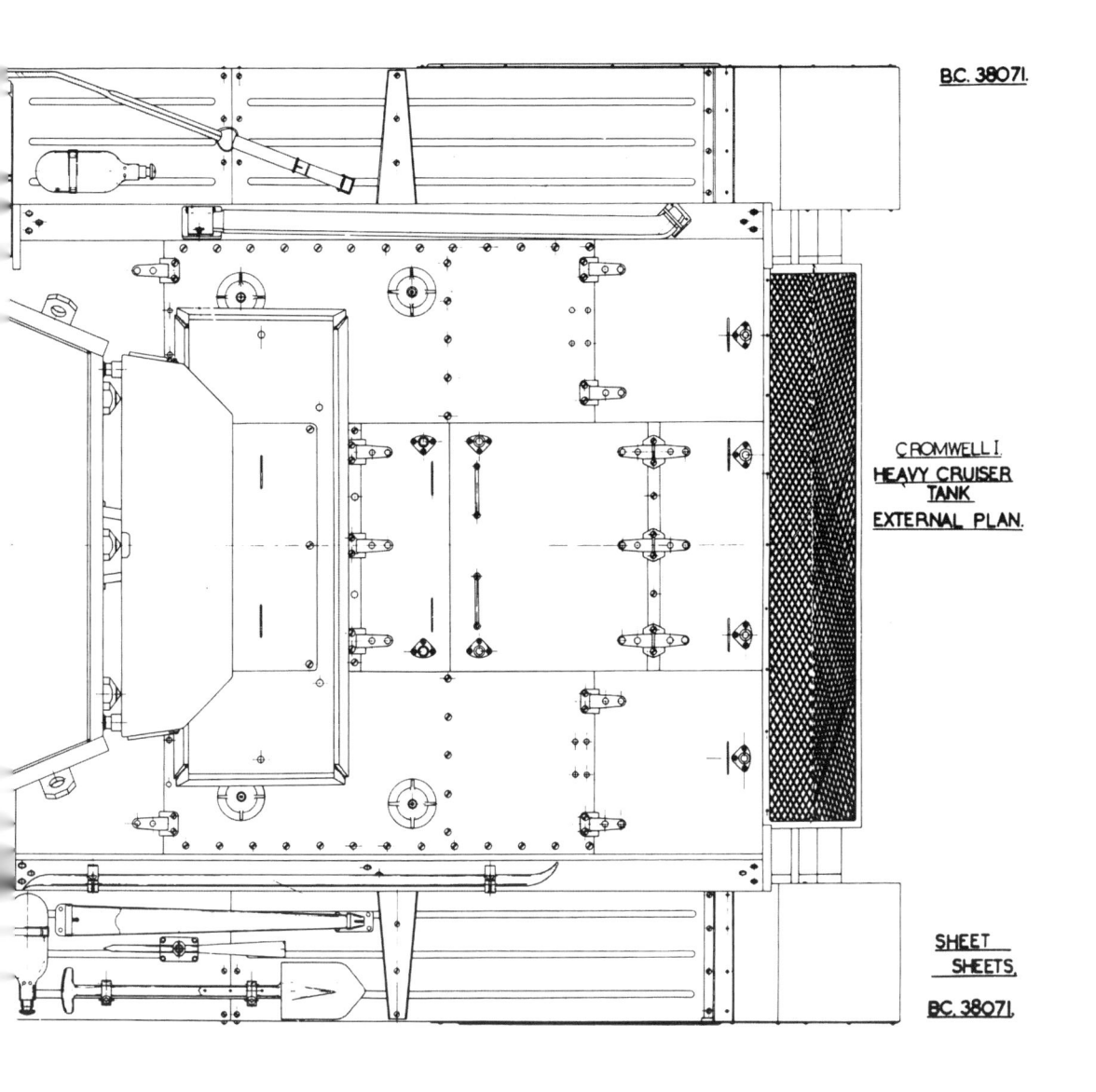

CROMWELL I.
HEAVY CRUISER
TANK
EXTERNAL PLAN.

SHEET
SHEETS.
B.C. 38071.

CROMWELL TANK

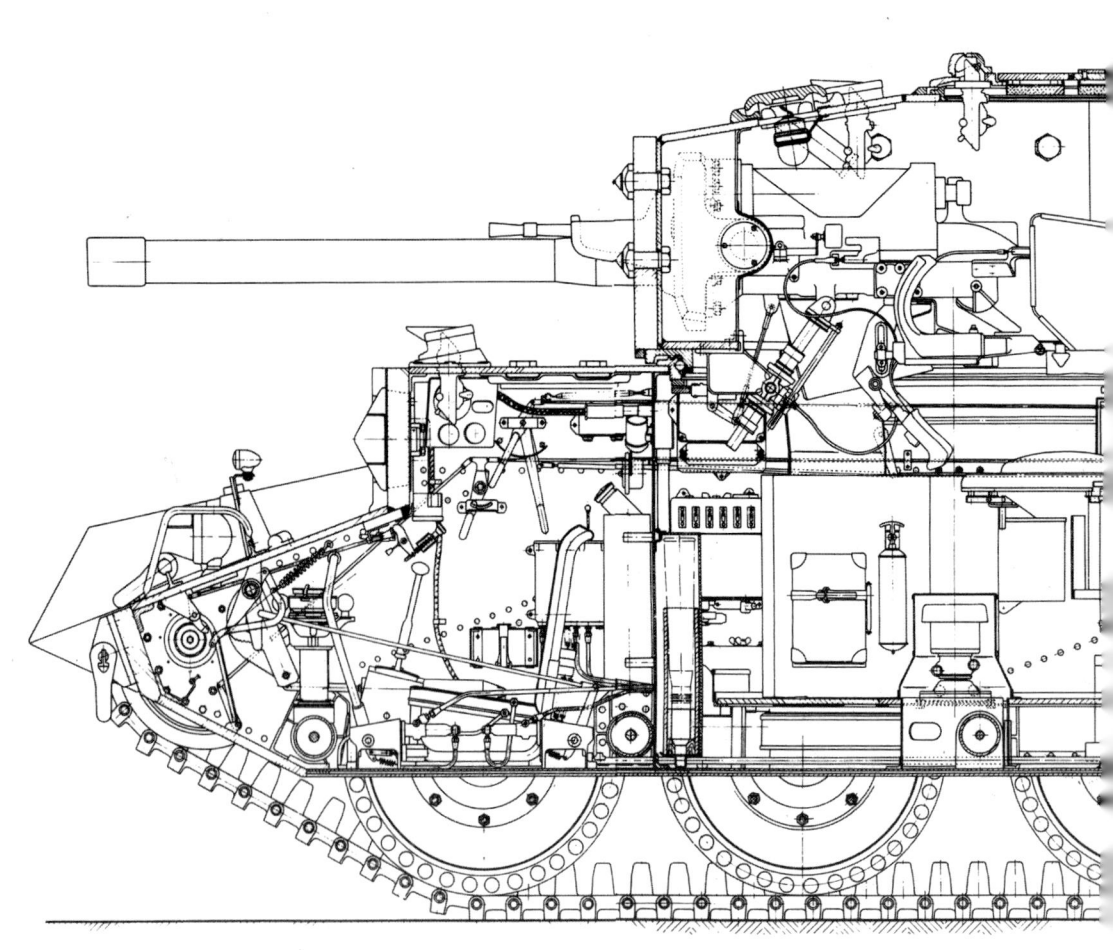

CROMWELL I HEAVY CRUISER TANK.   LONGITUDINAL SECTION.

VEHICLE HISTORY AND SPECIFICATION

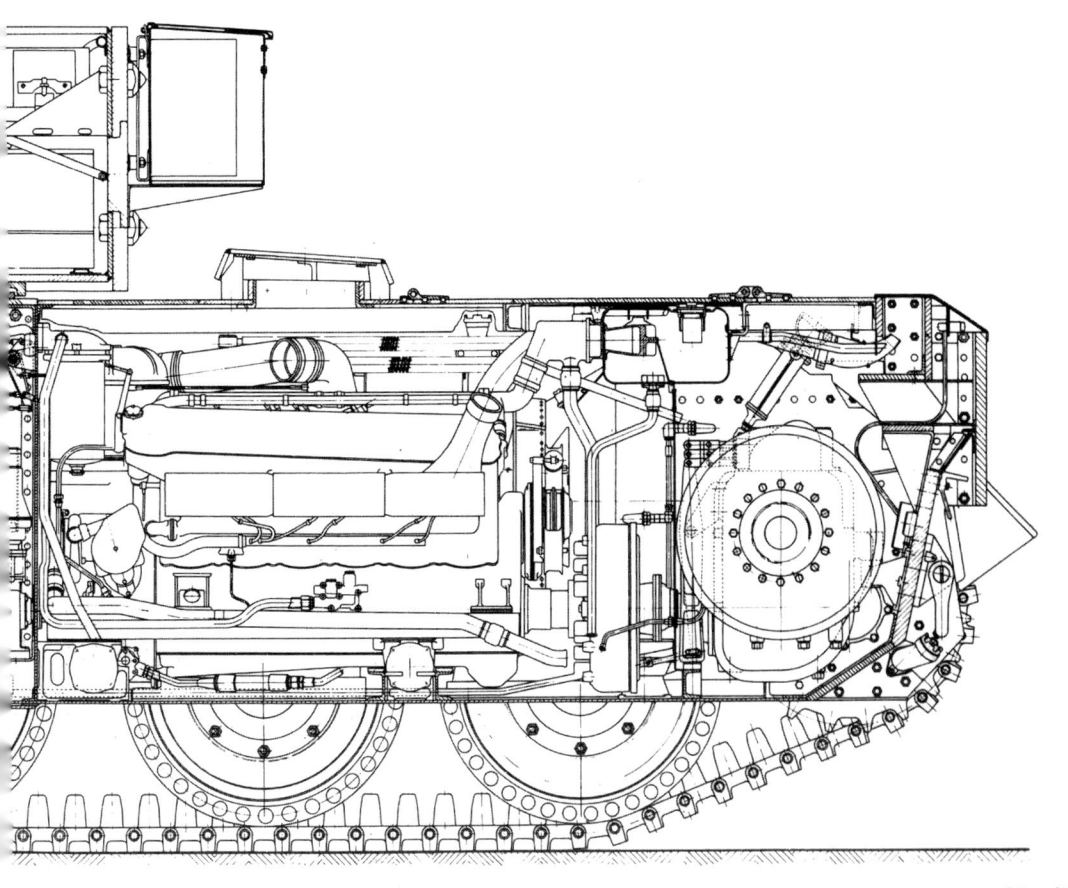

BC.38071.

CROMWELL TANK

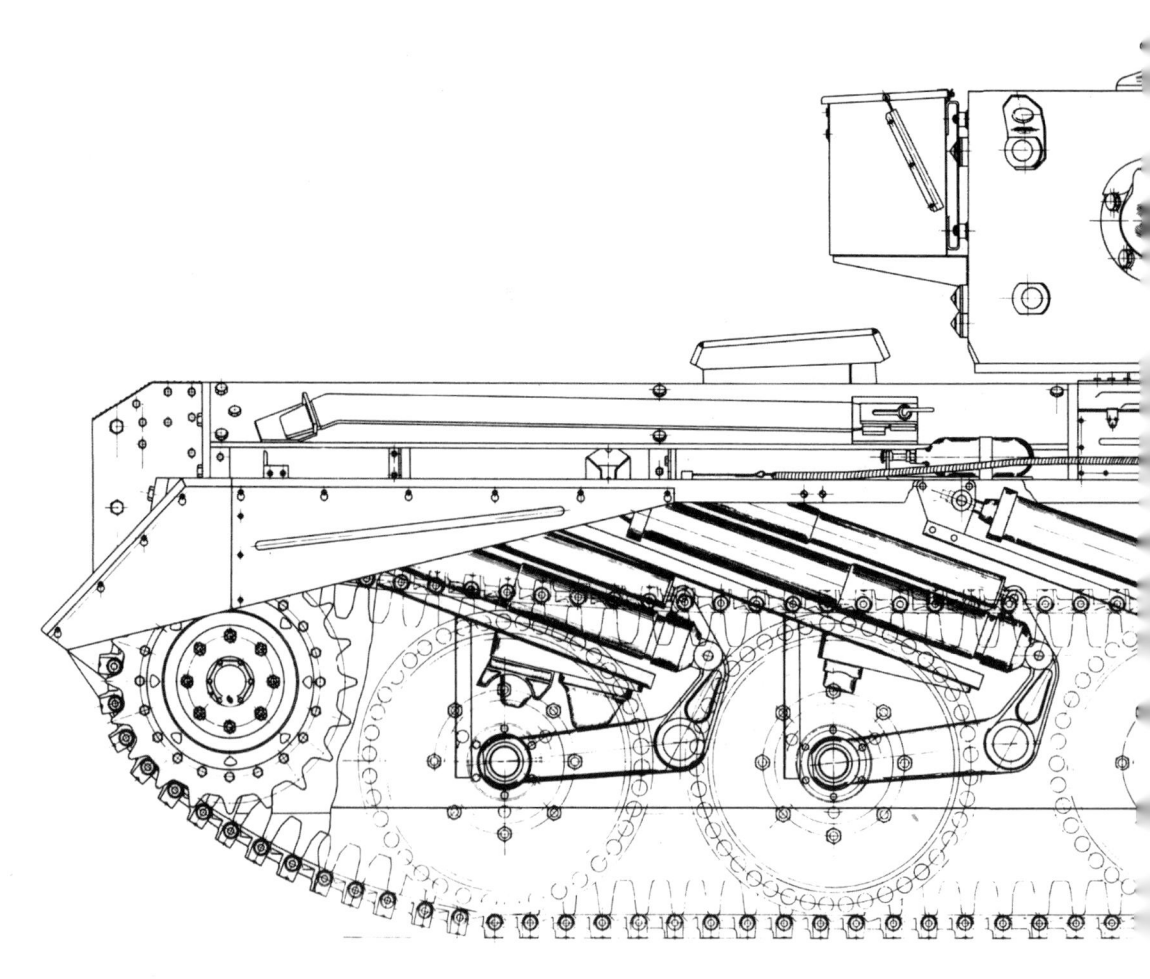

CROMWELL I HEAVY CRUISER TANK —

VEHICLE HISTORY AND SPECIFICATION

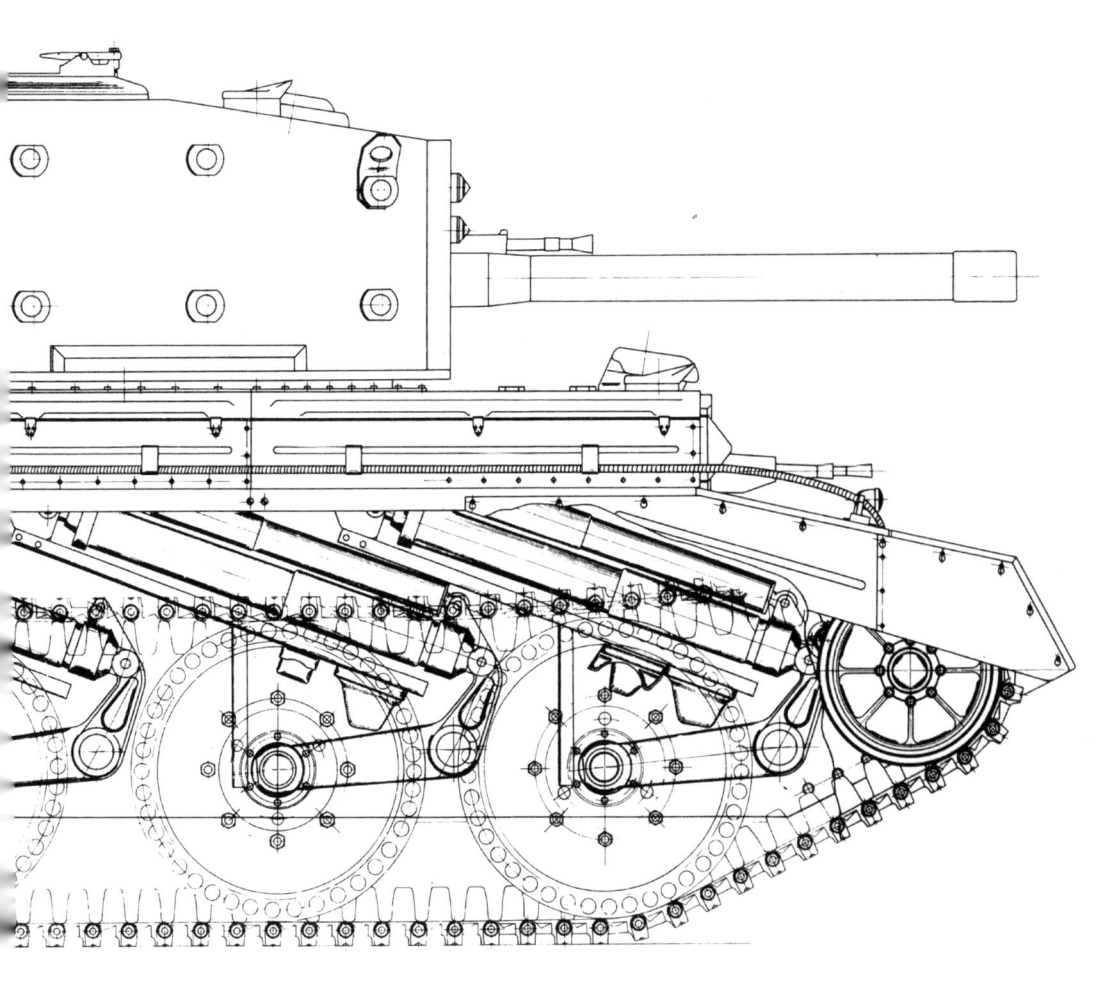

OFFSIDE ELEVATION WITH SIDE ARMOUR PARTIALLY REMOVED.

THANKS TO

The Tank Museum wishes to thank and acknowledge the following who kindly supported the crowdfunding campaign, which enabled this title to be republished in 2022.

Bradley Mitchell
Scott Parkinson
David Tabner
Andrew Smurthwaite
Frederick Brown
Stephen Birch
Kelvin Zhang
Jerald Marquardt
Trevor Wilson
Hans Johansson
Andrew Cadel
Steve Ellis
Bob Andrews
MSG Eddie M. Redfearn
Theo Hercules
Luigi Naruszewicz
Aaron Somerville
John Doyle
Howard Mitchell
Martin Jones
James J.G. Griffiths
Terry Hall
Steve Ellis
Ichikawa Tetsurou
Martyn Keen
Kirk Grainger
Chris Potter
Chris Swindells
Damian Brooks
John Kasawan
M.G.A. Weers
Andrew Downs
John Reeve
Peter Wilson
Philip Taylor
John Stanger
Edward Preston
Julian Davies
To Luka
Charles Taylor
Tancred Cassar
Ryan Allen
Joseph Jolley
Joanne Baker
Tom Achard
Andrew Speechley
Tom Grindall

Steven Bannister
Russ Spence
Peter James
Brendan Healy
WOII Bob Teasdale
R Hamps
Uwe Springhorn
Rocco Plath
Daniel Standen
Anthony J Bird
Kieron Weller
Adrian Harris
Mark Rogers
Rob Brunton
Andrew Morley Wilkinson
Niclas Lindberg
Gary Draper
Liam Young
Rhys Fouracre
Andrew Dickey
Kenneth Lilley
Kevin Dyke
Rick Williams
Richard Beale
Mark Osborne
Mark Guttag
Marcus Mosley
Elliot Wade
William Pointing
Brian Page
Peter Smith
Ralph Hart
Ashley Garrison-Brown
Andrew Philpott
Esler Jim
P.S. Waugh
Peter White
Robert Cousin
Stuart Butterfield
Mark Ryan
Joe Bristoll
Benjamin T. Richter
Paul James
Steve Stuart
For Oliver
Sean Harper
David Corran

Joseph Searles
Stephen Dickens
Steven Howes
Dr Stephen Pannell
Norman Salmon
Nigel Chappell
Mark Edmands
Penni Elton
Richard Curren
Michael Townsend
Chris Clements
Cok Martijn
Robert Harwood
Keith Dallimore
Rebecca Mill-Wilson
Jack Levai
Rasmus Rex
Andreas Kowald
Ben Lawrence
Tyler Steele
Sam Barratt
Oliver Austin
Matthew Walker
Connor Cane
John Wright
Mike Pratt
Paul Middleton
Martin Littlecott
David Woodside
Sean Day
David Makinson
David Byrne
Rodney Anderson
Warren Mason
Mark Reynolds
John Beck
Michael Hobbs
Anthony Roberts
Nick Hodges
Andrew Desborough
Brian Hitch
Simon Smith
Kieran Hall
Timothy Hills
Keith Terry
Connor Storey
Ben Williams

Andrew Ray
Anthony Fletton
Matthew Carn
Charles Paddick
Tizian Dähler
Adrian Chorlton
Leonard Decant
George S. Harbinson
Michael Patey
Steven Thornton
Richard Purvis
Nathanael Wood
James Cooke
Glenn Rose
David Pope
Andrew Tomlinson
Richard Lucas
Steven Blackburn
Simon Ashcroft
Steve Bastable
John Hunt
Keith Olding
Ian Creasy
Brendan Quinlan
Giles Morley-Loft
Paul Goffin
Carter Birchfield
Jack Porter-Lindsey
Clemens Doll
Matthew Charles Gray
Steve Hocking
Peter Marshall
Andrew Woodward
Ian McLaughlin
Alan Baxter
Fiona Kendall
Eddie King
Herman du Preez
Carl Doran
Marcel Tromp
Wayne Davison
Jordan Weaver
Andrew Gilbert
Lowell Wong
Adrian Pethick
Terence Plant
Michael Cooper

THANKS TO

Kenneth Goss
Chris Fitzsimmons
Russell Barnes
Gordon Chrisp
David Cole
Cameron Moeller
Paul Button
Richard Gibbon
Jeremy Double
Chris Naden
Adam Gilliver
Clive Bower
Keith Meachem
Connor Storey
Percy D. Boyles
Steven Dyer
Richard Featherstone
Paul Willms
Maurice Andrews
Chris Matson
Charlie Barker
Graham Green
Craig Smith
Robin McEwen
Nigel Heather
Simon Day
Gerald Pierson
Neil Illingworth
Stuart Greenhalgh
Mark Etheridge
Shaun Leeks
Shaun Poller
Mark Powell
Ryan Tennant
Jack Yates
John Hill
Christopher Thompson
Chris Mackay
Mark Paines
Phil Gray
Mark Jennings
Andrew Paul Cook
Quinten van Kasteel
Martin Campbell
Christopher Noble
Don More
Adrian Symonds
Jay Kaelin
Mark Brooking
Andrew David
Michael Green
Raymond Wong

Andrew Eatock
Paul Kerr
Lauren Child
Huw Williams
Oliver-Emil Pedersen
Geoff Housego
Neil Cooper
James Cutts
Luke Culley
Michael Schweizer
Scott Gill
Owen Fitzpatrick
Richard Brown
Jakub Masařík
Richard Burdett
David Crosbie
Matt Faiers
David Clark
Peter Paterson
Bradley Cameron
Andrew Peck
David Peck
Connor Coolbaugh
Winston Gould
Bryan Davis
Ian Hambelton
Robin van Dijk
Stephen Burkwood
Daniel House
Teresa Fletcher
Terry Drewett
Tim Wrate
M. Simpelaar
Paul Mutton
Christopher Pilags
Trevor Povey
Eero Juhola
Terry Marsh
David Cruickshank
James Hulme
Anthony Boyce
Paul Charlwood
Devon Spears
Jason Singleton
Nathan Schlehlein
Sean Morrison
Jason Hofer
Esker McConnell
Dave Batten
Anthony Grayson
Brian Silver
George G. Hill

Sarah Woodcock
Daniel J. Parker
Joshua Gibbons
Peter Patrick
Mark Barnett
Juha Honkanen
Stuart Mackenzie
Henry Tornetta
Robert Peach
Michele Petriello
Richard Tugwell
Ian Tong
Chris Saulpaugh
Carl Pfutzenreuter
Barry Curtis
James Smith
Alexander Ridler
Sven Soderberg
John Wells
Jeroen van Dijk
T. Hoult
Deverne Jones
Scott Harwood
Philip Kaye
John Allgood
Sander Vreuls
Bence Juhász
Paul Spandler
Andrew Osborne
Christopher Winkels
Colin Gibson
Ray Young
Philip McCarty
Ben Dummer
Michael Woong
Jonathan Nielsen-Moore
Robert Dickinson
Norman Jaffe
Eivind Helgetun
Matt Klotz
Eddie Jackson
Paul Bradley
Arron Chiswell
Thomas Stromberg
Alexander Carr
Edric Chang
Christopher Skelton
Steven Adams
Dougie Smith
Alan Mincher
Mark Ambridge
Friedrich Klett

Andrew Down
Chris Bridgman
Alan Hall
Graeme Bates
Paul Hachey
Mark Niblett
Robert Smith
Steven Parkes
Andrew Reilly
Alastair Boyles
John Tripi
Stewart Garnett
Stephen Booth
Tom Davidson
Robert Pilling
Brad Dunleavy
Keith Major
Ewan Spence
Mark Hook
Dafydd Lyons
Constantin Schreiber
Danny Hin
James Sherman
James Scrivener
Paul Baker
Richard Lunson
Graham Duff
Matthew Bell
Hannah Lightowler
Andrew Lind
Michael Carroll
David Corboy
David Howling
Steven Bromley
Gary Miller
Michael Gerus
Carson Thomas
Lance Garwood
Mark Arnold
Neil Smith
Paul Schoeman
Mark Hiles
Gert De Cuyper
Kevin Pennycook
Jacob Tierney
Paul Mullaney
Ian Reeves
Stephen Chopping
Mark Bolger
Harold Rutten
John Conran
Steve Sanders

CROMWELL TANK

THANKS TO

Pawel Czarnocki
James Flint
Robert Elder
Eric Hollis
Terence Brewer
Thomas Ruiz
Barry Canning
Erik Miller
Harry Grosvenor-Collis
Gordon Brown
Connor Green
James Taggerty
Ben Davies
Keith Stafford
Daniel Jerbi
Harry McKnight
Stephen Ayres
Bernard Wylie
Adam Mathwig
David Pyle
Mark Collins
Keith Walker
Tim Wisehart
Keith Dray
Alan Johnson
Colin Smith
Glenn Wilson
Graham Mellis
Alexander Delf
Mark Pugh
Adam Pascuzzo
Alexander Burnett
Nick Brown
Jake Martin
David Mason
Charles Walker
Alex Winchell
Stephen White
Philip Bateman
Richard Evans
David Leatherdale
Ashley Smyth
John Johnston
Justin De Lavison
David Lynch
Colin Avern
Rob Shipman
Jack Hewson
Mark Lechmere
Samuel Picardo
Aaron Ashbrooke
Jonathan Bordell

Darren Rolfe
Mark Towner
Diane Dowling
Simon Hodson
Jack Denley
David Pengilly
Nigel Ashcroft
David Preston
Christian Wall
David Julien Griebel
Richard Burdett
Steve Thomas
Dave Mylett
Harry Hennessey
Eoghan Jones
Michael Brydges
Mark Dorsett
Guillaume Galy
Hugh Thomas
Darren Baker
Paul Jones
John Bradshaw
Salvador Cadengo
Jacob Cain
Paul Turner
Josephine Drew
Richard Bradley
Steven Browning
Tony Kear
Nick House
Philip Moor
Howard Lindsay
John Gathercole
Andy Sacha
Annie And Michael
Martin Smith
Adrian Hampton
Per Ove Sekse
Christian Bieletzki
Grahame Bebb
Richard Stevens
Alan Batten
Stuart Gunner
Stuart Armstrong
Sam Vincent
Jürgen Hammann
Barry Richardson
Adam Rich
Johan Van der Bruggen
Liam Cooney
Ramsay Fergal
Cameron Van Den Hoek

Ian Raine
Jim Pascoe
Terry Veal
Derek Brown
Philip Newitt
Piers Burwell
Nigel Pollard
Chris Apletree
Nick Payne
David & Jill Mears
Martin France
Graeme Whiting
John Drover
Martin Reynell
Ian Clarke
Steve Percy
Mark Baird
James Dack
Paul Wilcox
Guy Walker
Simon Tankard
Josh Mounter
Stuart Marshall
Jonathan Vickers
Ildefonso Gómez Yáñez
Christopher Stokes
Hugh Maguire
George Price
Tracy Wood
David Adams
John Hodgkinson
Richard Palmer
Maj Gen D.H. Crook
Stuart Bestford
Thomas Williams
Julian Loewenthal
David Fraser
Peter Edmondson
Bã̦Rge
Andre Arild
Paul Perry
James Neal
Martyn Clark
Matthew M. Smith
Chris Payne
Shane Dale
David Alexander
Bruno Valerio
Sal Castellana
Matthew Hynett
David Adams
Nigel Walker

Rodolfo G. San Agustin Jr
Simon Barnes
Patrick Crelly
Louis Mcafoos
António Castelo
Mr Passfield
Steve Murphy
Cammie Lamont
Charles Odell
Gage W. Smith
Siyu Fu
Anthony Witham
Herminio Ramirez
Alan Marks
Joe Szul
Martin Killick
Craig McRobbie
John Parr
Mike Smith
Matt Davies
Debbie Thompson
Syd Coleman
Aaron Hutson
David Battson
Ian Merriman
David O'Reilly
Dwight Luetscher
Kevin Hopwood
Michael Woodcock
Colin Baddeley
Nathan Parker
Jake Owen
Hanqiu Jiang
Richard Morris
Douglas Wade
Steve Richard
David Ford
David Wright
Samuel A. Grant
Vlastimil Tkacik
Matthew Hadnum
Lindsay Turner
Stuart Humphries
Stuart Woods
Stephen Barber
Aaron Brown
Martin Tuck
Leslie Stephenson
Stuart Carter
Dave Malott
Stephen Brown
Lee Smith

THANKS TO

Andrew Shelley
Nick Goffin
Daniel Ogles
Chris Brook
James Turner
Harry Wilding
Eric Hede
Christopher Budd
Stephan Zadziuk
Vivian Symonds
Aaron Jackson
Andrew Robert Bevan
Christopher Wood
Alan Willcock
Glyn Lewis
Warren Fenner
Michael Corser
Alan Rhodes
Juergen Schaaf
James Glendinning
Albert Squires
Jeremy Witt
Andrew Dixon
Roy Griffiths
Jonathan Jones
David Shaw
Jeroen Vantroyen
Laurence Behan
Michael Earnshaw
Geoffrey Stobbart
Leonard Thomson
Mike Grant
Nigel Titchen
Anjan Saikia
Jack Rimmer
Andy Macrae
Jonathan Ireland
Martyn Sime
Alex Horton
Axel Lohmann
Gary Richardson
Stephen Laccohee
Malcolm McEwan
Krzysztof A. Edelman
Ian Appleby
Charles Jones
Iori Hicks
Chris Bill
Stephen
Steven Devlin
Steven Randall
Clough Derek

John White
William Allen
Phil Puddefoot
Anthony Antilles
Stephen Wilcox
Christopher Smith
Christopher Worsley
Martin Bürgisser
Michael Ball
Ian Williams
Rob Treen
Adam Crew
Jacob Grove
Gary Dhillon
Brian Siela
Kenneth Teeter
Benjamin Puricelli
Scott Atchison
David Butterfield
Louis Devirgilio
Kurt Zwick
Gary Stewart
Louis Powell
Nicholas Brodar
Michael Sanchez
Daniel Cosier
Martin Frost
Sam Lockwood
Keith Matthews
Ashley Connor
Chris Alexander
Michael Billings
John Tapsell
Andrew Penman
Justin Fischer
William Bradley
Jorrian Dorlandt
Gavin Bryant
George Warne
Kristian Wicks
Christopher Maher
Paul Gerrard
Steve Kummerfeldt
Chris Blackler
Richard Davies
Paul V. Scourfield
Sam Wild
Joe Seaman
Paul Cramer
Gavin Steff
Alan Long
Paul Wallis

Ian Sims
Jake Holden
Mark Cheyney
Christopher Clarke
Campbell Harris
Stephen Squirrell
Anthony Gaughan
Jennifer Maydon
Jeremy Budd
Patrick Bailey
Ron Blackman
Graham Mellis
Lachlan Harris
Felix Stiessen
James Peacock
Gary Coates
William Calvert
David Woodrow
Paul Watts
Göran Löwkrantz
Chris Heath
Alastair Monk
Andy Musgrove
Robert Pews
Tamila McMullan
Paul Newman
Jeffrey Moots
Michael Gettings
Bruce Ghent
Peter Kuonen
Tony Poulter
Jack Sharpe
Andrew Kenny
Elliot Goddard
John Patrick Doran
Jan Meyer-Kamping
Arran Hartley
Gordon Matthews
Derek Smith
Paul Turrell
Stuart Purvis
John Turner
John Kent
Robert Bayliss
Matthew Wassell
David May
Stuart Cooper
Timothy Stevenson
Shirley Stedman
Tony Edwards
Simon Cannon
Paul Flanary

Scott Batchlor
Steve Cartwright
Alexander Amini
Eleanor Billinghurst
Philip Castle
Steven Hopwood
Raymond King
Israel S. Gibson
Nick Jones
David Bottomley
Steven Marley
Nigel Chandler
Thomas Costall
Martin Deacon
Simon Paterson
Garry Bailey
Dr Lynn Gareze
Adrian Knight
Heidi Smith
Steven Boddy
Sean Ogden
Matthew Muraska
Michael Bishop
Daniel John Bright
Peter Dawson
Steven Harker
Jason Parfitt
Gary Davis
Matthew Dawson
Alex Tucker
Ben Couldwell
Stuart Shaw
Robert Parker-Bowen
David Young
James Underwood
David Britten
Jon Howes
Tony Waterhouse
Brian Smith
Graham Croft
David Cohen
Alfie Higgins
James Upton
Stephen Harvey
Catherine Chapman
David Evans
John Bateman
Shade Kelly
Richard St Cooper
Chris Standen
Anthony Meyers
Emily M. Hamilton

CROMWELL TANK

Kevin Page
Peter Frost
Rob Nichols
Peter Turner
James Stewart
Alexander Gibson
Ronald Lofthouse
Ian Crooks
Richard Lewis
Steven East
Matt Magee
Ian Kelly
Jeff Connolly
Paul Driscoll
Darren Hopkins
Robin Karpeta
Christopher Halford
Katy Moore
Carl Brodie
Mark Yates
Andrew Lowe
Dylan Ross
Aleksander Williams
Timothy Gray
Scott Liddell
Barry Walser
Kieran Caley
Neil Wiffen
Joyce West
Ian Griggs
Graeme Campsie
George Exon
Jeremy Bond
Simon Rilot
Rebecca Green
Chris Bray
Mark Meredith
Simon Gumbley
Robin Hardcastle
Ka Wo Au
Peter Piper
Dean Clark
Ashley Forster
Simon Jackson
Gary Burns
David Pepper
Glen Andrews
Maj R.D.B. Burgess HAC
Richard Bradley
Peter Everitt
Jolene Turner
Earl Nordgren
Jen Wilson
Andrew Butler
Robbie Macauley
Mark Jeffery
Kevin Bradley
Brian Burdette
Mike Howlett
Ian Clarke
Kevin Hazard
Tim Jones
Alistair Goodwin
Thomas Beck
Isaac Boots
Greg Kotecha
David Dibben
Dave Mitchell
Dominic Collins
Lee Greenwood
Deborah Schouten
Min Jung
David Reeves
Andrew Grayman
Clive Eastwood
Mark Knibbs
Zack Wright
Richard Mounstephen
Joe Taylor
Jeremy Fenby-Taylor
Tracy Gresty
Vance Chambers
Jean Grieten
Andrew Wood
Barclay Caras
Anthony Stewart
Joe Skinner
Chris Weston
Stuart Dobson
Joshua Bettinelli
David Crompton
Martin Clouder
Nik Johnson
Alastair Macfarlane
Mark Collins
Barry Sulliva
Kevin Mcalinden
 Gdsn 2665727
John Collier Coldstream
 Guards
Nicholas Ridley
Keith Skelhorne
Miller Watson
Matt Dawson
Thomas Foster
Cameron Liddle
Graeme Rigg
Nigel Fairhurst
Nicholas Nurden
Stuart Beaton
Matthew Sinn
Damian Van Velzen
David Shackleton
Brian Monument
Nathan Shine
Ian Price
Iain Longford
John Robertsom
Christopher Dunmill
Darren Partridge
Jan Schijff
Tim Marsh
Alan J Brown
Steve Barnes
Alec James
Neil Kedney
Mark Abbott
Jamie Goodridge
Andrew Noble
Paul Isles
Reuben Bale
Martin J. Quinn
Gareth Davies
Nick Crabb
Sebastian Shimmings
William Donnelly
Robert Rodden
Nick Vaughan
Phil Loder
Jacob Burnett
Stephen Rothwell
Mark Moore
Alec Graham
Gary Major
Graham Hurst
Mears Richard
Chris Reynolds
Matthew Perry
Charlie Trumpess
Andrew Hopkin
Ceri Thomas
John Harris
Mike Potter
Gary Hewings
Stephen O'Connor
Simon Harper
Wayne Symons
Jonathan Vardy
Roy Saylors
Clive Laws
Jesus Escudero
Ian McCormack
Chris Holt
Robert Dicken
Anthony Simmons
Steven Reid
Rodney Marshall
Ian Robinson
Tristan A. Cooper
Mark Smith
Phillip Heron
Anne Waite
Bruce Fritz
Nick Wood
James Killala-Ringwood
Panithi Itthithammaboon
Annabella McKenna
Werner Peters
Mark West
John Blackmore
Douglas Swanson
Kjell Arne Randen
Phil Jones
Bernard Pire
Daniel Ford
Alan Gould
Robert O'Connor
Richard Robson
Thomas Myers
Ramon Solar
Richard Bishop
Geoff White
Jyue Lim
Ian Uttridge
Melvin Avery
Huw Davies
Stephen Fleming
and Joel Fulcher.